ARTHURIAN STUDIES L

DIU CRÔNE AND THE MEDIEVAL ARTHURIAN CYCLE

Diu Crône (The Crown) is one of the most neglected of Arthurian romances, perhaps because it does not fit into the canon of orthodox Arthurian stories: it is Gawain, not Perceval or Galahad, who achieves the Grail, and Arthur is not a predestined, assured imperial figure but a ruler who struggles through reverses and challenges as he attempts to establish his authority. The author, Heinrich von dem Türlin, creates a figure who is much more credible than the superhuman achiever of the *Historia Regum Britannie* and the writers who followed Geoffrey of Monmouth, showing the initial vulnerability of the Arthurian order. The eventual triumph of the court and the accolade of the Grail are all the more dramatic in this context.

Diu Crône is a bravura performance which creates a compelling new foundation myth: Camelot is transformed from its initial state of factionalism, sexual betrayal and lack of morale under an inexperienced king to one of law, order and security symbolised by the supreme resourcefulness shown by Gawain in the unflinching service of Arthur, his liege lord. It reinvents the imaginative foundation of the Arthurian ideal, and demonstrates that the ideal maintained its appeal in Germany into the later middle ages.

Dr NEIL THOMAS lectures in the Department of German, University of Durham.

ARTHURIAN STUDIES

ISSN 0261–9814

Previously published volumes in the series
are listed at the back of this book

DIU CRÔNE AND THE MEDIEVAL ARTHURIAN CYCLE

Neil Thomas

D. S. BREWER

First published 2002
D. S. Brewer, Cambridge

ISBN 0 85991 636 7

D. S. Brewer is an imprint of Boydell & Brewer Ltd
PO Box 9, Woodbridge, Suffolk IP12 3DF, UK
and of Boydell & Brewer Inc.
PO Box 41026, Rochester, NY 14604–4126, USA
website: http://www.boydell.co.uk

A catalogue record for this book is available
from the British Library

Library of Congress Cataloging-in-Publication Data
Thomas, Neil, 1949–
    Diu Crône and the medieval Arthurian cycle / Neil Thomas.
        p. cm. – (Arthurian studies, ISSN 0261–9814 ; 50)
    Includes bibliographical references and index.
    ISBN 0–85991–636–7 (alk. paper)
    1. Heinrich, von dem Tèrlin, 13th cent. Krone. 2. Arthurian
romances – History and criticism.   I. Title.   II. Series.
PT1537.H35 K737 2002
831'.21 – dc21
                                                    2001043818

This publication is printed on acid-free paper

Printed in Great Britain by
St Edmundsbury Press Ltd, Bury St Edmunds, Suffolk

Contents

Acknowledgements

I am indebted to the Research Committee of the University of Durham and to the Arts and Humanities Research Board for financing an extended period of study leave which afforded me valuable time for writing. I have received valuable guidance in points of detail from the anonymous press reader and from Miss Linda Gowans. Thanks are also due to Dr Françoise Le Saux for her encouraging discussions and – for informal conversations more than twenty years ago in Regensburg – to Lewis Jillings, from whose work all students of the romance, none more than myself, have profited.

In a broader sense I should like to thank many colleagues and students both in Durham and in Reading for the interest they have shown in my project and the personnel at Boydell & Brewer for their helpfulness and courtesy. The book is published with the assistance of the Vinaver Trust.

Neil Thomas
Durham, January 2001

Abbreviations

ABäG	*Amsterdamer Beiträge zur älteren Germanistik*
ALMA	*Arthurian Literature in the Middle Ages*, ed. R. S. Loomis (Oxford: Clarendon, 1959)
ATB	Altdeutsche Textbibliothek
BBIAS	*Bibliographical Bulletin of the International Arthurian Society*
DTM	Deutsche Texte des Mittelalters
DVLG	*Deutsche Vierteljahrsschrift für Literaturwissenschaft und Geistesgeschichte*
GAG	Göppinger Arbeiten zur Germanistik
GLL	German Life and Letters
GRM	Germanisch-Romanische Monatsschrift
JEGP	*Journal of English and Germanic Philology*
MLR	*Modern Language Review*
MTU	Münchener Texte und Untersuchungen
OGS	Oxford German Studies
PMLA	*Publications of the Modern Language Association of America*
SM	Sammlung Metzler
WAGAPH	Wiener Arbeiten zur germanischen Altertumskunde und Philologie
ZfdA	*Zeitschrift für deutsches Altertum*
ZfdPh	*Zeitschrift für deutsche Philologie*

Introduction: the problem

The 30,000-line South German Arthurian romance, *Diu Crône*,[1] attracted the attention of scholars in the late nineteenth and twentieth centuries because it furnished numerous analogues to scenes occurring in other Arthurian romances written in Old French, Middle English and in medieval Latin. Throughout that period the German work tended to be used instrumentally as a resource for comparative studies by scholars whose primary interests lay elsewhere. In the last two and a half decades, on the other hand, there has been a growing interest in *Diu Crône* in its own right with the appearance of a number of substantial articles and books devoted to its exegesis. The results of this scholarly activity, whilst being welcome, have not always been uncontroversial, and the reviewer of a recent monograph complained of the 'unsatisfactory and contradictory interpretations' to which the romance had recently given rise.[2] Part of the problem may be that comparative studies of cognates and analogues have typically had a somewhat positivistic bias and have paid insufficient attention to the author's 'transgressive fantasy'[3] and the 'comedy and contrafactura' in which the romance abounds.[4] *Diu Crône* has more often than not been understood as a grand compilation or 'monster epic'[5] rather like Ulrich Füeterer's *Buch der Abenteuer* or the *Nüwe Parzifal* of Claus Wisse and Philipp Colin, works in which familiar motifs and even whole romances are appropriated according to a principle of maximum

---

1 Details concerning text, date and authorship are to be found at the beginning of the next chapter.

2 'Obwohl *Diu Crône* von der Forschung gewiß nicht vernachlässigt worden wäre, hat man sich doch aus diesem Text einfach noch keinen Reim machen können und nur höchst widersprüchliche und wenig aussagekräftige Erklärungsversuche vorgelegt'. (Albrecht Classen in a review of Johannes Keller's *Diu Crône Heinrichs von dem Türlin: Wunderketten, Gral und Tod* (Berne: Lang, 1997), *Seminar* 35 (1999), pp. 155–57, citation p. 155.)

3 Elisabeth Schmid, *Familiengeschichten und Heilsmythologie. Die Verwandschaftsstrukturen in den französischen und deutschen Gralromanen des 12. und 13. Jahrhunderts* (Tübingen: Niemeyer, 1986), p. 211.

4 Hartmut Bleumer, *Die 'Crône' Heinrichs von dem Türlin. Form-Erfahrung und Konzeption eines späten Artusromans*, MTU 112 (Tübingen: Niemeyer, 1997), p. 267.

5 M. O'C. Walshe, 'Heinrich von dem Türlin, Chrétien and Wolfram', in *Medieval German Studies Presented to Frederick Norman*, no editor (London: Publications of the Germanic Institute, 1965), pp. 204–18, citation 205. The work has also been termed 'eine postmoderne Wissens- und Mythencollage'. See Volker Mertens, ' "gewisse lêre". Zum Verhältnis von Fiktion und Didaxe im späten Mittelalter', in *Artusroman und Intertextualitat*, ed. Friedrich Wolfzettel (Giessen: Wilhelm Schmitz, 1990), pp. 85–106, citation 89. See also Mertens, *Der deutsche Artusroman* (Stuttgart: Reclam, 1998), pp. 185–204.

inclusivity.[6] Had Heinrich's methods been those of Wisse and Colin (who in the case of Chrétien's Continuations were commissioned to translate and amalgamate narratives which fail to harmonise with each other in their fundamental conceptions), it would make otiose any talk of a creative narrative structure in the accepted sense of 'a concept including both content and form so far as they are used for aesthetic purposes'.[7] However, despite some venial blemishes such as the double-naming of certain minor characters and some reversed narrative sequences (*hysteron proteron*)[8] such as are found in Malory and many other long medieval works, Heinrich's narrative organisation is a long way from mere compilation.[9]

Every literary text may be described in the Barthian sense as a cultural transaction terminating in a new tissue of past citations, and it might fairly be claimed that, like the modern writer Patrick Süskind, Heinrich von dem Türlin 'plunders dead authors'.[10] Yet *Diu Crône* is not simply a collage, and the question of intertextual relations will be submitted to a critical analysis in accordance with modern methodological principles.[11] In *Diu Crône* as elsewhere in Arthurian literature the re-writing of any given motif within a fresh context or combination gives a new sense to old material. Heinrich's preferred modus operandi was to recontextualise existing narrative traditions within a new imaginative framework so as to make old motifs appear new

6   Dorothee Wittmann-Klemm, *Studien zum 'Rappoltsteiner Parzifal'*, GAG 224 (Göppingen: Kümmerle, 1977), p. 129.

7   Rene Wellek and Austin Warren, *Theory of Literature* (Harmondsworth: Penguin, 1970), p. 141.

8   The name of the woman for whom Gawein retrieves flowers of youth is first named as Leigormon (line 6105) but later she is called Mancipelle (lines 21,095ff). Gawein reports on a number of exploits which he has not yet accomplished, whilst Riwalin 'recollects' that Gawein lost a rib and a spear to a lion at the 'castel a lit marveillos' (lines 6119–21) but in the description of the actual event no such loss is suffered: we are told after the combat that Gawein remained unscathed (lines 20,940–43).

9   On structure see Rosemary Wallbank, 'The composition of *Diu Crône*. Heinrich von dem Türlin's narrative technique', in *Medieval Miscellany Presented to Eugène Vinaver*, ed. F. Whitehead, A. H. Diverres and F. E. Sutcliffe (Manchester: Manchester U.P., 1965), pp. 300–20; Bernd Kratz, 'Zur Kompositionstechnik Heinrichs von dem Türlin', *ABäG* 5 (1973), pp. 141–53, and Marianne Glassner, 'Der Aufbau der *Crône* Heinrichs von dem Türlin. Handschriftengliederung und Werkstruktur', unpublished dissertation, University of Vienna, 1991.

10 The phrase is that of Gerhard Stadelmaeier, cited by Osman Durrani in 'The virtues of perfume, or the art of vanishing without trace: grotesque elements in Patrick Süskind's *Das Parfum*', in Neil Thomas (ed.), *German Studies at the Millennium* (Durham: Durham Modern Language Series, 1999), pp. 224–42, citation 225.

11 Although the romance is 'the product of preestablished structures, it is also a transformation of these structures and, as a result, a generic variant in its own right'. Ernst Dick, 'Tradition and emancipation: the generic aspect of Heinrich's *Crône*', in *Genres in Medieval German Literature*, ed. Hubert Heinen and Ingeborg Henderson, GAG 439 (Göppingen: Kümmerle, 1986), pp. 74–92, citation 78. Christine Zach's *Die Erzählmotive der 'Crône' Heinrichs von dem Türlin und ihre altfranzösischen Quellen. Ein kommentiertes Register*, Passauer Schriften zu Sprache und Literatur 5 (Passau: Richard Rothe, 1990), provides useful prolegomena for an assessment of the role of the French material.

again. Evidence of this has been found in his adaptation of the Rival Sisters dispute. Here the narrator supplies a political motive for the sisters' rivalries by adding material from *Yvain/Iwein* to the story which he found in *La Mule sanz Frein* and *Le Chevalier a l'Épée*.[12] Other transformations are not always so easy to discern, partly because of the sheer number of intertexts involved. Hence my first chapter will attempt to place *Diu Crône* in its wider European context, whilst summaries of the more important intertexts are provided in appendices so as to furnish readers with a convenient means of assessing my arguments about Heinrich's adaptations.[13]

The conjecture first put forward by Samuel Singer[14] that *Diu Crône* might be composed of two parts, that is, of an Arthur romance (up to line 13901) followed by essentially unrelated Gawein episodes, once thought to have some merit as a genetic theory, is in fact contradicted by Gawein's series of exploits against the giant Assiles (lines 5469–7659 and 9129–10,112) and by the Amurfina section (lines 7660–9128), sequences which are interlaced with Arthur's travails and which thus lie well within Singer's designated 'Arthurian' section. There is also no manuscript evidence for bipartition. The Vienna MS ends at line 12, 281 (*before* the end of Singer's 'Part One'). Moreover, whilst Arthur has a substantial challenge to face in the shape of the would-be usurper of his wife's favours, Gasozein, 'Crône I' celebrates Gawein's marriage, invalidating the argument for a strict unity of action centred upon Arthur.

Singer's analysis (never completely discounted)[15] is opposed not only by the way in which the Gawein and Arthur exploits are interlaced in 'Part I' but also by the way in which many of Gawein's ostensibly solo exploits are discharged on behalf of his liege lord. The 'hero' of the romance, it was long ago pointed out, is 'die Artusidee'[16] (the Vienna MS is entitled 'der werde künec Artus'). This idea is articulated through the twin biographies of Gawein and Arthur, the fate of both knights being interdependent since *Diu Crône* establishes a different relationship between protagonist and King than that which obtained in the 'classical' tradition of Chrétien and Hartmann. In *Erec* and *Iwein* two major framing scenes at Arthur's Court of Karidol are so positioned as to lend symbolic weight to the launch of the knight's career and to give regal validation to his later accomplishments. Arthur functions as an

---

12 Bernd Kratz, 'Die Geschichte vom Maultier ohne Zaum. Paien de Maisières, Heinrich von dem Türlin und Wieland', *Arcadia* 13 (1978), pp. 227–41.

13 In the summaries I have gone into some detail in order to show the *selective* nature of many of Heinrich's 'borrowings'.

14 Article on Heinrich von dem Türlin in the *Allgemeine Deutsche Biographie* 39 (Leipzig: Duncker and Humblot, 1895), pp. 20–22.

15 See Alfred Ebenbauer, 'Gawein als Gatte', in A. Cella and Peter Krämer (eds), *Die mittelalterliche Literatur in Kärnten*, Wiener Arbeiten zur germanischen Altertumskunde und Philologie 16 (Vienna: Halosar, 1981), pp. 33–66, here p. 37.

16 Luise Lerner, *Studien zur Komposition des höfischen Romans im 13. Jahrhundert*, Forschungen zur deutschen Sprache und Dichtung 7 (Münster in Westphalia: Aschendorff, 1936), p. 24.

unchallenged model of perfection against whom the efforts of individual knights may be measured. That structural model does not hold for *Diu Crône* because Arthur's status as an ideal monarch falls victim to constant challenge and it is typically by dint of Gawein's efforts, deployed in a representative capacity, that the King's honour is vindicated. Although he uses material found ready to hand in a number of disparate sources, Heinrich creates of them a new *maere* whose subject is not so much the biography of an individual protagonist as an account of 'Camelot' as an imagined institution. In the analysis to follow it will be shown that the narrative organisation of that story falls into the following thematic patterns, given here in tabular form as a point of departure for more detailed discussion in ensuing chapters:

PROLOGUE (lines 1–160)

PROBLEMS OF REGAL SUCCESSION (lines 161–5468)

1. Arthur laments the early passing of Uther and fears that he will be unable to live up to his father's example.
2. The shaming 'goblet test,' a test of honour administered by the emissary of King Priure according to which all Arthur's retinue, male and female, is found wanting.
3. Surreptitious defection from Court of Gawein and all but three of the other knights.
4. Emotional defection of Guinevere giving rise to the Gasozein–Arthur–Guinevere triangle.

GAWEIN'S INITIAL EXPLOITS AS A KNIGHT ERRANT
(lines 5469–10,112)

1. Gawein intercepts the emissary of King Flois heading towards the Arthurian Court to fetch help for his lord (presently besieged by the giant, Assiles), accepting the challenge in his own person on behalf of the beleaguered Flois.
2. Through his narration of various exploits portending Gawein's *future* career (*hysteron proteron*) Riwalin expresses a quasi-prophetic confidence in Gawein's ability to triumph in the Assiles campaign.
3. In the midst of that campaign Gawein succumbs to the powers of Amurfina yet manages to escape her sexual thrall when shown a plaque immortalising his erstwhile exploits as a knight committed to the furtheral of the chivaric enterprise.
4. Gawein returns to his knightly obligations and the successful accomplishment of the Assiles challenge.

RETURN OF THE MATURE GAWEIN TO COURT (lines 10,113–12,610)

His own emotional/moral dilemma resolved, Gawein returns to resolve the issue of the sexual triangle by compelling the would-be abductor, Gasozein, to relinquish his claim of a prior betrothal to Guinevere and to agree to a modus vivendi on terms favourable to Arthur. (Gasozein later consents to take another woman as his wife.)

PRELUDE TO THE GRAIL: THE REVOLVING CASTLE ADVENTURE AND FIRST PREMONITIONS OF THE GRAIL CHALLENGE (lines 12,611–14,926)

The ostensibly pointless escapade of Gawein's championing the cause of his wife's sister against the proper interests of himself and his own spouse has the advantage of bringing him to the favourable attention of the rival siblings' uncle, Gansguoter, whose accreditation and support he will later need in order to gain access to the Grail kingdom. This prolepsis, closely followed by a sequence in which Gawein gains his first apprehensions of the Grail (lines 13,935–14,926) erases the conventional distinction between *Crône* 'Parts One and Two'.

THE INTERVIEW WITH DAME FORTUNA (lines 14,927–16,496)

Gawein is said to gain Dame Fortuna's blessing for himself and Arthur – although subsequent reverses suffered by Gawein give little evidence of her practical support, and Gawein must largely be the author of his own salvation (and of that of the Court whose interests he represents).

THE TWO-FOLD GRAIL COMPLEX (lines 17,500–22,564)

1. Heinrich takes over the material of the Gauvain/Gawan adventures as found in the Grail romances of Chrétien and Wolfram, using this sequence as an ensemble to motivate Gawein's taking over the Grail quest from Angaras of Karamphi Castle (Chrétien's Escavalon) as a penance for his erstwhile killing of Angaras's brother.
2. The personal, penitential motive is then augmented by a more generally redemptive one when, in an innovation not represented in the source texts, Gawein saves a group of grieving widows (one in an apparently corpse-like condition) from the depredations of a huge Moorish aggressor. This episode foreshadows his final redemption of the spectral inhabitants of the Grail castle.
3. Gawein's redemption of the denizens of *Chastel mervillôs* represents an innovation over Gawan's freeing of the hostile Clinschor's prisoners in *Parzival*: Heinrich's magician figure, Gansguoter, is a benign figure

described as having entered into a *consensual* union with Uther's widow, Igern. Gawein's intervention in *Diu Crône* provides not so much a liberation as the opportunity for a strengthened dynastic cohesion when Arthur is reunited with his long-lost mother.

GIRAMPHIEL'S PSYCHOLOGICAL WARFARE (lines 22,565–26,090)

1. The morale of the Court is diminished by the 'glove test', a 'test of virtue' administered by an emissary of the hostile *fée*, Giramphiel, which only Arthur and Gawein 'pass'.
2. The Arthurians are tricked into relinquishing the magic talismans said to be necessary for the successful accomplishment of the Grail quest. All are cast down by the turn of events except Gawein who trusts to succeed without the magic requisites.

GANSGUOTER AND THE GRAIL (lines 26,091–30,000)

1. The courtiers recommend that Gawein and the Grail party should seek guidance from Gansguoter, who helps the knights to gain entry to the Grail kingdom and does away with the need for magical tricks by giving Gawein a hauberk able to neutralise hostile magic.
2. Gawein triumphs over Giramphiel's champion, Fimbeus (a combat in which Fortune is said to spread her favours evenly over both combatants).
3. Further counsel is received from Manbur, Gansguoter's sister and *châtelaine* of the Grail castle. Manbur advises that all but one of the magic talismans recently retrieved from the defeated Fimbeus should be returned to Court as proof that Gawein still lives and in order to annul Giramphiel's repeated attempts to spread rumours of Gawein's death.
4. The Grail king explains the genesis of the Grail curse and its associated 'wonders'. The 'undead' of the Grail castle are redeemed and Gawein receives an intact sword from the *altherre* as a sign of his success. Angaras, who originally imposed the quest upon Gawein as a penance for killing his brother, is conciliated by this outcome and agrees to enter the Arthurian ranks.

1

Text, Intertext, Polemic

Nu wil iu der tihtaere
Von künec Artûs ein maere
Sagen ze bezzerunge,
Daz er in tiutsche zunge
Von franzoise hât gerihtet,
Als er ez getihtet
Ze Karlingen geschriben las,
Wan er sô gelêret was
daz er die sprâche kunde.   (*Diu Crône*, lines 217–25)

(Now for your edification the poet before you will tell a tale of King
Arthur which he has translated from French into German just as he
found it written down in France – he being educated enough to understand the French language.)

Diu Crône is partially preserved in a number of manuscripts, the best
containing only just over a third of its 30,041 verses and only one having the
whole text.[1] It is thought to have been written in the Austro-Bavarian area but
the poor manuscript tradition together with the supra-regional lingua franca
in which it is composed[2] do not permit a precise localisation. Datings for all

---

[1] The only complete edition is that by G. H. F. Scholl, *Diu Crône von Heinrich von dem Türlin*
(Stuttgart: Bibliothek des Litterarischen Vereins 27, 1852, repr. Amsterdam: Rodopi, 1966).
Scholl's edition is inadequate. For emendations and for discussions of the edition and
manuscripts see Klaus Zatloukal, *Heinrich von dem Türlin: Diu Crône. Ausgewählte
Abbildungen zur gesamten handschriftlichen Überlieferung*, Litterae 95 (Göppingen:
Kümmerle, 1982); Werner Schröder, *Herstellungsversuche an dem Text der 'Crône' Heinrichs
von dem Türlin*, 2 vols (Mainz: Franz Steiner, 1996), and Arno Mentzel-Reuters, *Vröude.
Artusbild, Fortuna- und Gralkonzeption in der 'Crone' des Heinrich von demTürlin als
Verteidigung des höfischen Lebensideals* (Berne: Lang, 1989), pp. 1–7 and also pp. 322–26 for
further literature. There is also a new edition based on the best manuscript: *Die Krone
(Verse 1–12281) nach der Handschrift 2779 der Österreichischen Nationalbibliothek*, Altdeutsche
Textbibliothek 112, ed. Fritz Peter Knapp and Manuela Niesner (Tübingen: Niemeyer,
2000).

[2] Medieval German narrative poets using the medium of rhymed couplets typically drew
on a restricted linguistic corpus, a *Dichtersprache* based on the norms of Hartmann von
Aue and other literary predecessors. See Christopher J. Wells, *German. A Linguistic History
to 1945* (Oxford: Clarendon, 1985), pp. 116–22, and Hermann Paul, *Mittelhochdeutsche*

German romances of the high medieval period are conjectural, but *Diu Crône* was probably written about 1230.[3]

The author gives his name in the form of an extended acrostic on the initial letters of a sequence of verses: HEINRIKH VON DEM TVRLIN HAT MIKH GETIHTET (lines 182–216).[4] He also names himself less cryptically in the body of the text (lines 246–49; 8774; 10,443–44) but gives no information about his domicile, the name of any possible patron or any other composition. His reference to having previously treated the theme of a test involving a cup and mantle (lines 23,495–505) was once taken as evidence that he was the author of *Der Mantel*,[5] a much shorter work of just less than a thousand verses on the theme of a chivalric test, but the contention has not been sustained by recent scholarship.[6] Similarly, whilst it was once supposed that Heinrich came of a burgher family from St Veit an der Glan, and that he possibly stood in the employ of Duke Bernard of Carinthia (1202–1256), such identifications are now thought uncertain[7] – although the reference to a poet bringing the romance of *Erec* with him from Suabia (lines 2351–54) has continued to give rise to speculation that he may have lived in an Alpine region set apart from the main centres of literary activity in the medieval period.[8] Despite the

---

Grammatik, 21st edn revised by Hugo Moser and Ingeborg Schröbler (Tübingen: Niemeyer, 1975), pp. 14–17.

3 Werner Schröder, 'Zur Chronologie der drei grossen mittelhochdeutschen Epiker', *DVLG* 31 (1957), pp. 264–302, and 'Zur Literaturverarbeitung durch Heinrich von dem Türlin in seinem Gawein-Roman, *Diu Crône*', *ZfdA* 121 (1992), pp. 131–74.

4 A second acrostic, NIUWVELSE, was discovered by Bernd Kratz, 'Ein zweites Acrostichon in der *Crône* Heinrichs von dem Türlin', *ZfdPh* 108 (1989), pp. 402–05. Kratz speculated that this might point to a patron in the Baden bei Mühlheim or Öhringen region.

5 This was the view of Otto Warnatsch (ed.), *Der Mantel. Brüchstück eines Lanzeletromans des Heinrich von dem Türlin nebst einer Abhandlung über die Sage vom Trinkhorn und Mantel und die Quelle der Krone*, Germanistische Abhandlungen 2 (Breslau: Wilhelm Koebner, 1883). It was opposed by Bernd Kratz, 'Die Ambraser Mantel-Erzählung und ihr Autor', *Euphorion* 71 (1977), pp. 1–17.

6 For discussion of this point see Werner Schröder, *Herstellungsversuche an dem Text der 'Crône'*, vol. 1, pp. 14–16. The treatment of key Arthurian personnel differs in the two works: most notably, the figure of Kei is consistently denigrated as a social pariah in the *Mantel* poem whereas in *Diu Crône* he is given noble traits permitting him to act as the narrator's mouthpiece.

7 Ottokar of Styria's *Österreichische Reimchronik* (1301–19) mentions a prominent family surnamed von den Türlin in St Veit, the Carinthian seat of government in the thirteenth century, and a Heinrich von den Türlin is mentioned in a document of the year 1229. It is not impossible that this person (who may have been a notary at the ducal court) was the author of *Diu Crône*, but the surname von den Türlin was a common one in medieval Austria and, since the manuscript comes from Lienz in the Tirol, recent scholarship has moved away from identifying this particular bearer of a common name with the author of *Diu Crône*. See Bernd Kratz, 'Zur Biographie Heinrichs von dem Turlin', *ABäG* 11 (1977), pp. 123–67.

8 Lewis Jillings, 'Heinrich von dem Türlein. Zum Problem der biographischen Forschung', and Fritz Peter Knapp, 'Heinrich von dem Türlin. Literarische Beziehungen und mögliche Auftraggeber, dichterische Selbsteinschätzung und Zielsetzung', in A. Cella and P. Krämer (eds), *Die Mittelalterliche Literatur in Kärnten*, pp. 87–102 and pp. 145–87.

dearth of evidence for the poet's life, *Diu Crône* shows the impress of a vivid poetic signature on a number of internal grounds. Heinrich possessed an 'energetically fertile mind'[9] whose occasional sexual explicitness still has the power to shock.[10] He possessed a wide knowledge of both German and French literature and claims to have visited France (lines 217–25). Whether that claim is true or not, his knowledge of French Arthurian literature is unsurpassed by any other contemporary writer,[11] echoes of a wide variety of French works occurring with a frequency which makes the author's own claims to have derived his material from one source ('Ûz einem exemplar', line 29,970) by Chrétien de Troyes appear considerably too modest.[12]

Composed in an era when encyclopaedic collections of traditions of knowledge such as Thomas Aquinas's *Summa Theologica* or Vincent of Beauvais's *Speculum Naturale* were being produced, *Diu Crône* has been likened to a *summa arthuriana* in which 'Heinrich seems to have been intent on assembling an all-embracing corpus of Arthurian tales, somewhat like Malory'.[13] The protagonist's diverse biography has echoes of *Erec* and *Iwein*, *Parzival*, *Lanzelet* and *Tristan*. Many parts of the narrative have analogues elsewhere, but these are to be found dispersed in various narrative traditions. They range from the works of Chrétien de Troyes and the First Continuation, the Lancelot–Grail cycle (Prose *Lancelot*), a number of French Merlin traditions, the *Livre d'Artus* and *Perlesvaus* together with *La Mule sans Frein*, *Le Chevalier a l'Épée*, and the Didot *Perceval*. Further similarities of individual motifs are to be found with *l'Âtre Périlleux*, *Le Bel Inconnu*, *La Vengeance Raguidel*, a number of *lais* (*Tydorel*, *Lanval*, *Graelent*, *Le Lai du Cor*) and with the Latin romance *De Ortu Walwanii* and its French cognate, the fragmentary 'Enfances Gauvain', together with that romance which Gaston Paris claimed

---

9   Margaret F. Richey, 'The German contribution to the matter of Britain with special reference to the legend of King Arthur and the Round Table', *Medium Aevum* 19 (1950), pp. 26–42, citation 32.

10 Susann Samples, 'The rape of Ginover in Heinrich von dem Türlin's *Diu Crône*', in *Arthurian Romance and Gender, Masculin/Féminin dans le Roman Arthurien Mediéval/ Geschlechterrollen im mittelalterlichen Artusroman*, ed. Friedrich Wolfzettel (Amsterdam, Atlanta Ga: Rodopi, 1995), pp. 196–205.

11 Christine Zach, *Die Erzählmotive der 'Crône' Heinrichs von dem Türlin und ihre altfranzösischen Quellen. Ein kommentiertes Register*, Passauer Schriften zu Sprache und Literatur 5 (Passau: Richard Rothe, 1990).

12 References to Chrétien as source occur at lines 16,941, 23,046, 23,992. On the poet's professional self-understanding see Lewis Jillings, *'Diu Crône' by Heinrich von dem Türlein. The Attempted Emancipation of Secular Narrative*, GAG 258 (Göppingen: Kümmerle, 1980), pp. 142–84.

13 Marianne Wynn, 'The abduction of the queen in German Arthurian romance', in *Chevaliers errants, demoiselles et l'Autre. Höfische und nachhöfische Literatur im europäischen Mittelalter*, Festschrift für Xenja von Ertzdorff, ed. Trude Ehlert, GAG 644 (Göppingen: Kümmerle, 1988), pp. 131–44, citation 135.

as part of the French literary heritage, *Sir Gawain and the Green Knight*.[14] There are also possible echoes of the German heroic epic.[15]

The author shows a broad standard of humanist culture together with a knowledge of rhetoric and philosophical terminology which evidences a good awareness of the forms of learned discourse of his day.[16] The use of the scholastic terms *geômetrîe* (line 1119), *philosôphen* (line 303) and *dîaletike* (line 10811) is not recorded elsewhere in contemporary romance. Nor do we find the kind of elegant scorn for clerical quibbles expressed in a striking passage which urges that affairs of the heart are better decided by the parties involved than by the counsel of the great and good.[17] Like Chrétien de Troyes, Heinrich appears to have seen himself as a continuator of the Classical *auctores*[18] and there are a number of allusions to Classical traditions. He invokes the deities Minerva, Juno, Venus (lines 8288–91) and the Fates (lines 286–97) with further references to Fortuna[19] and Heil, on whom he confers independent mythological status as the son of the fickle goddess. Her depiction in *Diu Crône* enthroned with her son may have been inspired by iconographic tradi-

---

[14] *Histoire Littéraire de la France* (Paris: Académie des Inscriptions et Belles Lettres, 1888; repr. Nendeln/Liechtenstein: Kraus, 1971), p. 71. ('Nous ne possédons de ce roman qu'une version anglaise du XIVe siècle; mais il est extrêmement probable qu'elle ne fait que reproduire un poème français perdu.')

[15] See Georges Zink , 'A propos d'un épisode de la *Crône*' (v. 9129–9532)', in *Mélanges pour Jean Fourquet. 37 Essais de Linguistique Germanique et de Littératures du Moyen Age Français et Allemand*, ed. P. Valentin and G. Zink (Munich/Paris: Hueber, 1969), pp. 395–405; Bernd Kratz, 'Rosengarten und Zwergenkönig in der *Crône* Heinrichs von dem Türlin', *Medievalia Bohemica* 1 (1969), pp. 21–29 and 'Gawein und Wolfdietrich', *Euphorion* 66 (1972), pp. 397–404 and Annagret Wagner-Harken, *Märchenelemente und ihre Funktion in der 'Crône' Heinrichs von dem Türlin. Ein Beitrag zur Unterscheidung zwischen 'klassischer' und 'nachklassischer' Artusepik*, Deutsche Literatur von den Anfängen bis 1700, vol. 21 (Bern/Berlin/Frankfurt am Main/New York/Paris/Vienna: Lang, 1995).

[16] Karl Reissenburger, *Zur 'Krone' Heinrichs von dem Türlin* (Graz: Leuschner and Lubensky, 1879), pp. 3–18; Erich Gülzow, *Zur Stilkunde der 'Krone' Heinrichs von dem Türlin*, Teutonia 18 (Leipzig: H. Haeffel, 1914), and Peter Kobbe, 'Funktion und Gestalt des Prologs in der mittelhochdeutschen nachklassischen Epik des 13. Jahrhunderts', *DVLG* 43 (1969), pp. 405–57.

[17] Gasozein, the pretender to Guinevere's favours, claims in a speech bristling with well-aimed criticisms of legalistic obfuscations that the dispute between himself and Arthur over Guinevere should be decided by the goddess of love since her adjudications, he claims, remain uncorrupted by the sophistries of clerical arbitration (lines 10,803–30).

[18] Geoffrey of Monmouth had associated the Homeric world and medieval Europe by linking the beginnings of British history with the destruction of Troy whilst Chrétien de Troyes begins his *Cligés* with the assertion that the practice of chivalry had crossed from Greece to Rome and thence to France – a land which had effectively garnered the whole patrimony of ancient culture. See Adrian Stevens, 'Heteroglossia and clerical narrative: on Wolfram's adaptation of Chrétien', in *Chrétien de Troyes and the German Middle Ages*, ed. Martin H. Jones and Roy Wisbey (Cambridge/London: D. S. Brewer and the Institute of Germanic Studies, 1993), pp. 241–55.

[19] Whilst not all the gods and goddesses of the ancient world survived into the medieval period, the two-headed Fortuna, symbol of life's uncertainties, defied the imprecations of St Augustine to play an important executive role alongside the God of the Christian tradition. See Jean Seznec, *The Survival of the Ancient Gods* (New York: Harper and Row, 1960), and Max Wehrli, 'Antike Mythologie im christlichen Mittelalter', *DVLG* 57 (1983), 18–32.

tions of the Madonna with child,[20] this syncretic conception harmonising with ideas which the Middle Ages had inherited from Boethius's *Consolation of Philosophy* where the Christian God stands at the centre of a cosmic circle and Fortuna at its ring. There are also references to Natura, another allegorical figure who had developed from a background in Classical philosophy and Christian theology to influence vernacular literature.[21]

Although the presence of Fortuna might have appeared to contradict the Christian doctrine of Providence, common experience appeared to demand that some shows of obeisance be made to the ancient goddess so that the undeniable place of mutability in human affairs be acknowledged and formally represented.[22] The epistemological bases on which medievals erected their philosophical outlooks were at any rate more eclectic and less subject to normative regulation than was once supposed of 'the Ages of Faith'[23] and few writers of romance were as resolutely monotheistic as Orthodoxy might have preferred. Given a variety of possible approaches to the invisible realms and the traditional licence of literary expression, there was an often striking openness to other mythologies. There was clearly a spiritual and cognitive need throughout medieval Europe for non-orthodox explanations of things, as is shown by the rise of various proto-Protestant groups (not to speak of openly rationalist ideas circulating under the portmanteau term of Averroism). A mediated form of Celtic mythology and the 'Matter of Rome' with its distinctive pantheon of gods and goddesses were becoming familiar

---

20 Helmut de Boor, 'Fortuna in mittelhochdeutscher Dichtung, insbesondere in der *Crône* des Heinrich von dem Türlin', in *Verbum et Signum. Beiträge zur mediävistischen Bedeutungsforschung. Festschrift für Friedrich Ohly*, ed. Hans Fromm (Munich: Fink, 1975), 2 vols, vol. 2, pp. 311–28.

21 See G. D. Economou, *The Goddess Natura in Medieval Literature* (Cambridge, Massachusetts: Harvard U.P., 1972). The process began with philosophical meditations by scholars of the school of Chartres, namely, the *De Mundi Universitate* of Bernard Silvestris and the *Anticlaudianus* and *De Planctu Naturae* of Alan of Lille, finding later expression in the *Roman de la Rose* and Chaucer's *Parlement of Foules*. Natura, like Fortuna, had a delegated authority as the *vicaria Dei* or *mater generationis* and Bernard Silvestris described her in terms of an agency bringing order and refinement to the disorder of the material world.

22 The influence of Boethius was such that it became necessary for a metaphysical space to be allotted to Fortuna even in Christian cosmographies such as the seventh Book of Dante's *Inferno* (which features the capricious deity operating under God's jurisdiction).

23 To which G. G. Coulton preferred the term 'Ages of Acquiesence' (*The Plain Man's Religion in the Middle Ages* (London: Simpkin, Marshall, Hamilton and Kent, 1916), p. 5). From Tertullian to Bernard of Clairvaux there were 'fundamentalists' who placed their trust in Revelation and the letter of Scripture, finding the Church and the Academy to be irreconcilable institutions. Others, on the other hand (Justin Martyr, Clement of Alexandria, Augustine), appealed to the words of St Paul: 'The Word of God is the true light, which enlighteneth every man that cometh into the world' (John 1.9). In the Averroistic philosophy this saying could be amplified to imply that divine truths are apprehensible by all, without distinction of doctrinal affiliation, and that, ultimately, 'religion and Revelation are nothing but philosophical truths made acceptable to men whose imagination is stronger than their reason' (Etienne Gilson, *Reason and Revelation in the Middle Ages* (New York and London: Scribners, 1939), p. 43).

and some form of passive acceptance of non-Christian mythological systems not uncommon.

Since the idea of an autonomous Natura could, without a very clear Christian underpinning, be thought to smack of what later centuries would term deism, theological writers and most writers of courtly romance were reluctant to accord Natura a large place in their cosmology. Wolfram and Gottfried preferred the spiritually neutral term *art*, a non-personified term connoting 'essential nature'. Heinrich, on the other hand, shows considerably less hesitation about using the expression in the original sense of the *natura formatrix* of the Latin tradition, thereby implicitly putting God at one remove from his operations within a more mechanistically conceived universe.[24] *Diu Crône* (whose narrator in an enigmatic but suggestive self-disclosure describes himself as a 'child of the world')[25] has in fact been represented as a 'secular' work which 'betrays not only little apparent Christian motivation in the action, but also far-reaching erosion of an even conventional religiosity.'[26]

Heinrich implicitly defines himself as a professional writer of some discrimination by characterising his work as a 'well-wrought crown' ('wol gesmite(r) krône, line 29917) with a perfect number of jewels which gratuitous additions would only serve to disfigure (lines 29915–29980). His contemporaries appear to have appreciated his labours: Rudolf von Ems used the term crown as an honorific ('Allr Aventiure crone').[27] This positive verdict has not often been often endorsed in the modern period.[28] Nineteenth-century scholars valued the romance chiefly for its literary–historical utility, typically exploiting it as a quarry for analogues in the study of more highly regarded works of the medieval canon such as *Sir Gawain and the Green Knight*. *Diu Crône* therefore tended to become best known as an anthology for those motifs which had parallels in more favoured romances or which related to the putative Celtic background of medieval romance. Because of its sheer length, readers commonly chose to rely on summaries of its contents, a practice claimed to have 'given rise to the prevailing opinion that the author himself does not adhere to a strict plan'.[29]

---

[24] Nature (rather than the non-exercise of free will) is made responsible for moral lapses in women (4345–7); and rather perversely (it is implied) gives Lord Laniure daughters rather than a desired son (lines 7911–13).

[25] 'Ich heiz von dem Türlin/Der werlt kint Heinrîch' (lines 10,443–4).

[26] Jillings, *Diu Crône*, p. 185. But see also on this point Arno Mentzel-Reuters who cautions against use of what he sees as the anachronistic term 'secularism': *Vröude. Artusbild, Fortuna- und Gralkonzeption in der 'Crone'*, p. 112.

[27] See Franz Josef Worstbrock, 'Über den Titel der *Krone* Heinrichs von dem Türlin', *ZfdA* 95 (1966), pp. 182–86.

[28] See Volker Mertens, *Der deutsche Artusroman*, pp. 185–204 and Werner Schröder, 'Zur Literaturverarbeitung durch Heinrich von dem Türlin', pp. 131–74. For older criticism see Edmund K. Heller, 'A vindication of Heinrich von dem Türlin based on a survey of his sources', *Modern Language Quarterly* 3 (1942), pp. 67–82 and Erich Gülzow, *Zur Stilkunde* with their further references.

[29] Heller, 'A Vindication', p. 69. On the dangers of distorted readings resulting from exces-

It was once commonly assumed that the literary modus operandi of a 'post-Classical' or 'epigonal' author such as Heinrich consisted in the more or less arbitrary reintegration of predecessors' motifs into his own work, the frequent roll-calls of admired literary models being taken as evidence that later authors had little of substance to add to their predecessors' achievements. This understanding resulted in a rise-and-fall literary historiography of the German romances of the Middle Ages according to which, after Heinrich von Veldeke and Hartmann von Aue had established the genre, and Wolfram von Eschenbach and Gottfried von Strassburg brought it to perfection, 'it remained for the next generation to outbid the masters in the fantasy of their plots, the scale of their action or the exuberance of their diction'.[30] It is perhaps not too much to claim that until about a quarter of a century ago most scholars viewed *Diu Crône* as a more or less random collage of Arthurian motifs, a judgement still persisting in one strand of present-day discourse.[31]

Such a unidirectional understanding of an evolving literary tradition does less than justice to the healthy spirit of emulation which reigned among medieval poets. Behind the numerous pro forma humility formulae often lurked a competitive edge eager to cut through the medieval shibboleth of *auctoritas*. This is self-evident in the development of the medieval German lyric where Walther von der Vogelweide declined to be a mere continuator of the tradition of plangent eulogies to high-born ladies associated with Reinmar von Hagenau and Heinrich von Morungen. Yet by the same token Heinrich, in his ambition to write a Grail romance, was also tacitly vying with renowned predecessors, entering the lists alongside those many continuators who had attempted to bring closure to Chrétien's 'significantly unfinished'[32] *Conte du Graal* (c. 1180).

We do not possess the 'book' which Chrétien claimed to have received from Philip of Flanders and which he purportedly used as his source for his most celebrated work. All we know is that when Chrétien's uncompleted version breaks off both its heroes, Perceval and Gauvain, are engaged upon a quest for the 'grail' and that we do not know what the outcome might have been. Posterity was left to make its own efforts after meaning,[33] and by about 1225 four separate continuations were in existence. The First Continuation

sive dependence on summaries see Philippa Hardman, 'Scholars retelling romances', *Reading Medieval Studies* 18 (1992), pp. 81–101.

30 Paul Salmon, *Literature in Medieval Germany* (London: Cresset, 1967), p. 134. Fritz-Peter Knapp has a similar verdict: 'Heinrich hat als Nachgeborener der Klassiker des höfischen Romans sein Heil in der Antithese und in der Überbietung gesucht' ('Literarische Beziehungen', p. 172).

31 See especially Werner Schröder, 'Zur Literaturverarbeitung'.

32 The phrase is that of Nigel Bryant (trans.), *The High Book of the Grail. A Translation of the Thirteenth-Century Romance of 'Perlesvaus'* (Cambridge: D. S. Brewer, 1978), Introduction, p. 2.

33 See G. D. West, 'Grail problems I: Silimac the Stranger', *Romance Philology* 24 (1970/71) pp.

takes up the Gauvain story and leaves Perceval out of account. Gauvain witnesses a corpse on a bier and a broken sword which he is unable to mend and, besides omitting to ask about the Grail, he falls asleep before he has received an explanation of the Grail and its attendant mysteries. The Second Continuation turns to Perceval who is also only partially successful in his quest since a hairline fissure remains in the broken Grail sword as a token of his failing. It was not until the Third Continuation, by Manessier, that the story was brought to a conclusion when the sword was mended by a smith, finally permitting Perceval to assume kingship of the Grail.[34] A fourth continuation by Gerbert (occurring in the manuscripts as an interpolation between the Second Continuation and Manessier), also permits Perceval to mend the broken sword and become Grail king.

The difficulties experienced both by Chrétien and by many of his continuators in drawing this narrative to a conclusion have given rise to the suspicion that the medieval writers were drawing on traditions remote from their cultural horizons. The 'grail' (which in many Continental romances appears in a dual state, partly magic cauldron, partly Christian relic) may originally have been the kind of wondrous vessel encountered in Celtic fable whose mythical logic within the belief system of the ancient Britons was no longer perspicuous to later writers or to their audiences.[35] Whether Chrétien's source book reflected such ancient traditions is uncertain[36] but the similarities between the Grail knight's redemptive visit to a stricken castle and the Celtic mythological pattern of a chosen mortal being sent to restore a waste land to fecundity and its barren king to sexual vigour might suggest Celtic origins (with the possibility of Breton analogues as intermediaries to the Francophone world). How well such traditions would have been understood by Continental romance writers is unclear. In the event it was only the decisive intervention of Robert de Boron in his *Roman de l'Estoire dou Graal* (c. 1200) which clearly converted the 'grail' into the Holy Grail, drawing on New

---

599–611 and 'Grail problems II: The Grail family in the Old French verse romances', *Romance Philology* 25 (1972), 53–73.

[34] The torso was not known to medieval listeners in isolation. Chrétien and the Continuations, including the *Bliocadran* (containing the story of Perceval's parents) and the *Elucidation* (intended as a gloss on Chrétien's *Conte du Graal*), together come to a total of some 60,000 verses.

[35] For a discussion of this point see *Perceval. The Story of the Grail*, trans. Burton Raffel with Afterword by Joseph J. Duggan (Yale: Yale U.P., 1999), Afterword , pp. 293–307, esp. 294–96.

[36] See Madelyn J. Parins, 'Scholarship, Modern Arthurian', in *The New Arthurian Encyclopaedia*, ed. by Norris J. Lacy (Chicago and London: St James Press, 1991), pp. 402–11. To determine the precise point of origin of much early European Other World lore is not possible since, as Alfred Nutt pointed out a century ago, 'the attempt to discriminate modern national characteristics in the older strata of European folklore is not only idle but mischievous, because it is based on the unscientific assumption that existing differences, which are the outcome of comparatively recent historical conditions, have always existed' (*The Fairy Mythology of Shakespeare* (London: David Nutt, 1900), citation p. 24).

Testament Apocrypha and identifying the Grail with the chalice of the Last Supper, used to collect Christ's blood on the Cross.

This pious identification was to underpin much French thirteenth-century Grail literature including the influential Lancelot–Grail cycle, but the Christian interpretation of the Grail as a relic of the Last Supper, although it exerted considerable influence on posterity via the prose romances, was not followed by all medieval writers. So striking are some of the differences between many works conventionally brought together under the portmanteau title of 'Grail romances' that the usefulness of that taxonomic category must be in some doubt. The Middle English cognate of the *Conte du Graal, Sir Percyvell of Galles*, has no mention of the Grail and its hero 'receives no instruction in the use of weapons by an older man, does not meet with a woman lamenting the murder of a kinsman, is not thrown into a love-meditation by the sight of blood-drops in the snow (and) finds no hermit to point out the major sins of his past life to him'.[37] The theme of this version is essentially the young Percyvell's quest for vengeance on his father's murderer, and the protagonist (to whom the epithet *wilde* is liberally applied) is not required to undertake a prolonged journey of moral self-exploration, remaining little less gauche at the end of the romance as at its beginning.

The Middle Welsh form of the quest narrative, *Peredur*, also possesses no Grail in the sense of a holy vessel, for although the eponymous hero of the Welsh version witnesses a 'Grail-like' procession in which youths and maidens bear in a spear and silver salver, at the centre of the ritual is no dish, stone nor other relic but the severed head of the hero's cousin, slain by witches from Gloucester upon whom it is Peredur's task to seek revenge. Even in those romances where the Grail makes a formal appearance, its narrative importance varies. The writer(s) of the First Continuation disregarded Chrétien's cues concerning Perceval to concentrate on the deuteragonist, Gauvain, and, in the opinion of the text's editor, 'except for the one or two scenes in the Grail Castle, the First Continuation is merely a Gauvain romance which is in no significant way to be distinguished from the *Hunbaut*, the *Vengeance Raguidel, Gawain and the Green Knight*, or half a dozen others'.[38]

Regarding the German tradition,Wolfram von Eschenbach refers to his grail as a stone rather than as the vessel of Christian legend (possibly by analogy with the Alexander legend),[39] and avoids the mystical associations of the French tradition. Parzival's Grail quest, whilst being his supreme goal, is not his only one since he is faced with the task of harmonising two distinct

---

37 Maldwyn Mills (ed.), *Ywain and Gawain. Sir Percyvell of Gales. The Anturs of Arther* (London: Dent, 1992), Introduction, p. xix.

38 William Roach, *The Continuations of the Old French Perceval of Chrétien de Troyes* (Philadelphia: University of Pennsylvania Press, 1949), 5 vols, vol. 1, Introduction, p. xiii.

39 See Joachim Bumke, *Wolfram von Eschenbach*, 7th edn, SM 36 (Stuttgart: Metzler 1997), pp. 154–66.

legacies, each issuing its own imperatives. His father's *art* as a knight errant impels him toward the Arthurian arena, but his matrilineal link with the Grail dynasty leads him to develop more spiritual goals, and the romance tends towards the kind of gradualist solution of the God/World dichotomy which is made explicit in the narrator's final excursus.[40] Wolfram instrumentalised the Grail as a vehicle for his own, early form of *Bildungsroman* where he could project a moral vision in which the 'grail' is associated with an ecumenical form of Oriental kinship linked to the fabulous name of Prester John.[41]

It is difficult to disagree with the judgement that 'all that the Grails of medieval romance have in common is the function of indicating a goal worth striving for or preserving, and in content at least a modicum of sanctity'.[42] In composing a romance on the quest theme Heinrich von dem Türlin was hardly bound by the constraints of a normative tradition, and introduces a number of notable innovations. Contrary to Wolfram's precedent of permitting Parzival alone to accede to Grail kingship, Heinrich follows the example of the First Continuation by rejecting Parzival and choosing Gawein as his protagonist. His attitude to Gawein is particularly positive since, unlike the Gauvain of the First Continuation who fails to mend the symbolic fissure in the Grail sword, Heinrich's Gawein is granted an intact sword from the old Grail king as a sign of the unqualified success of his quest.

This endorsement of Gawein (a figure not known elsewhere in legendary tradition as a knight of special spiritual distinction) implies an ambition to make the quester a more worldly knight than Wolfram's Parzival or the Galahad of the French prose tradition. Where the French prose romances promoted a theory of conduct frequently deriving from Biblical typology, Heinrich seems to have been more influenced by the spirit of some of the post-Chrétien verse romances which represent more nearly the exigencies of contemporary chivalry.[43] Against notions of the Grail quester as an ascetic or mystic, Heinrich gives a provocative encore to the traditionally somewhat amorous knight who plays an honorific role in many of the verse romances but who in the contemporary prose tradition fails to understand the signifi-

---

[40] 'swes lebn sich sô verendet,/daz got niht wirt gepfendet/der sêle durch des lîbes schulde,/und der doch der werlde hulde/behalten kan mit werdekeit,/daz ist ein nütziu arbeit' (*Parzival*, ed. Karl Lachmann, 6th edn, with modern German translation by Dieter Kühn and Commentary by Eberhard Nellmann (Frankfurt am Main: Deutscher Klasiker Verlag, 1994), section 827, lines 19–24).

[41] See Ulrich Knefelkamp, *Die Suche nach dem Reich des Priesterkönigs Johannes, dargestellt anhand von Reiseberichten und anderen ethnographischen Quellen des 12. Bis 17. Jahrhunderts* (Gelsenkirchen: Andreas Müller Verlag, 1986).

[42] A. T. Hatto (trans.), *Parzival* (Harmondsworth: Penguin, 1980), Foreword, p. 8.

[43] On the more pragmatic spirit of the verse romances see Keith Busby, *Gauvain in Old French Literature* (Amsterdam: Rodopi, 1980); and Beate Schmolke-Hasselmann, *The Evolution of Arthurian Romance. The Verse Tradition from Chrétien to Froissart*, trans. Roger and Margaret Middleton with Introduction by Keith Busby (Cambridge: Cambridge U.P., 1998).

cance of the Grail in his preoccupation with the physical beauty of the Grail bearer.[44] Heinrich von dem Türlin in fact appears to have shaped his own romance in part as a literary counterblast to the French Lancelot-Grail cycle.[45]

That highly influential sequence was written approximately between 1215 and 1225/30 and three of its five major narrative sequences (the *Lancelot proper, Queste del Saint Graal, Mort Artu*) were translated into German shortly afterwards. We know nothing of the author(s) of this work, but it was probably inspired by Cistercian spirituality which would account for the work being composed in prose[46] and for the prominence of the warrior–saint figure who is its hero. The cycle demonstrates how the centrifugal forces of sexual passion and treachery unravel the slender threads which hold together the Arthurian kingdom. Amplifying the tradition of a sexual triangle involving Arthur, Guinevere and Lancelot found in Chretien's *Le Chevalier de la Charrete*, it assimilates that tradition to the Grail story,[47] subjecting the *affaire* to particularly rigorous moral scrutiny by revealing how Lancelot's illicit liaison with the Queen dooms his grail mission to a failure only partly redeemed by the success of his son, Galahad. Galahad's individual success can however do little to halt the final dissolution of the kingdom brought about by Arthur's discovery of the adultery and the ensuing division amongst the knights.

Although the cycle as a whole is by no means always consistent in ethical tone the *Queste* and *Mort* sections of the French cycle imply a critique of secular chivalry. By interlacing the Grail material with the worldly story of Lancelot and Guinevere it produces a creative tension between the two narrative traditions and through its tragic conclusion creates a negative exemplum which trumpets the superiority of the spiritual to the secular life. Gauvain, in his element at the Court of Arthur, fails to grasp the nature of the Grail quest and falls into vain acts of slaughter of his peers. Arthur also appears as an anti-hero. At first refusing to face up to the reality of Guinevere's adultery, when he does eventually become convinced of her failing he cruelly threatens her with the stake. Thereafter, whilst bowing to the Pope's decree that he should take his wife back on peaceful terms, he still pursues his destructive feud with Lancelot, so that the physical death of Arthur at the end of the *Mort* section appears to be heralded in some part by his moral degradation.

---

44 Fanni Bogdanow, 'The character of Gauvain in the thirteenth-century prose romances', *Medium Aevum* 27 (1958), pp. 154–61.

45 See Elizabeth Andersen, 'Heinrich von dem Türlin's *Diu Crône* and the Prose *Lancelot*; an intertextual study', *Arthurian Studies* 7 (1987), pp. 23–49.

46 From the early decades of the thirteenth century French romances in prose began to gain greater popularity than metrical versions, prose being widely regarded as being more acceptable than verse for the conveying of spiritual truths. See E. Jane Burns, *Arthurian Fictions. Rereading the Vulgate Cycle* (Columbus: Ohio State University Press, 1985), and Norris J. Lacy, *The Lancelot-Grail Reader. Selections from the Medieval French Arthurian Cycle* (New York and London: Garland, 2000), Introduction.

47 On this process see Elspeth Kennedy, *Lancelot and the Grail. A Study of the Prose 'Lancelot'* (Oxford: Clarendon, 1986).

Neither Arthur himself nor any one of his habitual company is shown sympathetically in a work which attempts a radical redefinition of chivalric values according to Cistercian norms. It is rather the *novus homo*, Galahad, a figure unknown to Arthurian tradition before the thirteenth century, who successfully embodies the new doctrine that the best life is the one which inheres in the spirit and dies to the flesh. This is why, having achieved the consummation of witnessing the transubstantiated Jesus Christ appearing from the Grail chalice and having no more need of life on earth, he is made to expire in mystic contemplation. Galahad, overcoming his opponents but not killing them, stands for the pacific principles of the Cistercian order and he alone of all the knights can see the Grail 'apertement'. With its strong doctrinal underpinning the romance delivers a resounding sermon on the vanity of the Arthurian ideal.

Popular in its native France, only nine manuscripts of the translated German version are extant, none of them complete, compared with the more than one hundred French copies. The negligible influence which the German translation exerted on subsequent German literature (unlike the French version, it was never printed) indicates that its reception in Germany was less enthusiastic than in its native land, a fact which may be related to the idiosyncratic German reception of the Lancelot story as a whole. The first known Lancelot romance, Chrétien's *Le Chevalier de la Charrete*, was not translated into German (although there is an echo of it in an episode of Hartmann's *Iwein*).[48] The German *Lanzelet* by Ulrich von Zatzikhoven (c. 1195) depends on a different source and shows no acquaintance with the famous triangular relationship between Arthur, Guinevere and Lancelot. Ulrich's Lanzelet, so far from being an ardent and tormented lover, is a carefree sexual adventurer (although his tally of four conquests has been explained genetically by the supposition that the hero attracted to himself a series of independent *contes* ending in sexual congress with each of the heroines).[49] He is described as one constitutionally incapable of languishing in love[50] and the romance fails to engage with the kind of principled questions about love in society which we encounter in the tradition inaugurated by Chrétien. German audiences will therefore have had no opportunity to become exercised by the morally problematical tradition of a Lancelot succumbing to Guinevere's charms and becoming guilty of a breach of faith to his liege lord. Where French audiences may have seen this unhallowed tradition as being in need of firm moral resolution, and may have responded positively to the albeit harsh judgement sounded in the larger cyclic version, the translated version may have fallen

[48] See Frank Shaw, 'Die Ginoverentführung in Hartmanns *Iwein*', *ZfdA* 104 (1975), pp. 32–40.

[49] *Lanzelet*, trans. K. G. T. Webster with an Introduction by R. S. Loomis (New York: Columbia U.P., 1951), Introduction, p. 9.

[50] 'der niht enweiz waz trûren ist', K. A. Hahn (ed.), *Lanzelet* with a 'Nachwort' and Bibliography by Frederick Norman (Berlin: de Gruyter, 1965), line 1341.

on stony ground because it would not have been an eagerly awaited sequel. In Germany the theme of adulterous passion and its consequences did not become firmly linked with the Grail story because of a different process of canon-formation by dint of the writings of Wolfram von Eschenbach, whose *Parzival* (c. 1210) became the accredited German recreation of the Grail theme from the early thirteenth up to the mid-eighteenth century.[51] Some account of this influential work, in which Wolfram chose to give prominence to fictional representations of contemporary experiences of the Crusades, will be necessary to provide further clues as to why Heinrich, whilst not following Wolfram slavishly, nevertheless may have been influenced by the more cosmopolitan ethos of the first German Grail romance.

The early decades of the thirteenth century were a time of spiritual flux in Germany and it appears that Wolfram, who was a layman according to the testimony of Wirnt von Gravenberg,[52] may have harnessed the glamour of the Grail tradition to launch independent conceptions of his own having less to do with ecclesiastical legend than with new attitudes to the crusading enterprise which emerged in the decades after the publication of *Li Contes del Graal*. When in 1187 Saladin succeeded in reconquering Jerusalem without recourse to indiscriminate slaughter, many Europeans began to see their sectarian foe as a humane people hardly deserving of the demonising opprobrium heaped upon them by the Church orthodox. The lyric poet Albrecht von Johansdorf registers a new mood of sobriety running counter to the earlier crusading conviction that 'God wishes it so' (*De le vult*). He reports that many crusaders felt that, if God really wished to relieve Jerusalem, he would have resources enough of his own to do so without having to compel mortal foot-soldiers to do his work for him. The courtly moralist, Thomasin von Zerclaere, also writing in the first decades of the thirteenth century, records the opposition and even frank scepticism encountered by preachers for the crusades. 'Why does God allow the Muslims to win so many battles?' was a common question which led some Christians to question their faith.[53] An index of this changing mood was the legend which arose claiming Saladin to have been a crypto-Christian who had received the accolade of Christian knighthood.[54]

Although precise dating is not possible, it appears that Wolfram would have been composing parts of his *Parzival* just after the abortive Fourth

---

51 Claudia Wasielewski-Knecht, *Studien zur Parzival-Rezeption in Epos und Drama des 18.–20. Jahrhunderts* (Berne: Lang, 1993).

52 *Wigalois. Der Ritter mit dem Rade*, ed. J. M. N. Kapteyn, Rheinische Hülsbücher zur germanischen Philologie und Volkskunde, 9 (Bonn: Klopp, 1926), lines 6344–6347.

53 Elizabeth Siberry, *Criticism of Crusading 1095–1274* (Oxford: Clarendon, 1985).

54 A fictional account of how Saladin was dubbed by the Christian knight Hue de Tabarie is contained in the short French romance, *Ordene de Chevalerie*. See *Le Roman des Eles* and *Ordene de Chevalerie*, ed. Keith Busby (Amsterdam: Benjamins, 1983). The reported event is apocryphal although it is known that Richard Coeur de Lion knighted Saladin's brother, al-'Adil.

Crusade of 1204. The Christian/heathen issue must have preoccupied him because the whole narrative frame which he placed about Chrétien's incomplete romance was trained on this issue. No unitary source is known for Wolfram's first two books, in which we encounter Feirefiz, the half-caste son of Parzival's father through his union with the Moorish queen, Belakane. Symbolically Feirefiz plays a major role since it is he who is chosen by his half-brother to accompany him on his redemptive visit to the old Grail king, Anfortas. Parzival's choice would count as a decidedly 'affirmative action' in present-day parlance since the old Grail king openly voices his opposition to the presence of the 'speckled' Feirefiz, a minority figure on two counts, being both a non-Arthurian and non-Caucasian.[55] Parzival, by disregarding the old king's prejudice, shows that *his* Grail kingship is to be run on more tolerant lines. When we learn in Wolfram's version (for which continuation there is no hint in Chrétien), that the future son of Feirefiz and the Grail bearer, Repanse de Schoye, is to be Prester John, the apocryphal king of the Orient (who, by dint of a forged letter circulating in western Europe had achieved notoriety by the middle of the twelfth century),[56] we may suppose that the somewhat open genre of Grail romance was here being appropriated to project an independent ecumenical vision.

The latter stages of Wolfram's *Parzival* have little to do with the ecclesiastical version of the Grail legend in which the Grail is the dish of the Last Supper. Wolfram's version is more concerned with his hero's slow maturation and with the theme of how non-Christians can be peacefully assimilated. This is a subject which we know to have been of interest to liberal contemporaries seeking a *modus vivendi* with Muslim adversaries. It became a popular literary motif, recurring in *Wigalois* (c. 1210–15 or later), the work of a self-confessed admirer of Wolfram, Wirnt von Gravenberg, and in the *Jüngerer Titurel* (c. 1270) the work of a Bavarian continuator, Albrecht. Although writing an independent romance with fresh material, Wirnt presented a vision of an ideal Christian state based on Wolfram's own conceptions where the idea that Wolfram adumbrates symbolically through the figures of Feirefiz and Prester John is glossed more literally when the eponymous hero, after having defeated the Muslim necromancer, Roaz, preaches to Roaz's pagan subjects and leads them towards acceptance of the Christian faith through mass conversions. Albrecht too, whose *Jüngerer Titurel* – a conflation and continuation of Wolfram's *Parzival* and *Titurel* – was accepted as being Wolfram's own work up until the modern period, continued to give currency to the conception of the Oriental priest-king.

In light of indigenous appropriations and augmentations of the Grail tradition, the German translation of the *Lancelot* was probably perceived as an intellectual foreign body. Encountering this Cistercian reconceptualisation of

---

[55] *Parzival*, ed. Lachmann , section 795, lines 17–19.
[56] See Knefelkamp, *Die Suche nach dem Reich des Priesterkönings Johannes.*

the Arthurian story, German audiences might well have balked at the whole-sale perdition of the *Mort Artu* and, rather like Malory's audiences at a later date, have found themselves resenting the knights being judged 'according to a set of religious principles we (and they) had no reason to suspect counted for so much'.[57] It is not then surprising that Heinrich rejected the implications of this 'anti-romance in which the (Arthurian) stage is set and so are the players, but all the accepted values are inverted'.[58] Yet he also denounces Parzival, Wolfram's protagonist, a crux which has puzzled students of *Diu Crône* for a century and a half[59] and which therefore requires considerably more explanation.

References to the character of Parzival in *Diu Crône* are relentlessly nega-tive. His failure to ask the question at the Grail castle in Wolfram's version (knowledge of which Heinrich presupposes in his audience) is adduced as the cause of his failure in the first of the tests of honour in *Diu Crône* (lines 2210–15) and his failing is thereafter dwelt on persistently. Parzival would have done better to keep to his rustic retreat, opines Heinrich in an allusion to Parzival's youth in rural Wales in Wolfram's version. He does not possess the heroic stature of Gawein whom he would have viewed as a god, continues Heinrich in a reference to Wolfram's passage where the unenlightened Parzival erroneously takes three passing knights to be gods and abases himself in front of them in an attitude of worship.[60] Previous generations of scholars sought to explain Heinrich's prejudice in genetic terms, claiming that he might have known only the early phases of Wolfram's romance which depict the hero's omission but not its rectification. A majority of modern scholars however think that Heinrich knew the whole of *Parzival*, a judge-ment which receives textual support from the otherwise sharp-tongued Kei's concession that the *mature* Parzival succeeded in making amends for his youthful faults (*Crône*, lines 24,607–15).

Heinrich's hostile reception of Wolfram's protagonist suggests that he chose to be selective in his perceptions, tactically overlooking the later stages of Parzival's maturation when, after the encounter with Trevrizent, Parzival not only asks the compassionate question but also all unbidden performs a second act of compassion in taking his 'heathen' brother Feirefiz to meet the Grail king in the final Book. The substantive issue for Heinrich is not compas-sion or the lack of it but what he sees as Parzival's lack of valour, that quality with which he liberally endows Gawein and which the old Grail king adduces as being the single factor which allows Gawein to succeed in the

---

57 Terence McCarthy, *Reading the 'Morte Darthur'*, Arthurian Studies 20 (Cambridge: D. S. Brewer, 1988), p. 43.

58 Pauline Matarasso (trans.), *The Quest of the Holy Grail* (Harmondsworth: Penguin, 1969), p. 15.

59 See August Zingerle, 'Wolfram von Eschenbach und Heinrich vom Türlein', *Germania* 5 (1860), pp. 468–79 and E. K. Heller, 'A vindication', p. 78.

60 *Crône*, lines 6372–6393; *Parzival*, 120, 27–121, 2.

quest where Parzival had failed.[61] By dissociating himself from the ascetic strain informing the standard French version and from the liberal ideology informing the standard German rendition of his material, Heinrich gives notice of an intention to write a version of the Grail story which honours Wolfram's deuteragonist considerably more liberally than his protagonist.[62] The implications of Heinrich's partisanship will be considered below where the attempt will be made to analyse the nature of the narrative which arose from this double rejection.

---

[61] *Crône*, lines 29,462–513.

[62] *Diu Crône*, it has been remarked recently, presents 'the most favourable portrayal of Gawein in German literature' (Bart Besamusca, article on 'Gawain' in *A Dictionary of Literary Heroes. Characters in Medieval Narrative Traditions and their Afterlife in Literature, Theatre and the Visual Arts*, trans. Tanis Guest (Woodbridge; Boydell Press, 1998), pp. 113–20, citation 117). On Heinrich's prejudice against Wolfram's Parzival see the special study of Ralph Read, 'Heinrich von dem Türlin's *Diu Krône* and Wolfram's *Parzival*', *Modern Language Quarterly* 35 (1974), pp. 129–39 and chapter 6 of the present work.

2

Arthurian Enigma

For while he linger'd there,
A doubt that ever smoulder'd in the hearts
Of those great Lords and Barons of his realm
Flash'd forth and into war: for most of these,
Colleaguing with a score of petty kings,
Made head against him, crying, 'Who is he
That he should rule us? Who hath proven him
King Uther's son? For lo! We look at him,
And find nor face nor bearing, limbs nor voice,
Are like to those of Uther whom we knew.

(Tennyson, *Idylls of the King*)

Before people began to believe in 'progress', patterns of perfection were invariably taken from one or other 'golden age' imagined to have existed in the past. Heinrich's predecessor, Wirnt von Gravenberg, exploited the legendary Arthurian era in ways which are indistinguishable from his use of the Carolingian age. His eponymous hero's subjects are commended to obey 'Karles reht'[1] in the same way as the narrator holds up the idealised morals of a fictional Arthurian culture as worthy of emulation. There is little awareness of an epistemologically distinct world inhabited by Arthur, and the equation of the two kings indicates that the same ontological status was assigned to Arthur as to Charlemagne. The nineteenth-century conception of historical truth as a form of philosophical absolute was a late development in European consciousness and many medieval writers would use pseudo-historical data opportunistically as it served their turn. Hence we may infer that the provenance of his material, whether 'historical' or otherwise, was of less moment to Wirnt's moralist narrator than its capacity to furnish him with fitting examples. If, like Hartmann von Aue, Wirnt had a notion of the cult of Arthur as a pious fraud,[2] he did not reveal it.

---

1   *Wigalois, Der Ritter mit dem Rade*, ed. Kapteyn, line 9554.
2   As suggested by the reserve in his reference to the fabulous king at the beginning of his *Iwein*. See *Iwein*, ed. G. F. Benecke and others with modern German translation by Thomas Cramer, 2nd edn (Berlin: de Gruyter, 1974), lines 1–20 and Hans Fromm, 'Komik und Humor in der deutschen Dichtung des Mittelalters', *DVLG* 36 (1962), pp. 321–39.

With the benefit of modern scholarship we can state that the fictionalised Charlemagne cycle was based on historical foundations; but it is uncertain whether there was even an historical nucleus to the Arthurian cycle. We do not know whether the figure described in the ninth-century *Historia Brittonum* and tenth-century *Annales Cambriae* was an historical or fictional figure – possibly a protective folk hero whom the chroniclers chose to locate in history. It is possible to posit a sequence for the development of the Arthur saga in which a fictional warrior became historicised and, through various pseudo-historical accretions, attracted to himself the victories of historical persons such as Ambrosius, the 'original' victor of the *bellum memorabile* at Badon.[3] This process of spurious historicisation, beginning in the early ninth century with the *Historia Brittonum*, would then have been continued by Geoffrey of Monmouth in his *Historia Regum Britanniae* of 1138 which played such a large part in the wider, Continental dissemination.

Geoffrey's 'pseudo-history of great imaginative power'[4] was the most influential literary product of the Anglo-Norman period. Its author refers to himself as a *Brito*, which in the twelfth century could mean a Welshman, Breton or an inhabitant of Cornwall,[5] and although we cannot be sure of Geoffrey's precise ethnic status, a rich vein of Celtic fancy appears to run through his sweep of nineteen centuries of insular history. Noting the relative silence about the period preceding the advent of the English in the works of William of Malmesbury and Henry of Huntington, Geoffrey asserts the Trojan pedigree of the Britons, bestowing on them as ancient and honourable a title as that of Rome itself. The author of British birth who writes ostensibly to call attention to the neglected kings of the indigenous people also produces a work pleasing to the Anglo-Norman ruling class[6] in that it maintains that the common ancestry of the various peoples of the Angevin empire is a branch of the Trojan stock which also founded imperial Rome.

Although Geoffrey's hero was in the strict sense Britain rather than Arthur, it was the large Arthurian section of his *Historia* which proved the most influential. It not only produced a powerful national hero for the inhabitants of these islands but also captured the wider European imagination. Geoffrey's *Historia* notoriously fails to meet modern standards of historiographical rigour, falling well below the standard of his sober colleagues William of

---

3   Oliver Padel, 'The nature of Arthur', *Cambrian Medieval Celtic Studies* 27 (1994), pp. 1–31.
4   Neil Wright, *The Historia Regum Britanniae of Geoffrey of Monmouth*, 2 vols (Cambridge: D. S. Brewer, 1985), vol. 1, Preface, p. xii.
5   A Breton lord, Wihenoc, founded a priory in Monmouth in 1075 and it is possible to imagine Geoffrey – who was appointed Bishop of St Asaph in 1152 – as being part of an influential Breton entourage.
6   The desire to flatter Norman overlords is evident in the multiple dedications of his volume to Robert of Gloucester, Waleran of Meulan and King Stephen who came to power after the death of Henry I in 1135. See Wright, xii–xvi.

Malmesbury and Henry of Huntington,[7] but despite or perhaps because of that inadequacy it became a fount of inspiration for Chrétien de Troyes and subsequent French and German writers of 'romances' (a fictional genre which Geoffrey's imaginative Latin prose epic had done much to anticipate).

At this 'Continental' stage of legendary development, with the British chieftain seamlessly inducted into the cultural milieu of feudal kings,[8] pretences to historicity are dropped. Once detached from his political role as a Hammer of the Anglian invaders, Arthur becomes a merely 'romantic' figure, his knights depoliticised and their feats 'dissociated from past and future (with) little attempt to place the particular events within Arthur's reign.'[9] In contradistinction to the more active, and thus ostensibly 'younger' Arthur fighting alongside his troops represented in the twelfth-century chronicles of Geoffrey and Wace, Arthur henceforth becomes a somewhat sedentary figure.

Although he is regularly festooned with honorific epithets, there is nevertheless in Chrétien's works a remarkable disparity between the author's formal panegyrics of the king and his actual conduct[10] – a disparity which the French author might possibly have made explicit had it been granted to him to finish his *Conte du Graal*. The king's irresolute conduct at the beginning of *Erec* (where he persists with arranging a beauty contest despite Gauvain's warnings that this could cause invidious divisions at Court) and his bizarre conduct in *Le Chevalier de la Charrete* (where he contrives to be both weak and over-rigid in his dealings with the hostile Meleagant)[11] lead to the suspicion that depictions of Arthur were beginning to draw on the negative tradition of the *rex inutilis*.[12] The somewhat paradoxical result of this trend is that the titular *fons et origo* of Arthurian chivalry becomes a somewhat déclassé figure rather like the Etzel of the *Nibelungenlied* (whose indecisive conduct in that epic would give few hints to the uninitiated that he had in an earlier, historical incarnation been the feared Attila of the Huns).

The process of 'epic degeneration' is common enough, but in the case of so highly vaunted a figure as Arthur the phenomenon would inevitably have led to cognitive dissonances amongst audiences led to question how the unimpressive Arthur had been able to achieve the status of role model of

---

7   The veracity of Geoffrey's work was called into question only decades after his death by William of Newburgh, who roundly accused him of lying. His claim to have translated his material from an ancient book written in the British tongue given to him by Walter, Archdeacon of Oxford, is widely taken to be a 'symbolic' use of language.

8   Chrétien enjoyed the patronage of both Marie de Champagne and Philip of Flanders.

9   Elspeth Kennedy, 'The narrative techniques used to give Arthurian romance a "historical" flavour', in *Conjunctions. Medieval Studies in Honor of Douglas Kelly*, ed. Keith Busby and Norris J. Lacy (Amsterdam: Rodopi, 1994), pp. 219–33, citation 219.

10 Hugh Sacker, 'An interpretation of Hartmann's *Iwein*', *Germanic Review* 36 (1961), pp. 5–26.

11 He lets himself be manoeuvred by Keu into allowing the seneschal to escort Guinevere to his enemy, Meleagant, which indirectly leads to her abduction.

12 Edward Peters, *The Shadow King. Rex Inutilis in Medieval Law and Literature* (New Haven and London: Yale University Press), esp. pp. 170–209.

feudal Europe. To be sure, the Galfridian conception story, with its mythic parallels[13] and its powerful narrative ingredients of unhallowed lust and physical metamorphosis, provided a stirring enough launch for the *infant* Arthur, but cannot have compensated entirely for the dearth of traditions involving the *young* Arthur. With such a frustrating gap at the heart of Arthurian tradition it is unsurprising that one of Heinrich's contemporaries, Der Stricker, in his *Daniel von dem blühenden Tal*, should aspire to foreground the biography of the king himself to tell something of those formative influences which were to lead to the king's later renown:

> ich kunde wol getiuten
> wes er (sc. Arthur) pflac in sîner jugent.
> ich weiz wol, ob ich sîne tugent
> mit worten gar her für züge,
> man spraeche, ich tobte alder lüge.
> dâvon wil ich lützel davon sagen
> und wil es doch niht gar verdagen.[14]

> (I could well tell you of Arthur's youthful deeds (but) I know very well that, if I were indeed to present his superlative qualities to you in words, people would say I was a madman or a liar. For that reason I shall say little about his early years – and yet I won't be silent on the matter altogether.)

These enigmatic words are commonly taken to be a bluff, for Stricker's *Daniel* largely concerns the help given by the eponymous hero to an already mature Arthur; yet there is nothing theoretically implausible about the desire for 'backward expansion' to fill in a legendary lacuna. The early thirteenth century was a particularly productive literary era 'when writers were no longer content to produce a series of unconnected romances as did Chrétien de Troyes, but wished to combine them in coherent groups, making them part of a larger scheme and filling in where necessary gaps in the tradition'.[15] The inspiration for a coherent scheme of romances appears to have lain with the Burgundian knight, Robert de Boron (composing between c. 1191 and c. 1212). Where Chrétien in his three self-standing Arthurian romances had made little attempt to explain the origins of the Grail or to produce a chronicle of Arthur's reign, Robert, using the resources of Church legend, set the 'Arthurian' era within a framework of universal story by initiating a trilogy

---

13 There may be Classical echoes in the conception story. According to Hyginus, whilst Amphytrion was away at war, the disguised Jupiter took his place in the bed of his wife, Alcmene, their union resulting in the birth of Hercules. See Rosemary Morris, *The Character of King Arthur in Medieval Literature* (Cambridge: D. S. Brewer, 1982), p. 34.

14 *Daniel von dem blühenden Tal*, ed. Michael Resler, ATB 92 (Tübingen, 1983), lines 52–58.

15 Fanni Bogdanow, *The Romance of the Grail. A Study of the Structure and Genesis of a Thirteenth-Century Prose Romance* (Manchester: Manchester U.P.; New York: Barnes and Noble, 1966), p. 1.

which tells the history of the Grail from apostolic times up to the time of Arthur. Of the trilogy, only the first part, the *Joseph*, or *Le Roman de l'Estoire dou Graal*, and 502 lines of the second part, the *Merlin*, have survived in their original verse form, but Robert's work was appropriated by successors who prepared the future downfall of the kingdom by introducing Oedipal conflicts into Arthur's past. These are fated to lead towards internecine tragedy, for whereas Mordred in Geoffrey's *Historia* was Arthur's nephew, he is recast as Arthur's incestuous son, making the king a hostage to the irresistible laws of *mescheance*.[16]

According to Robert, Merlin claimed the issue of the illicit union of Uther and Ygraine (Ygerne) and baptised him with the name Arthur, subsequently sending the boy to be brought up secretly out in the country with the knight Antor and his wife together with their son, Keu. Subsequent accounts relate how, thinking himself Antor's natural son, Arthur did not know of the existence of his three half-sisters (Ygraine's daughters by her first husband, the Cornish Duke Gorlois) of whom the eldest, Morgause, was married to King Lot of Orkney and was the mother of Gauvain. Following an uneasy interregnum after the death of Uther, Arthur asserts his right to kingship through the well-known sword-in-the-stone challenge. Not knowing the identity of the successful pretender, and disbelieving Merlin's reassurances as to Arthur's ancestry, Lot and other barons contest Arthur's right to kingship. At length however the rebel barons drop their opposition and Lot sends his wife, Morgause, as an ambassador to Arthur with his four sons, the eldest of whom is Gauvain. Not realising that she is his half-sister, Arthur makes love to her, prompting Merlin to predict that she would give birth to a son, Mordred, who would one day destroy his father and all his knights.

The full Lancelot–Grail sequence into which Robert's work was drawn evidences a reverse chronology where 'those parts of the cycle which deal with beginnings in narrative chronology tend in fact to be composed last in literary-historical chronology'.[17] Such is the case with the *Estoire del Saint Graal* and *Merlin* parts of the French *Lancelot* cycle which stand first according

16 The wider epic context is that Merlin prophesies that Mordred will be born on May Day, prompting Arthur to cast adrift all children born on that day, but Mordred escapes from the storm-tossed boat and is brought up by friendly fisher folk. Lot, reasonably assuming that Mordred had died in the storm, resumes his hostilities with Arthur, but is killed by one of Arthur's supporters, Pellinor, for which Gauvain takes revenge ten years later. On the concept of *mescheance* in contradistinction to moral culpability see Faith Lyons, 'La Mort le Roi Artu: an Interpretation', in *The Legend of Arthur in the Middle Ages. Studies Presented to A.H. Diverres*, ed. P. B. Grout, R. A. Lodge, C. E. Pickford and E. K. C. Varty (Woodbridge: D. S. Brewer, 1983), pp. 138–48, and Karen Pratt, 'La Mort le Roi Artu as tragedy', *Nottingham French Studies* 30 (1991), pp. 81–109.

17 Jane Taylor, 'Order from accident: cyclic consciousness at the end of the Middle Ages', in *Cyclification. The Development Of Narrative Cycles in the Chansons De Geste and the Arthurian Romances*, ed. Bart Besamusca, Willem P. Gerritsen, Corry Hogetoorn and Orlanda S. H. Lie (North-Holland, Amsterdam, Oxford, New York, Tokyo: Royal Netherlands Academy of Arts and Sciences, 1994), pp. 59–73, citation 65.

to the narrative chronology of the sequence but which were composed after the other three, being retrospective attempts to explain the sacred power of the Grail and to fill in details of Arthur's early education and accession to kingship respectively. Heinrich von dem Türlin also promises a new chronological perspective to tell of Arthur's earlier years in terms similar to but not identical with those of the French proto-histories:

> Uns ist dicke geseit
> Von maneger hant vrümekeit,
> Die Artûs der künec begienc.
> Wâ ez sich êrste anevienc,
> Daz ist ein teil unkunt,
> Ich wil ez aber ze dirre stunt
> Ein teil machen kunder
> Und wil iu doch dar under
> Sîner tugende anegenge sagen,
> Wie ez in sînen kinttagen
> Im aller êrste ergienge,
> Sîner tugende loblîcher strît,
> Den ime noch diu werlt gît.   (lines 161–74)

> (We have been told often enough of the valiant deeds performed by Arthur, but how things began is largely unknown. Now I will make matters a little clearer and tell of the beginnings of his knightly renown and of how he fared in his earlier years, how he contended for valour in ways which are still commemorated by posterity.)

Heinrich's promise to outline something of Arthur's earlier biography clearly arouses eager expectations, but, like Stricker, he has been suspected of bad faith. Many modern readers, when confronted early in the text with such vague details as that Arthur enjoyed the respect of all in his youth, that no failing of whatever sort was to be found in him, and that he acted as a role model to all future generations capable of responding to his example (lines 182–216), have at that point come to the swift conclusion that Heinrich had little or no new material at his disposal. Suchlike exordial matter, it has been objected, could have been culled from earlier romances such as the beginning of Hartmann's *Iwein* (lines 1–20), from which the lapidary praise of Arthur as one whose fame far outlived his death might have been taken, or else it could have been simply made up ad hoc.

The latter may well have been the case. That Heinrich should have been thrown back largely on his own resources to construct a story of Arthur's early reign is hardly surprising since only the most minimal data concerning the king's early life can be gleaned even from the chronicle tradition of Geoffrey of Monmouth and Wace. In fact, the details supplied by Heinrich concerning Arthur's loss of his father, Uther, and the contention that he underwent his knightly investiture and took his queen when he was only fifteen (lines 314–30; 423–24) do not add substantially to the information which we derive from a reading of the Arthurian sections of the *Historia Regum Britanniae* and of Wace's *Roman de Brut*. Heinrich's contribution here is indeed meagre.

It has, however, not been adequately noted that Heinrich's 'stage direction' cited above claims to tell us of Arthur's *kinttage*, a term which at the medieval stage of the language may refer to the period of young manhood[18] (in contra-distinction to its more restricted semantic range in modern German). Read with due attention to that chronological nuance, the verses cited above may be glossed as a promise to tell not so much of the boyhood deeds (which are indeed treated cursorily) but rather to develop the story of the young man who, we are told, had lost the father who was to educate him at the age of six (lines 313–15) and who has the responsibilities of a crown and a wife to contend with 'Nach vunfzehen jaren' (line 422). Those twin rites of passage, we are repeatedly told (lines 4807, 10777, 10933) had taken place 'seven years ago', which would make the Arthur of *Diu Crône* a man in his early twenties. Heinrich's aim is to narrate 'Sîner tugende anegenge' (line 170), that is, the youth's acquisition of adult chivalric qualities. In this aspiration Heinrich was on considerably firmer ground than Stricker whose knowledge of French tradition was considerably less and whose habit of assigning French names to characters was probably merely 'a conscious attempt to align his self-conceived work more convincingly with the French tradition (and) to induce audiences to accept more readily the assertion of a French source'.[19] Heinrich, by contrast, was deeply versed not only in Chrétien but also in the works of those successors which had already fleshed out many of Chrétien's narrative silences. Heinrich's narrative perspective is in fact somewhat similar to that of the anonymous continuator of the Prose *Merlin* who 'apparently felt the need for filling the gap between the youth and coronation of Arthur and his apogee'.[20]

In medieval literature 'the name "Arthur" comports a world, and any author who uses it means to evoke something of that world'.[21] Since in the course of previous literary tradition those regal qualities had typically been evidenced not through individualistic exploits but rather within the collective

---

18 In *Wigalois*, for instance, the testing messenger, Nereja, wishes at first to turn down the services of the eponymous young hero on the grounds that he is simply a 'kint', i.e. a young knight lacking the experience of Gawein, his father: 'si vorhte daz si ir arbeit/verlür von sîner kintheit/ durch daz er sô junc was'. See *Wigalois, Der Ritter mit dem Rade*, ed. Kapteyn, lines 1816–18; Matthias Lexer/ Ulrich Pretzel gloss M.H.G. *kint* as '*knappe, juncherre, aber auch nach dem ritterschlag, ja in der ehe können junge männer u. frauen noch kint heissen*', *Mittelhochdeutsches Taschenworterbuch* (Stuttgart: Hirzel, 1974).

19 Michael Resler (trans.), *Daniel of the Blossoming Valley*, Garland Library of Medieval Literature Series B, vol. 58 (London and New York: Garland, 1990, Introduction, pp. xxviii–ix.

20 Alexandre Micha, 'The Vulgate Merlin', in *Arthurian Literature in the Middle Ages. A Collaborative History*, ed. R. S. Loomis (Oxford: Clarendon, 1959), pp. 319–24, citation 322.

21 Rosemary Morris, *Character of King Arthur*, p. 2.

context of a knightly fellowship (to which Arthur contributes typically not through active military engagements but rather in an executive role), Heinrich must needs here be using Arthur's name in a metonymic sense as a portmanteau term referring not only to the person but also to the wider culture of 'Camelot'. Through use of Arthur's proper name the narrator would appear to announce his ambition to tell of the rise of the whole Court rather than simply of the person.

According to the terms of Heinrich's aside cited above (lines 161–74), *Diu Crône* is to be a biographical romance in the special sense that it will chart the young King's rise to his present (literary) preeminence. Since previous writers had bequeathed upon him no standard corpus of traditions about Arthur's early career, Heinrich would naturally have been obliged to resort to the only route open to him or indeed to any other contemporary writer: that of creating an imaginative form of 'De Ortu (Regni) Arturi' through the eclectic use of such traditions as *were* known to him. Fortunately for Heinrich, his work bears witness to a more than ordinarily extensive knowledge of various Arthurian traditions in both German and French which he seems to have been able to reforge in ways which advance at least a plausible claim to be charting an early period of a young king's reign. The attempt will be made to assess how Heinrich went about realising that claim, paying particular attention to ways in which he attempted to reorganise and reconceptualise the accepted sequence of Arthurian story.

A notable pendant to the lines 161–74 occurs in what appears to be a programmatic and possibly polemical excursus giving further notice of the ambition to tell a version of the beginnings of the Arthurian reign. In verses referring to the demise of the legendary kingdom, we are told that not even Arthur, however well blessed he had once been by Fortuna and the Fates, could resist indefinitely the unwelcome ministrations of that celestial power, Atropos:

> Daz hâte im vrouwe Clôtô
> Sô erteilet allen wîs
> Daz er werltlîchen prîs
> Vor aller werlde trüege.
> Ouch was vil gefüege/
> Vrouwe Lachesis dar an
> Daz sie den vadem lange span.
> Ich clage aber, daz Atropos
> Disen vadem niht verkôs
> Und in sô schiere abe brach
> Dar an der werlt geschach
> Ein unvertregelîcher schade;
> Nu sitzet eine ûf dem rade
> Ane erben vrowe Fortûne.   (lines 286–99)

(Lady Clotho had bestowed this upon him (sc. the gift of making people happy) so that he might enjoy greater worldly renown than all his peers. Lady Lachesis, too, was very generous to him in the way she span out the thread of his life. But I lament the fact that Atropos did not drop that thread, thereby causing this world an insupportable loss, for now Fortuna sits alone on her Wheel without an heir.)

The image of Arthur ousted from Fortuna's Wheel will have been inspired by the king's famous premonitory dream in the *Mort Artu* where, on the eve of the final battle, Arthur dreams that he has been dashed to the ground by Fortune's Wheel.[22] This conception of the Arthurian Court as one subject ultimately to the vicissitudes of (ill) fortune – which is essentially the theme of the *Mort Artu* part of the Lancelot–Grail cycle – clearly depended on knowledge of a more developed stage of the evolution of the Arthurian story than that utilised by Heinrich's more famous German predecessors. The death of Arthur, even though it was first narrated in the twelfth century by Geoffrey of Monmouth and Wace, did not exercise an immediate influence on the first wave of French romance writers and their German adapters. Literary preoccupation with Arthur's final battle and the downfall of the chivalrous kingdom due to marital infidelity and political treachery was not a theme treated by Ulrich von Zatzikhoven, Hartmann von Aue, Wolfram von Eschenbach or Wirnt von Gravenberg, all of whom typically foregrounded knights other than Arthur himself against a quasi-timeless Arthurian backdrop. It was only in later works such as the great Lancelot cycle and the Didot *Perceval* that the timeless spell of the Chrétien/Hartmann tradition was broken and a more naturalistic chronological perspective involving a rise and fall pattern introduced.

Since it is probable that both the above French works were known to Heinrich, it appears that he may have chosen to respond to the challenge of the more open, wider focus of the evolving legend by deciding upon a fresh perspective of his own for the developing subject of Arthur's biography. The elegiac tone of the verses cited above suggests that knowledge of the theme of the Destruction of Camelot may have kindled in him the determination to plan his own composition not as yet another *Mort Artu* derivative but rather as a more constructive literary experiment in which he would chronicle the rise of the Arthurian world. It is possible that *Diu Crône*, in which a considerable preoccupation with the Wheel of Fortune motif is evident and where Heinrich's Gawein in a sense 'regains' for his King the favour of Fortuna which Arthur lost in the course of the Old French prose cycle, may have been designed in some sense as a riposte to the tragic tone of the *Mort Artu*.

Since tragedy affronts desires for meaning and continuity, it was the prac-

---

[22] Ed. Jean Frappier, *La Mort le Roi Artu: Roman du XIIIe Siècle*, 3rd edn (Geneva: Droz, 1959, sections 176, 177.

tice of some medieval continuators to supply conciliatory endings to tragic works. Such was the case with the poet of the *Klage*, who constructed an imaginative sequel to the *Nibelungenlied* in which the literary ghosts of the old epic are laid to rest and hope for the future generated through the coronation of the son of Gunther and Brünhilde. Had Heinrich followed the example of the *Klage* poet and made the avoidance of tragedy his primary goal, it would place him retrospectively among that group of writers mocked by Wolfram for their facile preoccupation with Arthur as the perennial 'May King' ('der meienbaere man').[23] However, Heinrich's early narratorial aside lamenting Arthur's death at the hands of the Fates provides clear testimony of his sceptical attitude towards the myth of Arthur's physical return. Although Heinrich did not choose to *foreground* the Downfall of Camelot theme, he was clearly too well-versed in French tradition to escape the eschatological impli-cations of the *Mort Artu* theme and, albeit apprised of the fact that the thread of Arthur's life would eventually be severed, wished to leave the *Götterdämmerung* of the Arthurian world to other writers.

It becomes clear, however, that the author has no intention of composing a facile chronicle of chivalric idealism in which the imagined Camelot would represent the best of all possible courtly worlds. Arthur's status as an ideal feudal monarch is initially problematical and must first be established within the text itself. The king himself is shown to be painfully aware of this unfortu-nate state of affairs when he roundly curses the all-too abundant blessings bequeathed on him by his late father, Uther Pendragon. Arthur's funerary oration for his father reveals the profound feelings of inadequacy felt by a son who sees his father (*pace* the chronicle tradition of Geoffrey and Wace where Uther is a purely defensive warrior against the Saxons) as the great conqueror of many lands which have now fallen automatically and rather too effort-lessly under his own jurisdiction.[24] How could he, Arthur, ever come up to the standard of such an all-conquering forebear?

> Daz ist mîn sendiu riuwe,
> Daz er (sc. Uther) mich so gerîchet hat,
> Wan mîn lop dar an zergât.
> Disiu lant sint mîn eigen
> Von iu, vater, niht von mir.
> Sô ungelîche ziehen wir,
> Des muoz ich unwirde,
> Sô ich ze manne wirde,
> Dulden unde schande.

---

23 *Parzival*, ed. Lachmann, 281, 16.
24 On the social implications of the loss of a father in feudal society see Donald Maddox, 'Lévi-Strauss in Camelot: interrupted communication in Arthurian feudal fictions', in *Culture and the King. The Social Implications of the Arthurian Legend*, ed. Martin B. Schichtman and James P. Carley (Albany: State University of New York, 1994), pp. 35–53.

Bin ich disem lande
Durch reht ein lützel wert,
Ez enhete betwungen mîn swert,
Mich prîset cleines lobes wert.   (lines 398–411)

(I deeply regret that I acquired all my power from Uther since his prestige far eclipses my own. These lands, Father, are only mine through
you. Our ways are so palpably different that I shall have to endure
considerable dishonour when I come of age. Even though the law
assigns me some honour, I have not won it with my own sword, so
that honour is considerably the less.)

Despite some bland assurances that Arthur had been the ward of Fortuna in
his youth (lines 412–20), the early part of *Diu Crône* contains few suggestions
that his Court had invariably found favour with that deity.[25] On the contrary,
the early stages of the romance contain some intriguingly discordant
scenarios from which Arthur emerges not as a well-favoured paragon but
rather as a beleaguered king with feet of clay:

Born under a favourable star sign in the month of May, Arthur nevertheless
tasted tragedy at the age of six with the death of his father. On Christmas Day
seven years after his marriage and accession he arranges for a great tournament to take place to which many foreign kings and knights are invited. Although Guinevere is disappointed that her husband and his knights are not as
quick to tourney as their guests, presently Arthur, Erec, Lanzelet, Gawein and
the other knights throw themselves into the fray. Their exertions over, the
knights sit down to eat at the feast. To this Yuletide scene comes the emissary
of a distant ruler, King Priure, with a goblet having the power to discover any
hidden lack of integrity in man or woman by spilling tell-tale drops of wine in
their laps. Priure's representative says he brings it to Camelot on behalf of his
king to test whether the honour of Arthur's Court is as well-founded as is
commonly supposed. Should the test bring dishonour to the Court, says the
emissary, its good name could still be regained if a member of the entourage
could defeat him in combat. None of the courtiers except Arthur is able to
drink of the goblet without spilling its wine, a dishonour which is compounded when Kei is trounced when offering a knightly challenge to the emissary.

Following this reverse, Gawein surreptitiously leads away the majority of
the knights to take part in a tournament elsewhere, leaving the unsuspecting
Arthur with only the remnant of Kei, Gales and Aumagwin. After finding out
about the deception, Arthur angrily convenes a hunting expedition with his
remaining companions. The rigours of the season soon impel him to return to
Court where he warms himself by the fireside. There he is mocked by his wife

---

[25] Arthur's mortal enemy, Gasozein, claims with considerable justice that *he* is the recipient
of the Goddess's favour against Arthur (lines 4769–74), quite reasonably viewing his
ability to prove that he is the rightful consort of Guinevere as being evidence of Fortuna's
providential direction of his own life.

for soft ways which contrast unfavourably with those of a man 'known to her' who rides out lightly clad in all seasons singing love songs. Stung by the reproach, Arthur sets out again with the three companions in the freezing weather to find out if the stranger knight really exists. The latter turns out to be real enough and when challenged by Arthur's companions, proceeds to defeat the three of them despite his wearing no protective gear. To Arthur he agrees to reveal his name – Gasozein de Dragoz – and the fact that he was the first love of Queen Guinevere, whom he now reclaims as his own. To support his claim he reveals a magic ring received as a gift from Guinevere. After an inconclusive passage of arms Arthur and Gasozein arrange a later meeting when they would both be fully armed and able to contest fairly the issue of which man should possess Guinevere. Gasozein rides off but Arthur and his defeated knights, upset by their encounter, indulge in brittle raillery at each other's expense which threatens the cohesion of even that small group. A fresh solidarity is however found when Arthur confesses his fears about his wife to his fellows and informs them about the impending duel with the stranger. Shortly thereafter all the knights who had absented themselves from Court return with the exception of Gawein, who devotes himself to further solo exploits.

Read in the light of the narrator's early aside, the initial positioning of the satirical tests of chastity/nobility administered by the emissary of King Priure together with the rich and unblushing descriptions of the triangular relationship between Arthur, Guinevere and Gasozein tend rather to underline the rather hesitant beginnings from which the mature Arthurian order was obliged to emerge. For Priure's messenger in *Diu Crône* does not adhere to the common romance convention according to which a testing emissary comes to try preeminently one individual knight of the entourage (as does for instance Cundrie when she denounces the eponymous hero of Wolfram's *Parzival*). Rather do the messenger's tests (from which no single courtier is spared) serve to diagnose a far more widespread malaise throughout Arthurian ranks, the probative power of the tests themselves being maliciously augmented by Kei's acidulous analyses of each courtier's errant soul – all of which yields a moral profile of the whole Arthurian household glossed *in malam partem* by the misanthropic Kei – who here as elsewhere in contemporary literature appears to be half gratuitous court jester and half shrewd *merkaere*. Early on we are led to conclude that there is much that is amiss within an Arthurian Court which, when put to the test, turns out to be 'filled with liars, cheats, hypocrites, braggarts and the like'[26] – a theme which may have derived in part from a morally rigorous reading of the romances of Heinrich's 'classical' predecessors.

26 George Edward Harding, 'Tradition and creativity: narrative elements in Wirnt von Gravenberg's *Wigalois* and Heinrich von dem Türlin's *Diu Crône*', dissertation, University of Tennessee, 1985 (Ann Arbor: University Microfilms International, 1987), p. 121.

Neither Hartmann nor Wolfram portrays Camelot as a distant idyll whose values may safely be left unexamined, and an idealised view of the Court could hardly have seemed tenable to a writer so deeply versed in Arthurian tradition as Heinrich. The convention of a flawed hero inaugurated by Chrétien and followed by Hartmann had revealed potential tensions in the knightly system of values and a critical reader would inevitably have been prompted to ponder the problems to which adherence to those values gave rise. When the heroes of Hartmann and Wolfram are not involved in probing their own consciences, there are external critics enough to discover any lack of moral resolve: Hartmann's Iwein goes through the early part of his career in dread of the ever-watchful Kei's mockery, and Gawan also has to answer to the feared vigilante in *Parzival*.

Where Kei directs challenges to the Court from within its own ranks, the figure of an external challenger of the Court's integrity is an equally common feature of Arthurian fiction. When Cundrie condemns Parzival for his failure to ask the compassionate question at the Grail Castle, only his subsequent rectification of his omission can restore his honour. When Kingrimursel accuses Gawan of murder, his accusation is objectively false, yet Gawan, like Parzival, must still leave the Court to prove his honour since a knight's honour was a matter of public demonstration rather than a purely private affair. Medieval audiences were fond of 'moral laboratory work'[27] and Hartmann and Wolfram, whilst presenting us with a compelling picture of a well-meaning society, also show the wide gap between aspiration and reality within that fictional world.

Hence Heinrich's depiction of the Arthurian courtiers seems to be in part a response to his predecessors' critiques. He arraigns Gawein (for indulging in his youth in indiscreet sexual boasting in apparent mockery of one of his conquests, lines 1994–2000),[28] Guinevere, who in Heinrich's version is implicated in an adulterous affair not with Lancelot (as in Chrétien's *Chevalier de la Charrete*) but rather with the more shadowy Gasozein de Dragoz (lines 1273–92); Gawein's amie, Flori (lines 1293–1317; here named after the name of Florie in Wirnt's *Wigalois* rather than after Orgeluse, the name of his wife in Wolfram's *Parzival*); Laudine, the heroine of Hartmann's *Iwein* who, according to Kei's gloss at any rate, was responsible for causing Iwein to go

---

[27] John Burrow, *A Reading of Sir Gawain and the Green Knight* (London: Routledge and Kegan Paul, 1965), p. 160.

[28] Gawein's action appears to have been a serious offence and to have little in common with the situation in *Graelent*, *Lanval* and other *lais* where a knight infringes a more or less arbitrary taboo (*geis*) on speaking about his mistress in the 'fairy' domain. Rather does Heinrich's Gawein come closer here to the figure of Gauvain in the verse romance *Gliglois* whose 'amour vanité' (Schmolke-Hasselmann) leads to his humiliating rejection by the heroine of the romance in favour of his own page. See *Gliglois. A French Arthurian Romance of the Thirteenth Century*, ed. C. H. Livingstone (Cambridge, Massachusetts: Harvard U.P., 1932).

mad in the forest for love of her (lines 1341–60), Parzival's wife Blancheflur (again named after Chrétien, not after Wolfram's Condwiramurs, lines 1545–89) and Isolde (line 1598). Of the other male courtiers, whilst Arthur is diplomatically allowed to stand above reproach (lines 1897–1905) the rest show themselves to be corrupt in one degree or another. The more notable offenders are Lanzelet, arraigned not for his love of Guinevere (since the role of queen's lover is given to Gasozein in Heinrich's version and Lanzelet's own love is here called Janphie) but rather on the terms of an alternative tradition in which he yielded to the temptation of riding in a cart rather than brave thickets and thorns on his journey to do battle with Milianz (lines 2000–06); Erec, who had made things easy for himself by listening to the warnings of Enite (lines 2154–78); Iwein, who had been given unfair help by his lion companion (lines 2183–92), and Parzival, who had abandoned the Grail king to his pain, for which he had already been denounced by 'the maiden in the tree', a reference to Wolfram's Sigune (lines 2208–24).

Many of the 'sins' supposedly discovered by the goblet (which pours wine in suitably varied quantities over the fallible courtiers) and explicated by Kei have a laboured air and in some cases appear to have been trumped up to serve a comic purpose. It is however probable that the narrator, whilst expecting his audiences to take some of the peccadilloes imputed to individual heroes and heroines with a pinch of salt, nevertheless wished them to take the overall symbolic charge against the Court more seriously, for Heinrich portrays Kei as an 'all-licens'd fool' whose criticisms often meet their mark (lines 1521–44, 1723–77). Although a good number of Kei's strictures are fatuous, the image of the whole Arthurian household falling subject to the lacerations of one of its own number is remarkable, and it is particularly notable that, after the departure of Priure's messenger, the invariably poor verdicts on the Arthurian courtiers yielded by the test appear to be 'confirmed' when Gawein succeeds in inciting all the knights bar three (Kei, Gales and Aumagwin) to give King Arthur the slip to attend a tournament elsewhere. This act of juvenile delinquency (Gawein instructs his co-conspirators with boyish histrionics to call off the escape if they should be intercepted by the king, lines 3222–56) appears at the literal level to be equally as trivial as some of the supposed shortcomings on which Kei had dilated. Yet it was precisely the institution of the court feast (to which considerably more than culinary meaning was attached in medieval culture) which feudal rulers frequently chose to bind the nobility to themselves,[29] and this striking scene of defection, placed towards the beginning of Heinrich's Arthurian chronicle,

[29] Joachim Bumke, *Courtly Culture. Literature and Society in the High Middle Ages*, trans. Thomas Dunlap (Berkeley, Los Angeles, Oxford: University of California Press, 1991), p. 209.

evidences at the symbolic level 'a telling sign of the court's lack of cohesion'.[30]

Corroboration for that contention and for the conclusion that we have here an image of knights voting with their feet against their inactive King may be found in what appears to be an occurrence of the same motif complete with an unambiguous moral gloss in *Perlesvaus*, a romance in all probability known to Heinrich in some form. In the French romance, Arthur descends into an ignoble inactivity, the shame of which leads his peers to desert him and his wife to feel alienated from him, the knights consenting to return to Court only after Guinevere has compelled Arthur to go on a penitential pilgrimage to give evidence of a renewed spirit of chivalry:

> (Arthur) 'commença a perdre le talent des largesses que il soloit fere. Ne voloit cort tenir a Noël, ne a Pasques, ne a Pentecoste. Li chevalier de la Table Reonde, quant il virent son bienfet alentir, il s'en partirent e commençirent sa cort a lessier [. . .] La roïne Guenievre en estoit si dolante qu'ele ne savoit conroi de li meïsme.[31]

> (Arthur began to neglect his wonted largesse, not wanting to hold court at either Christmas, Easter or Pentecost. When the knights of the Round Table witnessed the king's good qualities dwindling in this way, they began to drift away from his Court. Queen Guinevere was so cast down that she could hardly contain her grief.)

In *Perlesvaus* it is clear that Arthur's fault comes very close to that of his legendary peer, Erec, namely *recreantise/verligen*, except that in this case the forthright Guinevere, unlike the infinitely more diffident Enide, has no hesitation about telling her husband of the 'grant vergoigne' which she sees enveloping their rapidly denuded court, at the same time lacing her denunciation with a clear directive to her husband to win back the respect and admiration of the defecting knights.

The impression of a fledgling court suffering internal divisions and descending into culpable inactivity is also a dominant image of the early sections of the German work, and that image is underscored when Heinrich's Guinevere, like the queen in *Perlesvaus*, takes it upon herself to berate her

---

30 Jillings, *Diu Crône*, p. 36.
31 *Le Haut Livre du Graal, Perlesvaus*, ed. William A. Nitze and T. A. Jenkins, 2 vols (Illinois: University of Chicago Press, 1932–7), vol. 1, lines 69–73. Beate Schmolke-Hasselmann has pointed out instances of this same motif occurring in other French verse romances (*Hunbaut, Li Chevaliers as deus epees, Les Merveilles de Rigomer*) where the knights are regarded as the very symbols of royal power. 'In the verse romances the king strives by every available means to bind the knights to his court, in order to avoid the development that has already taken place in the contemporary prose romances, where all the knights have departed on a quest and where this is one of the factors in the downfall of Arthur's kingdom' (*The Evolution of Arthurian Romance. The Verse Tradition from Chrétien to Froissart*, trans. Margaret and Roger Middleton (Cambridge: Cambridge U.P., 1998), pp. 72–5, citation 75).

husband for his soft ways. In *Diu Crône*, Guinevere's reproach is made all the stronger by the note of sexual reproach[32] conveyed through her invidious comparison of her husband's warming himself by the fireside with a knight who rides through the woods night and day singing her praises with only the most minimal clothing to fend off the winter cold:

> Ouch sît ir zwâre niht so heiz
> Als ein ritter, den ich weiz,
> Den ich niht nennen wil,
> Er ist aber bekant vil;
> Wan im daz îs und der snê
> Niht mêre entwelt denn klê
> In deheiner sîner reise,
> Wan in des vrostes vreise
> Ze deheiner zît nimmer tuot
> Dan sumers blitze und bluomen bluot.   (lines 3395–3404)

(In truth you are not so hot as a knight known to me whom I will not name, although he is very famous. His journeys are no more impeded by ice and snow than they are by clover, for he is as little afflicted by the terrors of frost as he is by the heat and scents of summertime.)

What makes the sense of reproach more vivid is the fact that, quite unlike some of Kei's more trumped-up calumnies, it is depicted as being the involuntary outburst of an irascible and somewhat wilful woman who swiftly comes to regret the acutely wounding effects of words which had clearly been all too revealing:

> Artûs sich nider seic
> Und erkom von dem worte.
> Ouch gerou es sie vil harte,
> Daz sie sich sô sêre
> Wider ir selbes êre
> Dô het übersprochen
> Und sô gar zebrochen
> Wîbes zuht unde ir scham.   (lines 3429–36)

(Arthur slumped down shattered by these words. Guinevere was also now contrite about having spoken so hastily to the detriment of her reputation and in such a way as to compromise the decorum proper to a woman.)

---

[32] The situation in *Diu Crône* is considerably more serious for Arthur than the scene in *De Ortu Walwanii* where Guinevere prophesies that an *unknown* knight will approach Camelot with the capacity to eclipse her husband in valour. In the German version the third party is an all too well-known sexual rival, a 'Mann-Vorher' bringing a serious sexual (as opposed to merely military) challenge to the reputation of the Court.

Guinevere's shocked realisation that she has spoken out of turn impels us to conclude that that she had meant what she had said, and that the motif of the provoking spouse is here made to compound the theme of Guinevere's emotional defection.

The Celtic analogues of the widespread Abduction of the Queen motif typically have a supernatural dimension, presenting the pretender to her affections as an Other World prince come to claim his fairy bride. Such notions hark back to ancient mythological conceptions of a two-way traffic between the world of mortals and the denizens of the invisible realms.[33] Guinevere's claim in *Diu Crône* to have enjoyed a prior betrothal in an Other World coheres with the logic of the older, semi-mythological version of the abduction of Guinevere motif which Heinrich favours and for which there is a precedent in the Breton *lai* of *Tydorel* (where a Breton queen, having no child by her husband, conceives Tydorel through a union with a supernatural lover).[34] Unlike the triangular scenario of the Prose *Lancelot* which 'emits no ring of ancientness' and which presents the queen's lover as being one of her husband's own knights, Guinevere's lover in *Diu Crône* bears a greater resemblance to the supernatural prince of more ancient tradition in which Guinevere is 'a fairy queen ravished from her supernatural husband by Arthur of this world, and therefore subject to raids which the Other World would regard as rescues, but which to the Arthurian world – and the narrator's – appear as abductions'.[35]

The tradition most commonly found elsewhere in romance is that of Chrétien's *Le Chevalier de la Charrete*. Here the Arthurian courtiers are challenged by King Meleagant with the boast that he holds many of Arthur's subjects captive in his kingdom of Gorre, but the initial motif of Guinevere being claimed by the Other Worldy prince is eventually eclipsed by the more 'modern' theme of the queen's adultery with one of her husband's own men. Here, once Lancelot has slain the more mysterious pretender, he himself falls prey to Guinevere's charms and the story then takes a different turn focussing on Lancelot himself and his failure to resist the queen. Even Geoffrey of Monmouth's *Historia Regum Britanniae* no longer reflects the most ancient stratum of tradition since here the adultery is described naturalistically as being related to Arthur's long absences in his Roman campaigns against Lucius Hiberius, during which Guinevere forms a sexual relationship with the regent, Mordred.

Heinrich almost certainly knew the *Charrete* and sources of the Lancelot–Grail cycle, and so it is all the more remarkable that in *Diu Crône* the

---

33 On this point see Leslie T. Topsfield, *Chrétien de Troyes. A Study of the Arthurian Romances* (Cambridge: Cambridge U.P., 1981), pp. 15–16.

34 For a comparison see Christine Zach, *Die Erzählmotive der Crône*, pp. 349–53.

35 Kenneth G. T. Webster, *Guinevere. A History of her Abductions* (Milton, Massachusetts: Turtle Press, 1951), p. 126.

name of Lancelot is not given in the context of the betrayal episode (for the earlier chastity test would have given Kei ample opportunity to dilate on the famous adultery had that been the narrator's plan). In place of the famed Lancelot Heinrich chose the more obscure, semi-mythic figure of 'Gasozein', the brother of 'ein rîche fei' (line 10,500) who fights without armour and in whom the knight Gales perceives uncanny features.[36] Although Gasozein has undeniably modern traits such as his singing songs of love, he also bears characteristics of the mythical Summer King in his preternatural resistance to the cold in mid winter.[37] There is a possible resemblance to early Celtic versions of the abductor figure such as the Old Irish *Etain and Mider* where Etain, who had once been married to Mider in a former existence in the Celtic Other World, but loses consciousness of that event when she joins the world of mortals. Guinevere may likewise have been in this sense 'a fairy who dwindled into a wife',[38] having been originally the imagined inhabitant of another sphere to which her former fairy betrothed attempted to return her.

At any rate the Guinevere of *Diu Crône* gives the rather shifty impression of one strenuously repressing memories of a former life in her attempt to maintain her position within the Arthurian order. It is for that reason that she repeatedly attempts to discredit Gasozein's claims that she had been delivered to him in early youth by the 'night spirits' ('nahtweiden', line 4840).[39] According to her supernatural admirer, it is Arthur who is the usurper and he the 'reht amis' (line 4838), a claim for which he adduces trenchant testimony in the shape of a magic belt made originally for her lover, Fimbeus of Karlin, by Giramphiel, the sister of the goddess Fortuna.

This belt (which has the property of conferring Fortuna's perpetual favours on its owner) had once been won for Guinevere by Gawein, but Guinevere had given it to Gasozein, which is why he offers it now as proof of his credentials. The gift of the girdle to Gasozein 'can hardly be seen as an innocent gesture, in view of the fact that a woman's belt was recognised as a

---

[36] At one point Gales speculates that Gasozein (who refuses to reveal his name) might be little more than a fantastical delusion ('troges bilde', line 3566) or, alternatively, that he might be a wild man beyond the ken of the courtly world: 'Dehein mensch ist sô wilde/ daz sich erzeige en solhen wîs' (lines 3567–68). A 'Gosangos' whose love is not reciprocated by the queen occurs in the *Livre d'Artus*. See Frank W. Chandler, Martin H. Jones, *A Catalogue of Names in the German Court Epics. An Examination of the Literary Sources and Dissemination, together with Notes on the Etymologies of the More Important Names*, King's College London Centre for Late Antique and Medieval Studies (London, 1992).

[37] Rosemary Wallbank, 'Heinrichs von dem Türlin *Crône* und die irische Sage von Etain und Mider', in *Die mittelalterliche Literatur in Kärnten*, ed. Cella and Krämer, pp. 251–68.

[38] Rosemary Wallbank, 'An Irish fairy in Austria; Vrou Giramphiel and Lady Fortune in *Diu Crône*', in *Connections. Essays in Honour of Eda Sagarra on the Occasion of her Sixtieth Birthday*, ed. Peter Skrine, Rosemary E. Wallbank-Turner and Jonathan West (Stuttgart: Hans Dieter Heinz, 1993), pp. 285–96, citation 285.

[39] In Ulrich von Zatzikhoven's *Lanzelet* Valerin similarly claims that he was betrothed to Guinevere before she was of marriageable age (ed. Hahn, lines 4966–5360).

symbol of chastity when on, but of sexual favours when off.'[40] To Gasozein's damning testimony Arthur has no effective counter-claim, and the pretender's account is given strong support by the later reaction to the news of Guinevere's own brother, Gotegrin. He, unpersuaded by his sister's denials, abducts her and narrowly fails to execute her for the dishonour which he supposes her to have brought down upon their family (lines 11037–607); it is only *force majeure* which compels Guinevere, brought into a judicial ring where she is intimidated by the crush of Arthur's troops, to deny that she had ever known Gasozein.

It might appear that this form of resolution of the Arthur/Guinevere/Gasozein affair is scarcely satisfactory and that Gawein's negotiated solution to the Gasozein problem does little to dispel the query overhanging Guinevere's adultery raised by the testing goblet and compounded by the queen's immoderate praise for the dauntless *Minnesänger*. There is abundant evidence in the witness of Gotegrin's spy (who infers from the queen's physical gestures that she loves Gasozein rather than Arthur) that Guinevere had not always been the exclusive sexual property of her husband. Gawein's appearance as a *deus ex machina* saving Guinevere's face might then seem rather to underscore the fragility of a marriage blighted by imperfectly repressed memories and held together more by the diplomacy of a third party than by any internal strength. Yet the choice of the older model of the sexual triangle involving the Other World pretender, Gasozein, rather than Lancelot, together with the decision to place his challenge for Guinevere in the first decade of the King's reign (the Guinevere of the Lancelot–Grail cycle is fifty years old) are positive factors giving the adultery motif in *Diu Crône* a different implication from that which adheres to it in the Arthurian chronicles of Geoffrey and Wace, the Didot *Perceval* and the cyclic romance of Lancelot.

Whereas in those works the triangle forms a terminal episode leading to the ultimate tragedy, Heinrich's retelling draws on a more ancient form of sexual challenge *not yet linked cyclically with the theme of the Downfall of Camelot*. The same motif in *Diu Crône*, situated within Heinrich's imagined beginnings of the Arthurian order, becomes detached from the 'canonical' account where Lancelot, the ostensible saviour of the queen, betrays his trust to Arthur. The Gasozein plot is not coupled with associations of the decadence of the Court so that, although the logic of the adultery story combined with dissension amongst the Arthurian courtiers might lead us to anticipate an Arthurian Armageddon by analogy with the *Mort Artu*, Heinrich's initial

---

40 Marianne Wynn, 'The abduction of the queen in German Arthurian romance' in *Chevaliers errants, demoiselees et l'Autre: höfische und nachhöfische Literatur im europäischen Mittelalter Festschrift für Xenja von Ertzdorff*, ed. Trude Ehlert, GAG 644 (Göppingen: Kümmerle), pp. 131–44, citation p. 137. For this reason Gawein in *Wigalois* advises Guinevere to return the gift of a magic belt to King Joram so as not to sully her (sexual) honour (ed. Kapteyn, lines 370–83).

placement of an episode elsewhere placed in a final position allows scope for the processes of reconciliation and rehabilitation superintended by Gawein.

Heinrich's version of the triangle is a rewrite of the Lancelot/Guinevere story which attempts to fill hermeneutic gaps in Arthurian tradition (as known to his countrymen and women) by imagining how the course of events might be redirected if the rescue of the Queen had been transferred not to Lancelot but to the more sexually self-disciplined Gawein, a protagonist able to 'steer the course of Arthurian history away from the path of destruction'.[41] In modern parlance he was constructing an 'historical counterfactual'.[42] In order to make his new story convincing, however, it was necessary to rehabilitate Gawein from the unfavourable impression he had made in the early stages of the romance, where his sexually insulting conduct to a lady of the Court and his desertion of his liege lord revealed distinctly unmessianic qualities of emotional immaturity and irresponsibility. The means by which that rehabilitation is conveyed will form the subject of the next chapter.

41 Elizabeth Andersen, '*Diu Crône* and the Prose *Lancelot*', p. 46.
42 Niall Ferguson, *Virtual History. Alternatives and Counterfactuals* (London: Picador, 1997).

3

The Formation of a Saviour

The romance hero appears in some lights to be a 'character'; he passes through stages of innocence, ignorance, inadequacy and irresponsibility. His illumination is progressive and can be charted. And this suggests inner growth; it suggests, in short, a 'character' with its inner laws, its inner life. But this might still be misleading because the growth from innocence to maturity is preconceived and there is only a limited degree of interaction between him and the world around him. The 'character' of a romance-hero is rather a rehearsed interior monologue than a meaningful and unpredictable dialogue with the outside world'.[1]

The depiction of Gawein in the early stages of *Diu Crône* hardly corresponds to his customary image in the verse romances. Though successful in the second of the tests of virtue visited upon the Court (lines 23,599–604), he acquits himself no more gloriously than any other courtiers in the first. Where in the 'classical' romances of Chrétien and Hartmann he acts as the standard-bearer of the Arthurian order, here he not only fails King Priure's test and absconds with the Court's vital manpower but also, unlike his companions, fails to respond to Arthur's summons to rejoin the Court by February (lines 5451–64). Heinrich clearly did not at first elect to reproduce an exemplar of *triuwe* and may have used his own invention to create his transgressive younger Gawein from typical images of anarchic young aristocratic males, possibly of the sort dubbed *iuvenes* by Georges Duby,[2] distilling an individual biography from a set of typical features.

In a romance which he announces as being an account of the early part of the Arthurian world, the 'early' Gawein appears as a knight with some distinctly juvenile character traits. In his portrayal of this younger Gawein prior to the Assiles and Amurfina sequences, Heinrich must have rejected notions of what has been termed Gawein's 'pre-formed character', that is, of the normative force of the mature Gawein found in the romances of his

---

1   John Stevens, *Medieval Romance* (London: Hutchinson, 1973), p. 170.
2   'Dans la France du nord-ouest au XII siècle: les "jeunes" dans la société aristocratique', *Annales ESC*, 19 (1964), pp. 835–46.

predecessors.[3] The idea that the later Grail quester and the earlier deserter and sexual harasser could be one and the same person (in moral terms) is opposed by the ways in which Heinrich strove to suggest a form of progress representing his quester becoming 'slowly wise', the evolution of the individual character matching the overarching aim of charting the ascent of Camelot itself.

Some French verse romances of the early thirteenth century purport to delve back to an imagined era when the personnel of the Arthurian kingdom were negotiating youthful rites of passage. This is the case in the fragments of 'Les Enfances Gauvain',[4] where Gauvain is obliged to rise from anonymous beginnings to make a name for himself, and likewise in the Latin cognate *De Ortu Walwanii*, where his cognomen is significantly *puer sine nomine*.[5] In other French verse romances Gauvain is presented in somewhat burlesque tones as a cadet figure whose inexperience marks him out as one in need of vigorous testing. In some romances his youthful foibles attract a degree of narratorial raillery. This is the case in *Hunbaut*, where Gauvain's immature and unreliable conduct falls well beneath the standard of the eponymous hero, and in *Meraugis de Portlesguez*, where his philandering leads to his having to promise that he will not stay two successive nights in the same castle lest he compromise the good name of its maidens and ladies. The teasing/testing tone is also present in the two short French verse romances appropriated by Heinrich to initiate Gawein's proving in *Diu Crône*: *Le Chevalier à l'Épée* and *La Mule sans Frein*.[6]

The first of these, cognate with the Tempation scene in *Sir Gawain and the Green Knight*, tells of Gauvain's encounter with an ill-famed knight who offers him the favours of his daughter for the night, supposing that a magic sword which had previously protected his daughter's virginity would put an end to the hero. But the sword, which had slain previous wooers, gives Gauvain only a flesh wound, which the father takes as a sign that the knight standing relatively unscathed before him must be the best knight in the world, whereupon he makes over both his daughter and his realm to him. In a sudden turnabout, however, the daughter opts for another knight encountered by chance on the journey back to Camelot with Gauvain (it is implied that she is dissatisfied with Gauvain's performance in the bedchamber). Although

---

3   The term 'präformiert' was used by Christoph Cormeau, *'Wigalois' und 'Diu Crone'. Zwei Kapitel zur Gattungsgeschichte des nachklassischen Aventiureromans*, MTU 57 (Munich: Artemis, 1977), *passim*.

4   'Les Enfances Gauvain: fragments d'un poème perdu', ed. Paul Meyer, *Romania* 39 (1910), pp. 1–32.

5   *The Rise of Gawain, Nephew of Arthur/ De Ortu Walwanii, Nepotis Arturi*, ed. and trans. Mildred Leake Day (New York: Garland, 1984).

6   *Two Old French Gauvain Romances*, ed. R. C. Johnston and D. D. R. Owen (Edinburgh and London: Scottish Academic Press, 1972).

Gauvain defeats the pretender, he refuses to take the girl back, deserting her by the wayside as he launches into misogynistic tirades.

The second short narrative poem, one of whose episodes corresponds with variations to the Beheading Test in *Sir Gawain and the Green Knight*, tells of how a maiden comes to Court to petition for a champion to take her mule as a mount with which to retrieve her lost bridle. Keu volunteers for the task but the animal takes him into such infernal regions that he balks at the challenge. Gauvain then volunteers for the task, the mule taking him beyond the terrain traversed with Keu to a revolving castle. Here a *vilain* the colour of a Blackamoor challenges him to the beheading game (the outcome being the same as that of the Middle English poem). After further challenges including some against wild animals, Gauvain is presented with the bridle by the lady of the castle and the populace rejoices that he has killed the dangerous animals. Yet this second romance too brings humiliation for the hero and also has a bathetic ending: the girl for whom he had retrieved the bridle and who had promised him her hand in marriage should he succeed, duplicitously withdraws her promise to the consternation of Gauvain, Arthur and Guinevere.

In *La Mule sans Frein* we are not told why the bridle was important to the younger sibling (beyond the cryptic hint that it was 'mauvaisement [. . .] tolu', line 80), and Heinrich's making it into a bridle of sovereignty able to confer supreme power on its possessor was probably a logical amplification derived from the Rival Sisters story in *Yvain/Iwein*. He will then have harmonised the various traditions to comply with the demands of verisimilitude and a realistic chronology.[7] He must also have deleted the burlesque endings of both the shorter romances and integrated the material into a richer moral context, making his ensemble into an ethical challenge for Gawein with echoes of the problematics of *Erec* and *Iwein* in ways which will be analysed below.

Heinrich's extended sequence is embedded in an 'Arthurian' adventure where Giwanet, a page of the besieged Flois of Effin, proceeds to seek help from Arthur and is by chance intercepted by Gawein, who accepts the challenge without demur, so giving notice of the possibility of a rehabilitation from his erring ways.

In the midst of a flirtation of Gawein with Sgaipegaz, the daughter of Blandukors (an ally of Flois whom Gawein helps against the giant, Assiles) a female messenger arrives from Lady Amurfina demanding that Gawein

---

7 Boll calculated the chronology of the first 14,000 lines spanning the time from Christmas (Priure's challenge) to June and the formal celebrations of the double wedding (Gawein/Amurfina, Sgoidamur/Gasozein), adjudging it 'as perfect as a medieval writer, or, for that matter, a modern writer could make it'. See Lawrence L. Boll, *The Relation of 'Diu Krone' of Heinrich von dem Türlin to 'La Mule sanz Frain': A Study in Sources*, Catholic University of America Studies in German 11, repr. (New York: AMS Press, 1970), pp. 9–11, citation 11. (Whether Heinrich had a French source which had already combined the two stories remains uncertain.)

should join her in her distant land without delay. Despite his obligations and present sexual entanglement, Gawein responds to Amurfina's summons with keen sexual anticipation, to the acute consternation of Sgaipegaz and Blandukors' family. (Whilst there is no mention of a prior betrothal with Amurfina we do learn that Gawein had once visited her land when he had defeated her father, Laniure of the Serre, the combat being etched on a commemorative plaque in Amurfina's possession.) When he arrives in her land she enlists him in a territorial dispute with her sister, Sgoidamur. This conflict had arisen because Laniure (who left no male heir) gave a bridle of sovereignty to his two daughters, the presumption being that they would share power. Amurfina, however, being the older sister, wanted to exercise authority over the younger Sgoidamur and stole the bridle in order to be able to occupy the throne unopposed. The theft moves Sgoidamur to resort to Arthur for help and Amurfina to preempt her by gaining Gawein as her champion.

Having gained Amurfina's realm, Gawein can hardly wait to enter her bedchamber. Notwithstanding the sexual thrall in which the beautiful Amurfina holds the knight, she additionally makes him drink a love potion whilst a further device in the shape of a threatening sword above her bed ensures that Gawein will remain eternally faithful to her. Becalmed in an erotic paradise, Gawein is said to resemble 'a second Arthur' in his sedentary ways. Due to the effects of the love potion, Gawein thinks he has been the Lord of the Serre for thirty years. In truth, however, his sojourn with Amurfina lasts only fifteen days. At this point he sees a decorated bowl immortalising his victory over her father and this, contrary to Amurfina's wishes, serves to revive memories in him of his office as knight errant and of his immediate obligation to help the victims of Assiles, to which obligation he now returns. After defeating Assiles, and returning to the Arthurian Court where he saves Guinevere from the depredations of the pretender, Gasozein, the Rival Sisters theme is resumed. The girl searching for the bridle of sovereignty, Sgoidamur, is here the younger sister of Amurfina. A sequence of events ensues similar to that occurring in La Mule sans Frein, but here the villain of the French poem is the noble Gansguoter, uncle of the sisters, who reveals to the hero that the bridle was Gawein's anyway through his marriage to his niece, Amurfina. Despite the ostensible futility of his exertions, Gansguoter reassures him, he had covered himself in glory. Gawein accepts the plaudit with good grace whilst Sgoidamur accepts that 'her' champion, Gawein, is in fact her sister's husband and agrees to be married to Gasozein instead.

In order to groom Gawein as a saviour figure it would have been necessary for his initial delinquency to be made to yield to a mode of conduct more consistent with the role which he plays in his future Grail quest. It appears that it was the marriage to the wryly named Amurfina which Heinrich chose to initiate Gawein's critical moral shift, heralding an important shift from irresponsible *iuvenis* to mature, married knight. Whilst the goblet test had revealed an early sexual indiscretion, two other sexual liaisons are mentioned before he meets his future wife. Besides Sgaipegaz there is report of a relationship with Flori (line 1294). Whilst the liaison with Sgaipegaz is depicted as being only a brief infatuation (being nipped in the bud by the arrival of Amurfina's messenger), the name of Flori(e) in Arthurian story suggests a more settled relationship.[8] For Florie is in *Wigalois* the name of Gawein's wife whom he eventually deserted (rather in the same way that Iwein forsook Laudine because of a compulsion to return to the world of armed combat). Wirnt glossed over the potentially discreditable aspects of that desertion in order to be able to introduce both Gawein and Florie as suitable parents for his protagonist. He therefore attributed Gawein's failure to return to Florie to his loss of a talismanic belt granting him access to his wife's magically enclosed kingdom. Despite this attempt at exculpation, however, it would have appeared to those acquainted with the similar narrative contained in Hartmann's *Iwein* that the morally problematic issue of Florie's desertion is side-stepped and Wirnt's praise of Gawein's 'stoicism'[9] in reconciling himself to his exclusion something of a non-sequitur.

The desertion in *Diu Crône* may have caused contemporary audiences to have remembered Gawein's undischarged marital obligations to Florie in *Wigalois*.[10] If so, then they would certainly have seen some satirical humour in the way that the tough-minded Amurfina contains the traditionally errant Gawein so effectively within the bonds of matrimony. Unlike Laudine with Iwein or Florie with Gawein, she refuses to rest content with marriage vows alone, and when Gawein eventually returns to the Assiles campaign she presses upon him a picture of a golden padlock on a shield so that all should know its owner was married.[11] Although Gawein and Amurfina are described as being ablaze with love for each other (lines 8116–18), the perhaps justifiably distrustful Amurfina still causes Gawein to drink a love potion in

---

8   In *Diu Crône* she is described as related to Arthur and as the second most important lady at Court next to Guinevere (lines 1294–98).

9   Dô er mit vrâge daz bevant
        daz niemen mohte in daz lant
        vor den hôhen bergen komen,
        als er die wârheit hêt vernomen,
        dô teter als der biderbe man,
        der sich des wol getroesten mac.   (*Wigalois*, ed. Kapteyn, lines 1203–9)

10   The desertion scenario is one for which medieval audiences would have had long memories, as is confirmed by the adult Feirefiz's refusal to forgive his father, Gahmuret, for having deserted his mother, Belakane, even though that event had taken place in his distant youth (*Parzival*, ed. Lachmann, section 750, lines 15–30). On this point see Alfred Raucheisen, *Orient und Abendland. Ethisch-moralische Aspekte in Wolframs Epen 'Parzival' und 'Willehalm'*, Bremer Beiträge zur Literatur und Ideengeschichte 17 (Frankfurt: Lang, 1997), pp. 90–92.

11   'Ze dienen einem wîbe
        Und anders deheiner
        Mit niht, wan ir einer'   (*Crône*, lines 9109–11).

the attempt to ensure the durability of his affections (lines 8617–94). A further deterrent to any trifling with her affections appears in the shape of a magically suspended sword having the power to ensure that any would-be claimant to Amurfina's hand harbours only honourable intentions, or else the sword would attack the false suitor (lines 8504–40).

The hanging sword motif, which the narrator confesses that he is treating rather freely (lines 8515–16) is indeed a rather arch modification of the similar episode occurring in *Le Chevalier a l'Épée*. There the sword plays the considerably less discriminating role of deterring any and every sexual adventurer (being blind to how 'honest' any suitor's intentions might be) and is not credited with the 'mind-reading' powers of the sword in *Diu Crône* which, capable of divining the faintest portion of 'unstaete', forces the intemperate suitor to become constant and loyal in his attentions. The reproving, educative powers of the sword are described in the following terms in the German version:

> Swer der meit solt ligen bi
> Und ze deheinr unstaete
> Sie iemer iht gebæte
> Oder wolt betwingen
> Mit ungevüegem ringen
> Mit willen oder sunder danc,
> Als er denne mit ir ranc,
> Sô sleif ez ûz der scheide
> Und half dirre meide,
> Daz ir von ime niht gewar,
> Unz im der muot ze stæte gar
> Ze ir stuont und ze triuwen.   (lines 8517–28)

(If anybody were to lie with the girl and wish to make her unchaste either by persuasion or through brute shows of force, the sword would slip from its sheath at that very moment, ensuring that no hurt would be inflicted on her until the wooer's heart became constant and faithful to her alone.)

In a witty gloss on the French tradition the sword is made to deprive Gawein of his potency as he advances upon Amurfina (lines 8585–87), causing the hero to bemoan his waning sexual powers to his soul (lines 8600–06), whereupon the sword, perceiving that Gawein has entrusted his love to his soul (rather than to more fleshly parts), acknowledges his new, 'spiritual' form of love and withdraws to its scabbard.

In the French version the father submits his daughter to the sexual attentions of a succession of suitors, the voyeuristic nature of this custom being evident in his forbidding her to extinguish the candles in the bedchamber, whilst the sadistic component of his bent is to get the sword to kill his daughter's suitors. Anticipations of a morally satisfying finale are mocked when, although the evil host duly surrenders his daughter to Gauvain, the same knight is swiftly jilted by her. Heinrich on the other hand appears to have honed the sword as a moral instrument compelling sexual fidelity in order to keep his hero in line – for after the sword test Gawein does indeed remain true to Amurfina. Though Heinrich clearly knew the burlesque form of the test contained in *Le Chevalier a l'Épée* he must have resisted the sexually deviant tone of a version in which the sword has more to do with sado-masochistic titillation than with virtue.

Although the German narrator might have wished to show Gawein's marriage as an event representing a change in his protagonist's character tending toward the stage of dependable *vir gravis*, there would inevitably have been dangers to this project, already revealed in some dark references to the fate of Solomon in love (lines 8430–66). Gawein's journey to Amurfina's land, like the journeys of Iwein to Broceliande or Gauriel to the land of Fluratrône in Konrad von Stoffeln's *Gauriel von Muntabel*, is a distant reflection of a journey into the Celtic Other World.[12] In the Middle Ages the easy acceptance in the older mythology of a two-way traffic in and out of other-worldly locations had fallen under the influence of Christianising notions and a misogynistic interpretation of the erotic allure of *fées* as 'aspects of a struggle between the world of chivalry and another, hostile world'.[13] On this view, intercourse between a knight and a *fée* came to be seen as emblematic of a surrender of personal autonomy to atavistic, 'pagan' impulses. Hence the conclusion of Hartmann's *Iwein* (where the eponymous hero forsakes his Arthurian peers to rejoin Laudine) appears to have been felt disquieting by contemporary audiences[14] and, I have suggested elsewhere, to have been 'corrected' by Konrad von Stoffeln in his *Gauriel von Muntabel* (c. 1280).[15]

Gauriel tells of how the lovesick hero is so taken with his fairy mistress that he performs acts against the interests of his peers at her behest, but at the conclusion of the work Konrad brings his errant hero and his fairy spouse back into the Arthurian circle in the attempt to provide a corrective to the socially disruptive ending of *Iwein*. This closure may have been planned so as to counteract the implication that the affections of an Arthurian knight could be alienated by a foreign amazon. The conclusion of *Gauriel* comes closer in spirit to Hartmann's *Erec* than to his *Iwein*, and the fictional figure of Erec is appropriated to motivate the new conclusion when, as one of the hostages whom Gauriel is compelled to abduct from the Arthurian Court at his mistress's behest, he advises Gauriel to return to Karidol, citing to him the moral of his own experience:

---

12 Jillings, *Diu Crône*, p. 62.
13 Jillings, 'The abduction of Arthur's queen in *Diu Crône*', *Nottingham Mediaeval Studies* 19 (1975), pp. 16–34, citation 16.
14 See Christoph Gerhardt, 'Iwein-Schlüsse', in *Literaturwissenschaftliches Jahrbuch der Görres Gesellschaft* 13 (1972), pp. 13–39.
15 Neil Thomas, 'Konrad von Stoffeln's *Gauriel von Muntabel*: a comment on Hartmann's *Iwein*?', *Oxford German Studies* 17 (1988), pp. 1–9.

> ein man sol ein vrumen lîp
> niht lân verderben umbe ein wîp
> noch durch ein liebez anesehen.
> Mir was vil nâhe alsô geschehen
> In den selben zîten
> Dô ich vrowen Enîten
> Von êrst ze hûse sazte;
> Ir liebe mich entsazte
> Von manlicher wirdikeit.[16]

(A knight should not let himself be corrupted by the fair appearance of a woman. Such a thing almost happened to me when I took Lady Enite as my wife. For love of her I almost forfeited my knightly honour.)

Gauriel thereupon takes his colleague's advice, convinces his inamorata of the courtly doctrine of *mâze* enunciated by Erec and tells her that he must repair his relationship with the knightly world in order to be able to see their sexual union in a broader perspective:

> geleiste ich daz, sô bin ich vri,
> daz ich niemen niht ensol,
> sô zime ich hie ze herren wol.   (lines 2951–53)

(If I achieve that then I will be free, owe no moral debt to any man and be a fine and fitting lord.)

The two lovers then forsake their enclosed domain and return to Court, Gauriel to perform penance for Guinevere for having abducted his brother knights, his mistress symbolically renouncing her opposition to Arthurian chivalry through her willingness to accept the welcome of her husband's knightly peers, leaving us to infer that she has become socially integrated as a courtly *vrouwe*.

Heinrich appears to have pursued a similar narrative strategy as Konrad von Stoffeln. Both *Diu Crône* at this point and *Gauriel von Muntabel* are genetically related to the *Iwein* story pattern, yet they both appear to enlist the authority of *Erec* to correct the somewhat dubious moral of the *Yvain* story pattern. If 'fairy mistress stories in Celtic and elsewhere are apt to end with the happy return of the hero to live with his supernatural wife',[17] neither Konrad nor Heinrich brook this form of closure. Heinrich shows himself to be aware that a knight's marriage could all too easily result in an 'Emanzipation

---

16 *Gauriel von Muntabel: eine höfische Erzählung aus dem 13. Jahrhundert*, ed. Ferdinand Khull (Graz; Leuschner und Lubensky, 1885), lines 2890–98. On the place of this romance in German Arthurian tradition see *Der Ritter mit dem Bock. Konrads von Stoffeln 'Gauriel von Muntabel'*, ed. Wolfgang Achnitz (Tübingen: Niemeyer, 1997), pp. 195–232.

17 A. C. L. Brown, 'The Knight of the Lion', *PMLA* 20 (1905), p. 674.

von der Artusrunde'.[18] Therefore, whilst permitting Gawein to marry Amurfina, he nevertheless denies him the right to assume kingship in her realm, devolving that duty on to Gasozein, the husband of the younger sister, Sgoidamur. By this self-denying ordinance, Gawein sets himself free to escort his new wife back to Karidol, henceforth to be their marital abode.[19]

The exogamous marriage of any Arthurian knight would have caused ethical and diplomatic problems, but with Gawein the old problem of love versus knightly honour would have presented itself in a particularly acute form. In his case there would have been strong audience expectations that he should remain at Court as the King's second-in-command.[20] According to traditional literary images of Gawein he was the disinterested champion of all ladies rather than the exclusive partner of one. In Hartmann's *Iwein* he expresses himself fairly curtly on this point to his brother knight, voicing his fear that Iwein's liaison with Laudine could annul the two friends' perfect community of chivalrous interests.[21] From Gawein's point of view, Iwein's overriding obligation is to Arthur and he shows scant regard for the two lovers' contract of marriage. Discounting Laudine's moral claim on her husband, he translates Iwein's dilemma into a straightforward command-ment that a knight should not succumb to the temptation of *verligen* like Erec[22] but rather subordinate the claims of his sexual life to the imperatives of his knightly avocation.[23] Similarly in *Diu Crône* Kei blames Laudine for Iwein's troubles and simply obliterates the moral problem of the desertion by asserting that there was no case against Iwein to answer:

> Her Îwein wist die triuwe wol,
> Ob man ez allez sagen sol,
> Dô er durch ir gaehen zorn
> Haet nâhe sînen lîp verlorn
> In einem walde durch ir minne

---

18 Alfred Ebenbauer, 'Gawein als Gatte', in *Die mittelalterliche Literatur in Kärnten*, ed. A. Cella and P. Krämer, pp. 33–66, citation 35.

19 When the absent Gawein is later presumed dead, Amurfina is present at Camelot to join in the chorus of lament with the other courtiers (lines 17,173–313).

20 Wirnt von Gravenberg solves the dilemma of Gawein's marriage by the device of allowing Gawein to lose the magic belt which prevents him from returning to his wife's magically enclosed realm. This allows his hero to return to his Arthurian peers with sorrow as a virtual widower but with a clear conscience. Wolfram von Eschenbach on the other hand can permit Gawan to marry Orgeluse since he was taking the romance genre into new terrain where the Grail kingship was to exert the major authority in an implied new dispensation in which the defence of Camelot was no longer a supremely critical issue. On this point see Ebenbauer, 'Gawein als Gatte'.

21 *Iwein*, ed. Benecke, lines 2804–06, 2909–12.

22 Gawein says of Erec: 'wan daz er sichs erholte/sît als ein rîter solte/sô waere vervarn sîn êre/der minnete ze sêre' (lines 2795–98).

23 *Iwein*, lines 2791–94. Cf. also the unequivocal sympathy for Iwein voiced by Arthur (lines 3239–48) and by the narrator (lines 3249–60).

Im selben ze ungewinne,
Dô er verlôs die sinne.   (lines 1354–60)

(To tell the truth my Lord Iwein was being perfectly loyal when his
lady's quick temper almost lost him his life at the time when, for love
of her, he suffered the devastating experience of losing his wits in the
forest.)

In his portraiture of Gawein as a married man Heinrich attempted to do
justice to images of Gawein already generated by literary predecessors. He
achieves this fine balance by making his future Grail quester into a supreme
exemplar of courtly moderation in the well-nigh oxymoronic shape of a
monogamous knight errant. Having put down narrative markers for
Gawein's good name as a faithful married man, Heinrich continually strives
to stress his hero's continence, avoiding reference to his once errant sexuality.
This is borne out by comparative readings in the Castle of Wonders sequence,
the one large section based on a unitary narrative sequence occurring in the
works of two literary predecessors, namely the so-called 'Chrétien-Wolfram
adventures' (Crône, lines 17,500–22,564; Conte du Graal, lines 4816–6216,
6519–end; Parzival, Books 7–8, 10–14). Here comparisons with the other
versions will be made in order to show how Heinrich's adaptation under-
scores both Gawein's sexual continence and his growing readiness to undertake the Grail quest.

Chrétien's incomplete Gauvain section was chosen both by the author of
the First Continuation and by Heinrich as the sequence in which the obligation to quest for the Grail would be transferred to Gauvain/ Gawein (rather
than to Perceval/Parzival). It is also a series which abounds in some broad
sexual humour. Having arrived at the castle of Escavalon (Wolfram's
Schampfanzun, Heinrich's Karamphi) Chrétien's Gauvain is greeted in direct
and amorous terms by the sexually assertive daughter of the castle (called
Antikonie in Wolfram's eighth Book); but the couple are interrupted in their
dalliance by a vavassor who berates 'Antikonie' for reciprocating the affections of the very man who had supposedly killed her father, the late king of
Escavalon. In Diu Crône, by contrast (which represents a hybrid form), the
renamed Seimeret does not, like the heroine of Chrétien and Wolfram, enter
into a dalliance with Gawein but rather suggests the distinctly more decorous
game of chess with her new male companion. Meanwhile, the figure of
Orgeilleuse/Orgeluse, renamed Mancipelle by Heinrich, is introduced rather
late in Diu Crône (lines 21,095ff) as a waspish but rather weak and bloodless
substitute for the more concretely realised Proud Lady of the sources.

The impression repeatedly given is that Heinrich sought to avoid the issue
of sexual entanglement in this sequence. Where for instance Wolfram creates
considerable dramatic and sexual tension out of the rebarbative attitude of
Orgeluse towards Gawan and out of the latter's dogged determination to
retain his patience (and continence) towards her until she can be conciliated,

Heinrich's hero is a married knight, and in that state ambiguous sexual tensions are to be studiously ignored, it is implied. Heinrich certainly does not enlist such tensions to generate narrative interest here: Seimeret ('Antikonie') has no emotional involvement with Gawein, nor does Mancipelle (who, under the name of Orgeluse had eventually become Gawan's wife in Wolfram's version), and the overall impression is one of bowdlerisation. The rather bland modus operandi of the later author is at any rate different from the emotionally more satisfying methods of his German predecessor, who modifies and augments various cues from Chrétien's version in order to foreground the theme of (male) sexual abuse. Heinrich, by contrast, steers well clear of Wolfram's thematic innovations, as can be observed most clearly by contrasting his colourless treatment of Chrétien's warring lovers story (dubbed Obie and Meljanz in Wolfram's seventh Book) with that of Wolfram himself.

In Chrétien's version of that story 'Obie' provokes her would-be lover into engaging in combat with her father in order to gain her love, a provocation which clearly extenuates Meliant's later attack. Wolfram on the other hand, pursuing the theme of male sexual aggression, deprives his Meljanz of any hope of extenuation when he makes him decide unilaterally and with premeditation to besiege Obie's father (Chrétien's Tybalt, Wolfram's Lippaut) in order to abduct his daughter. Wolfram blackens Meljanz's character yet further by letting him associate with Meljacanz (section 343, lines 19ff), absent in the corresponding part of the *Conte du Graal* but familiar from his traditional role as Guinevere's abductor (Meleagant) in the Lancelot romance and of whose character a squire reports to Gawan:

> ez waere wîb oder magt,
> swaz er dâ minne hêt bejagt,
> die nam er gar in noeten:
> man solt in drumbe toeten. (*Parzival*, section 343, lines 27–30)

(Irrespective of whether the woman was married or not, whatever love he took, he took by force, for which he deserves the gallows.)

The narrator even indulges in quips to underline the sexual tension between the couple, observing with feigned incredulity that he (the narrator) could never have summoned up the reserves of well-nigh preternatural patience displayed by Gawan, but would rather have forced her to submit to his sexual will without ceremony (section 601, lines 11ff and 604, 4ff). When Gawan returns the droves of young women formerly imprisoned by Clinschor, Keye mockingly insinuates that Gawan has come upon the equivalent of a private harem:

> 'got mit den liuten wunder tuot.
> wer gap Gawan die frouwen luot?'
> sus sprach keye in sime schimpf. (*Parzival*, section 675, lines 13–15)

('God performs miracles for some people. Who gave Gawan all these women?' asked Kei with his customary malice.)

Finally, the sexually assertive figure of Antikonie (unnamed in Chrétien) is as amorous and direct in Chrétien's version as she is in Wolfram's, but only Wolfram adapts the words of the knight who interrupts their play to accuse the male partner of violating the daughter of the house:

> 'owe unde heia hei
> mins herrren den ir sluoget,
> daz iuch des niht genuoget'
> irn notzogt och sin tohter hie'   (*Parzival*, section 407, lines 11–19).

(Woe and shame on you. It isn't enough for you that you have slain my lord. Now you are violating his daughter.)

In Chrétien's version on the other hand the *affaire* is reciprocal and it is the female partner who is denounced by the knight for accommodating her father's supposed murderer: 'fame, honie soies tu!' he shouts, concluding contemptuously in a misogynistic tirade:

> 'Mais tu iez feme, bien le voi;
> Que cil la qui siet dalez toi
> Ocist ton pere, et tu le baises!'[24]

('But you are a woman as I can well see. He killed your father and now you are offering him your body!')

Wolfram uses a number of narratorial quips to, as it were, tease and challenge his hero to adhere to a superior set of sexual standards. He continues the theme of sexual abuse when we hear that the captives in *schastel marveile* have been subject to an unwilling sexual segregation by the evil magician Clinschor (the benign 'clers sages d'astronomie' of Chrétien, Heinrich's Gansguoter). Heinrich's treatment of the 'Obie'–'Obilot'–Meliant–Tybalt story (*Crône* lines 17,500ff, renamed by Heinrich Flursensephin, Quebelplus, Fiers of Arramis and Leigamar respectively) does not on the other hand significantly alter the substance of Chrétien's account, except that both the lover, Fiers, and the father, Leigamar, are defeated by Gawein and both are 'surrendered' to Quebelplus, the minor, to do with as she wishes. In an equally ironic twist the older sister, Flursensephin, becomes the sexual property of Gawein who, being already married, very properly hands her over to be married to his companion in arms, the Breton Quoikos, a character innovation whom Heinrich uses with some forethought to give a decorous, marital resolution to the squabble.

---

24 *Le Roman de Perceval ou Le Conte du Graal*, ed. Keith Busby (Tübingen: Niemeyer, 1993), lines 5861–63.

Heinrich's treatment of sexual relations in this section of the text is then a little pro forma. Whilst Chrétien treats amorous by-play exuberantly and Wolfram reshapes Chrétien's narrative data to give expression to the theme of sexual abuse, Heinrich seems to have treated the series in a somewhat sanitised fashion, a procedure which may have been something of a self-denying ordinance on the part of an author whose graphic and protracted depiction of Gasozein's earlier sexual assault on Guinevere (lines 11,608–746) has earned him something of a reputation as a medieval pornographer. In the sequence directly under consideration here, however, he may have wished to exercise a measure of restraint because he possibly saw this sequence as a fixed ensemble of exploits which was (eventually) to precipitate Gawein towards the Grail.

If such were the case then he may have felt justified in having viewed Chrétien's sexual humour and Wolfram's deepening of the emotional terms of reference as side issues irrelevant to and even detrimental to the main issue of preparing his protagonist for the Grail quest – an issue which for him lay buried underneath the extraneous details of what he seems to have regarded as a sequence somewhat lacking in unity of action. If such was Heinrich's thinking, then his modus operandi bears some similarity to that of the author of *Perlesvaus* in which, once Gauvain has determined upon the Grail quest, he abjures his old, philandering ways, and indeed so convincingly that three young women out for some sexual sport conclude to their dismay that their chaste interlocutor, who eschews his customary 'luf talkynge', can only be a 'counterfeit' of the real Gauvain.[25]

The thematic core of the Gauvain sequence in the *Conte du Graal* for Heinrich was then clearly perceived to reside not in its sexual content but rather in an early episode where Gauvain is accused by the knight Guigambresil of having murdered his master, the old Lord of Escavalon. Gauvain is arraigned for having slain him unchivalrously, that is, without having issued a due knightly challenge and his blustering response to the accusation appears to give at least prima facie support to the case of his accuser:

> 'Mais se je rien mesfait eüsse
> Au chevalier et jel seüsse,
> Molt volontiers pais en queïsse
> Et tele amende l'en feïsse
> Que tot si ami et li mien
> Le deüssent tenir a bien.
> Et si il a dit son outrage,
> Je m'en desfent et tent mon gage
> Ou chi ou la ou lui plaira'.   (lines 4779–87)

25 'Par Dieu, fet l'une a l'autre, se ce fust cil Gavains qui niés est le roi Artu, il parlast a nos autrement, e trovissions en lui plus de deduit que en cestui; mes cist est un Gavains contrefez'. *Perlesvaus, Le Haut Livre du Graal*, ed. by Nitze and Jenkins, vol. 1, lines 1259–61.

(But if I were to have wittingly given any offence to this knight I would most earnestly plead for peace and make such reparations as both his kin and my own might approve. But what he says is an outrage and I give my pledge that I will defend myself either here on the spot or in another place of his choosing.)

Wolfram, revealing himself at the outset to be no bona fide continuator of Chrétien, appears to take over the initial premise of a homicidal Gawein when Kingrimursel (Chrétien's Guigambresil) accuses Gawan of murdering his lord, but by the beginning of the eighth Book it emerges that Gawan did not commit the act – another knight (Ehkunat) is now arraigned all unheralded as a villainous *deus ex machina* and Gawan is therefore exonerated. The potential cause of conflict being defused, the motif of the Grail quest (maintained pro forma by Wolfram when the knight Liddamus maliciously proposes that the quest be transferred from Vergulaht to Gawan) descends to the status of a blind motif. That is, the fortunate clearing of Gawan's good name has at the same time the unfortunate consequence of bringing about his narrative marginalisation, an impression which is confirmed when the adapter of what was already a *Doppelroman* introduces a third hero in the shape of Parzival's pagan half-brother, Feirefiz, to accompany Parzival on his final visit to the Grail castle. Parzival's choice, made over the heads of all other knights including Gawan, allows the two formerly estranged brothers to approach the Grail together and so give effective symbolic expression to an ethical vision to which Gawan was irrelevant, namely, that which forms the main focus of Wolfram's *Willehalm*: a rapprochement between sectarian adversaries. It is clear that this preconceived theme, originating in Wolfram's first two Books where the circumstances of Feirefiz's mixed-religion parentage are introduced, was all along to be given precedence over the granting of any larger role to the figure of Gawan, who plays an essentially subordinate role in *Parzival,* albeit an extensive one.

Wolfram confers on Gawan a function appropriate to his secondary status, namely, that of being an opponent of rape and sexual abuse, this being an independent theme which Chrétien hints at but which Wolfram emphasises through a number of substantial modifications to his French source. Heinrich, by contrast, used the sequence largely as a means to an end – that of leading his hero towards the goal which he had inevitably failed to attain in Chrétien's incomplete romance. He cannot therefore have found much of interest in Wolfram's amplifications of the love theme or in the subordination of Gawan in the interests of furthering an idiosyncratic vision of positive Orientalism. Such extravagant innovations, had he taken his cue from them, would have led him far from his own concerns. His reasons for setting special store by a motif peremptorily annulled by his German predecessor may be further clarified through observation of some fundamental moral and structural differences between *Parzival* and *Diu Crône.*

The Gawan sequence presented Wolfram with an opportunity to create a more or less independent romance in which he portrayed his second hero essentially as a sexual saviour figure with a quick sympathy for the damaged sexuality of Orgeluse and of the captive youths and maidens of *schastel marveile*. The skill with which Wolfram reconceptualises this whole sequence cannot however obscure the fact that there is a *lectio facilior* which he fails to address. This is that, with Gawan exonerated, there is no barrier to his Grail adventure, so that 'the audience naturally' expects that the romance will turn to an account of Gawan's adventures in this search. They might also expect the flower of Arthurian knighthood to succeed where Parzival had failed'.[26]

Such is precisely the neglected theme to which Heinrich devoted his efforts, using this sequence as a preparatory narrative stage in the course of which his hero must prove himself to be a faithful married knight and worthy prospective Grail quester. For that reason it was necessary to 'unsex' the potentially compromising figures of Seimeret and Mancipelle to ensure that his future Grail quester would be able to pass the second test of virtue where he had failed the first on account of a sexual offence. In *Parzival*, the old Grail king, Anfortas, is punished with a symbolic wound in the genitals for 'serving' Orgeluse, and it is Wolfram's prospective new Grail king, the eponymous hero, who, rejecting the selfsame Orgeluse's advances out of loyalty to his wife, comes to establish his superior credentials with regard to the holding of the sacred office. It seems likely that Heinrich, seeking a similar degree of moral rectitude for his own protagonist, will have invented *ex nihilo* the figure of 'Quoikos' to ensure that his hero's monogamous record is kept intact when Gawein's due sexual prize, Flursensephin, can be honourably handed over to the Breton comrade in arms. Having already redeemed Gawein's sexual reputation earlier in his narrative through the marriage with Amurfina, Heinrich makes sure thereafter that a line may be firmly drawn under it – the better to focus concentration on the primary theme to which other incidents now become subordinate, namely, the Grail quest, the somewhat elusive nature of which is intimated to Gawein at various stages in the narrative.

---

26 Bonnie Büttner, 'Gawan in Wolfram's *Parzival*', unpublished dissertation, Cornell University, 1984, p. 108.

4

Visions of Apocalypse and Salvation

> Although Bosch's works are often complicated in their imagery, they are
> likely to be properly understood if we search in them for an overall theme
> consonant with the world in which the artist worked [...] Life then was one of
> sharp contrasts, understood by people in the light of dogmas of the Pre-Refor-
> mation Church. The climate of thought was largely conditioned by a pessi-
> mistic view of man's fate in the world, in which the power of evil seemed to be
> driving him relentlessly towards his damnation.[1]

Marvels (*wunder*) take on a variety of forms in medieval romance. The immediate origins of many marvellous traditions lay in the romances of Chrétien
de Troyes, some elements doubtless springing from his own imagination but
many representing a metaphorical palimpsest of older mythological lore
upon which Chrétien superimposed a twelfth-century cultural overlay. Heinrich has a similar store of *le merveilleux*[2] but some sequences, in which Gawein
perceives uncanny scenes of irremediable human destitution, appear to
derive from a different source than the *matière de Bretagne* tradition. Many
elements of these rather macabre 'Wunderketten' appear to resemble Biblical
apocalyptic more closely than they do the putative mythological substratum
of the *matière de Bretagne*. The first two sequences (lines 13,935–14,903;
15,997–16,495) are interspersed with a visit by Gawein to the palace of
Fortuna (Vrou Saelde, lines 15,823–931) and appear to present visions of apocalypse and salvation juxtaposed.

En route to a tournament in the company of the other knights, Gawein
becomes detached from his fellows and in a vacant mood supposes that he
hears the sounds of his companions' jousting, then witnesses a maiden riding
up with a dead knight (a scene similar to that occurring in Wolfram's *Parzival*
and *Titurel* where Sigune mourns the slain Schionatulander). He then
witnesses an old woman behind whose eyes burn vivid flames and a giant

---

[1] Hieronymus Bosch, *The Garden of Earthly Delights*, ed. John Rowlands (Oxford: Phaidon,
1977), p. 1.

[2] We encounter for instance in *Diu Crône* a magic ball of string with which a knight may pull
himself across a lake (lines 15,649ff), magical fluid employed to solidify quicksand (lines
14,440ff), a magic cloak (lines 15,248ff), a magic fountain with life-protecting qualities
(lines 26,6290ff) and a plethora of narcotic and amatory preparations.

sacking a castle and forcing its unfortunate female inhabitants into the flames (lines 14,267ff). In a yet more grotesque vignette, a boy pierced through the eyes by arrows holds a fan which wafts a fiery breeze (line 14,373). Other sights include that of a naked maiden unsuccessfully attempting to drive scavenging birds away from the wounds of a chained giant (lines 14,122ff), a black knight with a decapitated woman's head in his hand pursued by another knight and yet another decapitated male figure lying with a dog cut in two (lines 14,198ff). Gawein eventually comes to a castle unknown to him but where he is recognised by the inhabitants (lines 14,568ff). In its chapel where he goes to pray Gawein sees a sword appearing before him on a golden chain, only to disappear from view. The sword is succeeded by two 'disembodied' gloves with a spear streaming with blood as if a knight were reaching out from the wall. Going now from the chapel into the hall of the castle (lines 14,739ff) the hero witnesses what appears to be a spectral 'grail'[3] procession (although it is not named as such) which involves four maidens carrying lighted candles followed by another maiden with a crystal vessel containing fresh blood. All five walk up to the grey-haired host who is given the blood to drink. Gawein is unable to find out the import of these strange occurrences, but finds out that the old host has recently died. Just as he hopes to find out more the next day, he finds himself alone in the open air outside the castle walls.

The *Wunderketten* have commonly been seen as abounding in gratuitous enigmas[4] and many details defy precise exegesis. It cannot for instance be decided with any degree of certainty if the bound giant being gnawed by vultures is meant to represent Prometheus[5] or whether the old woman with fire behind her eyes whipping a Blackamoor is the Whore of Babylon from the Apocalypse or else simply a part of Heinrich's 'inventory of terror' innocent of typological links.[6] And are the six hundred knights being cut down by sword and lance meant to represent members of the Arthurian entourage or that of the Grail?[7] These spectral pageants, appearing to exist in a different dimension to that inhabited by the protagonist (or else imposing

---

3 In Chrétien and his continuators there is always a set order of personnel: a vassal with a lance, two further vassals with candles, a lady with the Grail and another lady with a silver platter. The sequence is only slightly varied in *Diu Crône*.

4 Gawein's experiences have been compared with the literature of the fantastic or with the Gothic novel of a much later era by Ernst Dick, 'Tradition and emancipation: the generic aspect of Heinrich's Crône', in *Genres in Medieval German Literature*, ed. Hubert Heinen and Ingeborg Henderson (Göppingen: Kümmerle, 1986), pp. 74–92, especially 84–92.

5 See Johannes Keller, *Diu Crône, Wunderketten Gral und Tod*, pp. 66–70.

6 Keller 73, and for a different view Mentzel-Reuters, *Vröude; Artusbild, Fortuna- und Gralkonzeption*, p. 258.

7 Keller, *Diu Crône*, pp. 56–62.

themselves on his inner eye)[8] introduce details which remain as puzzling as the paintings of an Hieronymus Bosch or Alfred Kubin. Their broad import can however often be gauged from an intertextual comparison with motifs occurring in parallel narrative traditions.

The term *merveille* in Old French was sometimes used in a restricted sense with the powerful if somewhat vague connotation of a nameless, unhallowed horror. In Chrétien's *Conte du Graal*, Gauvain is warned by a ferryman standing before the Castle of Wonders to be on his guard in this abode of the dead 'Car c'est une terre salvage,/Tote plaine de grans merveilles' (lines 7464–65). The title of the French romance, *Les Merveilles de Rigomer*, which refers to the baleful enchantments surrounding the castle of Rigomer[9] and the sinister portents which knights encounter when approaching it, has a similar negative resonance. 'Wonders' of this kind are encountered by the unfortunate Lancelot in that romance when he hears sounds of hunting horns in a forest, suggesting the Wild Hunt (*exercitus furiosus*) and its phantom forms of unconfessed dead and unbaptized child deaths caught in a purgatorial limbo.[10] In *Diu Crône*, a similar scene (also called a 'wunder', line 27,468) occurs in a short sequence where Gawein hears a blast from a horn and a group of knights surrounded by flames as hot as those blown in a blacksmith's forge (lines 27,370–27,458). Many other such wonders witnessed by Gawein contain the motif of fire, suggesting hellfire or else (since the terms were not precisely differentiated in vernacular literature)[11] the flames of purgatory. This conception was probably inspired by the spirit king, Lar, in Wirnt's *Wigalois*, who languishes in a limbo from which he, like the old Grail king in *Diu Crône*, is permitted remissions.

---

8   Gawein is described as having entered a trance-like state in which he becomes blind to his physical environment:
> Nu gienc ein wec bî ime eneben,
> Der in von sîn gesellen truoc:
> Dar ûf er sîn ors sluoc,
> Daz ez sich des nie verstuont:
> Alsô die liute alle tuont,
> Sô sie in gedenken sint,
> Dâ von sint sie schiere blint.   (lines 13,940–46)

9   In this case the dangers warn of the sirens whose sexual allure has the power to rob knights of their wits and to consign Lancelot to an ignominious *val sanz retor* in the kitchens of its castle. See Wendelin Foerster and Hermann Breuer, *Les Merveilles de Rigomer*, 2 vols (Dresden: Niemeyer, 1908–15).

10 Jakob Grimm, *Deutsche Mythologie*, 2 vols (Göttingen: Dieterische Buchhandlung, 1854), vol. 2, pp. 760–68.

11 In Hartmann's *Erec*, when Erec releases Enite from the obligation to tend their horses, she is relieved to be free of what she terms 'the torments of Hell' ('hellewîze', line 3652). Modern theological distinctions between the punitive fires of Hell, the purifying and expiatory fires of Purgatory, and the probative fires of Judgement are late rationalisations. See Jacques Le Goff, *The Birth of Purgatory*, trans. Arthur Goldhammer (Chicago: Chicago U.P., 1984), especially pp. 39–43. On the development of the doctrine of remission see Marcus Landau, *Hölle und Fegfeuer in Volksglaube, Dichtung und Kirchenlehre* (Heidelberg: Winter, 1909).

Whether the time of purgatory was earthly or eschatological was a matter of debate in the period 1150–1300 when Christendom was engaged in redefining the map of its spiritual universe. The scenes involving Lar and his troupe of lost souls in *Wigalois* show that purgatory could be conceived in terrestrial terms (or else that purgatorial conditions might at least be apprehensible through a breach in the normal space–time continuum). In cases where living beings were permitted apprehensions of dead souls, the souls were imagined as possessing a material likeness (*similitudo corporis*) which allowed them to be seen (and so that punishment could be inflicted upon them as if corporeal).[12] At a time when the greatest reality would in any case have been imputed to the world of ideas,[13] there already existed a widespread popular belief in 'the existence and power of supernatural beings who were generally invisible but always nearby.[14] The 'ghosts' witnessed by Gawein in *Diu Crône* would have been lexicalised as *species umbraticae, similitudines,* or *quasi corpora*.[15]

The location of many of Gawein's spectral encounters is described as barren and scorched,[16] linking it with the familiar motif of the Waste Land.[17] From the time of the Church Fathers to that of Gildas and Geoffrey of Monmouth it was a commonplace to explain a blight on a kingdom as evidence of divine punishment. Playing upon the medieval belief in the interdependence of the moral and the material universe, stories containing the Waste Land motif account for the blight by adducing some irredeemable human wickedness which had exerted a baleful influence on the material world, only to be redeemed through the good offices of a knight-messiah. In

---

12 The spatialisation was taken quite literally, so that it was thought that Gehenna would have to be sixty times the size of Eden in order to receive the greater number of sinful deceased.

13 Hiltrud K. Knoll, 'Studien zur realen und ausserrealen Welt im deutschen Artusroman (*Erec, Iwein, Lanzelet, Wigalois*)', doctoral dissertation, University of Bonn, 1966.

14 Jean-Claude Schmitt, *Ghosts in the Middle Ages. The Living and the Dead in Medieval Society,* trans. Teresa Lavender Fagan (Chicago and London: University of Chicago Press, 1998), p. 2. In Germanic tradition these were the quasi-physical doubles (*hamr*) that survived after death; in Norse mythology the often malevolent dead were called *draugr*: the Middle Ages was influenced by such concepts together with the great pneumatic tradition of Antiquity to which Augustine was heir.

15 In Marie de France's *Espurgatoire Saint Patrice*, ed. Michael J. Curley (Binghampton: University of Binghampton Press, 1993), souls are described as having foreknowledge of their fate either through *revelaciün*, or *avisiün* or by *dreite conscience* (lines 65–68): 'Els veient espiritelement/ço que semble corporelement' (lines 77–78).

16   Dô warn sie komen in ein lant,
    Daz was allez verbrant
    Ganz gar unde wüeste:
    Swer dâ wesen müeste
    Der het den lîp gar balde verlorn:
    Dâ wuohs weder gras noch korn,
    Niht wan hecken unde dorn.   (lines 14,115–21. Cf. also lines 28,619–28)

17 In the First Continuation the Grail realm is frequently termed a *roialmes destruis* and in Wolfram it is called a 'waste' (*Parzival*, ed. Lachmann, section 250, line 5).

both the *Conte du Graal* and *Diu Crône* the lance and Grail are symbols of destruction, possibly emblematic of death itself.[18] As long as the Question remains unposed, a fatal influence issues from the Grail, for, it has been contended, 'at the very heart of the Grail legend there lies a grave ambivalence in that the relics of the Last Supper and passion are made to appear responsible for the malefic enchantments and perils afflicting King Arthur's kingdom [. . .] the sacred lance and the sword of King David, "the sword of the spirit", appear at times in the light of weapons of vengeance and Nemesis'.[19] Many legends of the Grail preserve the old sense of the intensely harmful potential of holy objects, but little sense of ambivalence would have been felt since in medieval terms 'a thing is not sacred because it is good. It is sacred because it contains mysterious and awesome power.[20] This is precisely the quality possessed by the Grail in *Diu Crône* where it represents a curse of which the *Wunderketten* give ghostly intimations. This is not a 'pervertierte Gralkonzeption'[21] but arguably a logical response to the premise widely taken for granted by many of Heinrich's contemporaries that they were living in a 'monster-ridden environment [. . .] sometimes almost reminiscent of Hieronymus Bosch'[22] and ruled over by a punitive deity.

If this world of spectral 'marvels' is one that we have largely lost [23] it is because of the Early Modern 'decline of Hell'[24] and the growing disinclination to believe in curses inflicted by a vengeful deity, together with the 'demythologisation' of the Christian legacy which has led to a considerably reduced theological commitment to the doctrines of both hell and heaven.[25] Yet despite the fact that 'the furious troop of Hellequin has been chased from our culture',[26] the logic of the tradition is as clear today as it was in the Middle Ages, a sure sign of which is that the terms of the original discourse have been preserved in metaphorical form. Now as then 'ghosts' of countless

---

[18] It is reported of the bleeding lance that it has the power to destroy the whole land of Logres (*Conte du Graal*, 7538–45) and Ulrich Wyss argues that the Grail represents death in *Diu Crône*: 'Wunderketten in der Crone', in *Die mittelalterliche Literatur in Kärnten*, ed. A. Cella and P. Krämer, pp. 269–91. For the iconography of death in the Middle Ages see George Henderson, *Early Medieval* (Harmondsworth: Penguin, 1972), pp. 73–96.

[19] Pauline Matarasso, *The Quest of the Holy Grail*, Harmondsworth: Penguin, 1969, Introduction, p. 13.

[20] Richard Cavendish, *King Arthur and the Grail. The Arthurian Legends and their Meaning* (London: Paladin, 1980), p. 177.

[21] Johannes Keller, *Diu Crône,Wunderketten, Gral und Tod*, p. 61.

[22] Dennis Nineham, *Christianity Medieval and Modern. A Study in Religious Change* (London: SCM Press, 1993), p. 235; although there is evidence of some softening of attitudes by the twelfth century. See Colin Morris, *The Discovery of the Individual* (New York: Harper and Row, 1973.

[23] See Peter Dinzelbacher, 'Mittelalterliche Vision und moderne Sterbeforschung', in *Psychologie in der Mediävistik*, ed. J. Kühnel, H.-D. Mück, Ursula and Ulrich Müller, GAG 431 (Göppingen: Kümmerle, 1985), pp. 9–45.

[24] D. P. Walker, *The Decline of Hell* (London: Routledge and Kegan Paul, 1964).

[25] Colleen McDannell and Bernhard Lang, *Heaven: A History* (New Haven and London, Yale U.P., 1988).

[26] Schmitt, *Ghosts in the Middle Ages*, p. 227.

murdered souls[27] languish who will not 'rest' until the unfathomable mysteries of human iniquity have been properly understood and confronted.[28]

Medieval literature, in harmony with Christian theology, traced the cause of all present woes back to an original sin. The 'Elucidation' (a short early thirteenth-century work purporting to provide an exegesis of Chrétien's *Conte du Graal*) has the parable of a past Arcadian era when maidens at wells would serve drink to wayfarers from golden goblets. Matters changed when the evil Amangon and his men deflowered the maidens and carried off their vessels. After this event the land of Logres became desolate and the Court of the Rich Fisher could no longer be found. (Arthur's knights went forth to redress the wrong, Gauvain and Perceval being successful in this endeavour). The most fully worked out application of this metaphysical logic in Old French literature is the Balain story in the *Suite du Merlin*.

The Balain and Grail narratives, 'related to each other as introduction and conclusion to the Enchantments of Britain',[29] tell of a story of human sin the after-effects of which can be expunged only by the most sublime effort of redemption. Balain, called the *chevalier mescheant*, falls foul of an ancient form of justice[30] according to which he becomes an unwitting yet culpable sinner in the stamp of an Oedipus or Gregorius,[31] and plunges himself and his Arthurian peers into deep misfortune after his administration of 'le cop dolereus par coi li roiames de Listenois (=Logres) est tornés a dolur et a essil'.[32] This Dolorous Stroke is part of a complex of disasters: Balain's sword breaks when he kills his own brother. Thereafter he accidentally but illicitly seizes a holy lance with which he stuns the good King Pellehan, causing the castle walls to crumble, the country to become waste and its inhabitants either to die or to walk round like living dead.

The figure of Parzival in *Diu Crône* is functionally comparable to Balain in

---

[27] The troupe of the dead was often imagined as an army of the dead (*exercitus mortuorum*), a sort of infernal double of the feudal army, and 'in the twelfth century there was a relationship between the increasing prevalence of the furious army of the dead and all the contemporary measures being taken to rein in the feudal system and to limit its wars and devastations' (Schmitt, *Ghosts in the Middle Ages*, p. 100).

[28] Society still harbours collective phantoms such as Auschwitz, Katyn, and more recent ones too numerous to mention whose victims 'continue to break open the doors of guilty indifference and forgetting' (Schmitt, *Ghosts in the Middle Ages*, p. 227).

[29] A. C. L. Brown, 'The bleeding lance', *PMLA* 25 (1910), pp. 1–59, citation 50.

[30] 'When anyone sins without knowing it against one of God's commandments concerning things which must not be done, he will be considered guilty and will be held accountable for his deed.' (Leviticus 5.17)

[31] Due to the self-confirming quality of medieval conceptions of Providence, to be unlucky was to be sinful in some unrevealed way. If the wicked man encountered adversity this was a punishment from God. If a godly man was smitten then he was being tested and tried. The correct reaction on the part of a believer smitten by ill fortune was therefore to search her/himself in order to discover the moral defect which had provoked God's wrath, or to eliminate the complacency which had led the Almighty to try him.

[32] *Merlin*, ed. Gaston Paris and Jacob Ulrich, 2 vols (Paris: Firmin Didot, 1888), vol. 2, p. 57.

that his sin is presented as a terminal episode whose effects cannot be undone by the original perpetrator. Here the old Grail king (who is himself a corpse like the stricken inhabitants of Logres in the *Suite du Merlin)* tells that a relation of Parzival had committed the sin of Cain against one of his kinsmen, bringing misfortune down upon the heads of the whole family. Parzival himself, as a member of the same kin, is the legatee of a stigma which persists indefinitely since Parzival was not courageous enough to ask the redemptive question on reaching the Grail castle (lines 29,484–513). This dolorous offence not only perpetuates the torment of the old Grail king and his retinue (as in Wolfram) but also – since it is hinted that Parzival's failure occurred not in a distinct 'Grail realm' but at Arthur's court[33] – it may be supposed to damage the whole Arthurian kingdom where the offence occurred.

In Wolfram's version Parzival's failure to ask the compassionate question at the Grail castle is a tort which falls outside Arthurian jurisdiction. Heinrich on the other hand is closer to Malory who saw no disjunction between knighthood and the Grail in his *Tale of the Sankgreal,*[34] (hence Wolfram's Arthurian/Grail dichotomy remains unproblematised in *Diu Crône).* The effect of this is that Parzival's failure signals a crisis not merely for himself, but for the whole Court under whose aegis the omission occurred. This wider effect is confirmed by the words of the maiden calqued on Wolfram's Sigune[35] in whose plaint the death of her *ami* and the unredeemed Arthurian world are fused. Unlike her Wolframian prototype, Heinrich's Sigune figure does not attribute her lover's death to her own folly for having sent him off on a life-endangering *service d'amour*[36] but to the unfortunate Parzival's omission, from which all other disasters are said to flow (lines 13989–14030). The terms of the maiden's lament in *Diu Crône,* unlike those of Wolfram's Sigune, bear a greater similarity to the more comprehensive reproach of Wolfram's Grail messenger, Cundrie. Cundrie's condemnation of the whole Arthurian household *(Parzival,* section 315, lines 1–15) remained a blind motif in Wolfram but it is picked up again and problematised in *Diu Crône:*

> Daz er in ungevrâget liez,
> Noch alsô sêre riuwet mich;

---

33 The Grail is housed at Gornemant (line 14,001), a name which had previously been associated with Arthur's lands (line 3304). It is also said to be located at Katerac (line 9023), a castle belonging to Amurfina. The final location of the Grail, which is something of an 'ubiquitäre Instanz' (Ulrich Wyss), is described as 'Illes ûf der habe' (line 29,683).

34 Mary Hynes-Berry, 'A tale "breffley drawne oute of Freynshe" ', in *Aspects of Malory,* ed. Toshiyuki Takamiya and Derek Brewer (Cambridge: D. S. Brewer, 1981), pp. 93–106.

35 The mourning female figure and her slain lover whom Gawein encounters in the first visionary sequence correspond to Sigune and Schionatulander in Wolfram's *Parzival* where Sigune appears in a similar *pietà* role.

36 'Ich hete kranke sinne/daz ich im niht minne gap' *(Parzival,* section 141, lines 20–21). On Sigune's guilt see Bernhard Rahn, *Wolframs Sigunedichtung* (Zurich: Fretz and Wasmuth, 1958), p. 79.

Daz künec Artûs velschet sich
Und die tugentriche ritterschaft
An dirre traegen gsellschaft,
Ez entuoc niht ir magenkraft.   (*Crône*, lines 14,003–08)

(The fact that Parzival left without posing the question still causes me sorrow. Because of that omission King Arthur and his knights are dishonoured – and all through one knight's pusillanimity. Their power is no more.)

Since the whole Arthurian company is implicated in the dishonour, the Grail quest is presented as an 'Arthurian' challenge in which the survival of the Court is at stake. The *Wunderketten*, reinforcing a number of more conventional apocalyptic warnings that the Court will fall without Gawein's military prowess, show in spectral form the fatal effects of the curse and remind the protagonist of unfinished business at the Grail castle. They are only visionary admonitions since Gawein is as yet powerless to intervene and, consistent with the metaphysical logic of a narrative rooted in ancient conceptions of messianism and the mythology of death, the hero must at first content himself with these initiatory forms of *descensus*[37] as a preparation for his final challenge. Only the last of the *Wunderketten* (lines 28,606–29,009) makes clear the precise nature of the task awaiting Gawein when another flaming, demonic figure whipping on a group of naked, defenceless women ceases his assaults upon Gawein's approach, whereupon the whole company gives joyful thanks to Gawein as their redeemer and expires before him (line 28,665). The benign euthanasia bestowed upon these tormented souls by Gawein's charismatic presence foreshadows his final liberation of the *altherre* and his other 'undead' companions at the Grail castle.

It may initially seem remarkable that the wonders with their cryptic summons for the need for salvation do not diminish their force after the goddess Fortuna (Vrou Saelde) grants Gawein her own form of salvation. When that knight arrests the motion of her notorious wheel and receives her assurance of prosperity for the Arthurian Court, we might suppose that a signal benediction were taking place. Yet strangely the encounter would seem to point rather to her powerlessness and the consequential futility of attempting to conciliate her. Although Gawein is described as being in pos-

---

[37] Much of Gawein's career has been termed a 'Strudel von Descensusabenteuern' (Matthias Meyer, *Die Verfügbarkeit der Fiktion. Interpretationen und poetologische Untersuchungen zum Artusroman und zur aventiurehaften Dietrichepik des 13. Jahrhunderts* (Heidelberg: Carl Winter 1994), p. 124). Even the realm of Amurfina is, especially from the point of view of Gawein's anxious peers, a *Minne-Totenreich* (Meyer, p. 89). The same applies functionally to the island of flowers at Colurmein where Gawein has to stick himself through the foot to escape its narcotic effects (sleep being traditionally the mythical brother of death). On the knightly quest as *descensus* see Ernst Dick, 'Katabasis and the Grail epic: Wolfram von Eschenbach's *Parzival*', *Res Publica Litterarum* 1 (1978), pp. 57–87.

session of Fortune's favour even *before* he gains his audience with her[38] his approach to her palace is anything but the straight path we might expect for one of Fortune's favourites. On the contrary, he needs to execute the most determined stratagems to traverse the hostile territory of Saelde's sister, which appears to be the only gateway to Fortuna's realm of Ordohorht.

When Gawein passes through this dangerous terrain, we are told that he had once incurred the couple's wrath by wresting from Fimbeus a magic belt encrusted with a miraculous jewel of sovereignty. This had been wrought by Lady Fortuna and given to her sister who had in turn passed it to Fimbeus in order to protect him in battle. Ostensibly under Fortuna's tutelage Gawein is able to make his way through the hostile land. However, her support conspicuously has no power to stop Giramphiel trying to take her revenge for the theft since she gives him the false information that the land of Fortuna is guarded only by a small dragon where in fact it is a large one (in the event the beast almost costs Gawein his life). Making his escape from the fiery breath of the enormous dragon, he gains the palace of a helping maiden, Siamerac of Lembil who gives him instructions for reaching Fortuna's realm of Ordohorht: Gawein must cast a ball of thread over the lake before her castle and pull himself over the water to her stronghold. Having reached Fortuna's palace in this way, he finds her, in accordance with traditional iconographic conventions, beautiful on her right hand side but loathsome on the left. On Gawein's entrance, however, her wheel stops rotating, whereupon the goddess, her son, Heil, and other stricken inhabitants of her palace become as well-formed on both sides of their bodies as they had once been only on their right side. The goddess now promises perpetual good fortune to Gawein and to his king but, before he even reaches the perimeter of her realm, Gawein encounters a second 'Wunderkette' in the form of volcanic storms which threaten to engulf him and against which he requires the additional help of a third party, Aanzim. Whilst making his escape he also receives heart-rending requests for help from various victims of oppression to which he would have responded had not another emissary of Fortuna, Samaidien, warned him not to become involved with helping others. Such interventions, she asserts, would be as detrimental to the welfare of the Arthurian Court as was Parzival's erstwhile failure to pose the required question at the Grail castle.

Just as Hartmann through his invocation of 'der höfische got' implied a desire to co-opt the Christian God as a perennial support for the ambitions of courtly society, Heinrich's personification of Fortuna as a *fortuna stabilis* might seem to represent an attempt to portray the goddess as a Christian guardian angel functionally equivalent to Christian Providence, a conception for which there were ample precedents in courtly narrative.[39] However, this

---

[38] On the occasion of an earlier danger we are informed: 'Wolt sîn dâ hân vergezzen/ Fortunâ, sô waere er tôt' (lines 14,985–86).

[39] Cf. Hartmann's *Erec*, ed. Leitzmann, lines 2438–39 : 'Saelde und grôze werdekeit/ die hâte

conception is so undermined by the bathetic, almost farcical depiction of Gawein's dealings with the goddess that we might suspect parody. The dialogue between the pair is strangely brief and laconic, her greeting hardly going beyond the conventional (lines 15,870–930). The manner in which she and those on her wheel are transformed by Gawein's entrance does not even make clear whether Saelde herself was behind the metamorphosis or (and this is the *lectio facilior*) Gawein brought redemption to his supposed redeemer (the reactions of the unfortunates on Fortune's wheel with their songs and obeisances to their deliverer make Gawein, rather than the goddess, appear the author of their salvation):

> Als nu Gâwein in den sal trat,
> Dô stuont stille daz rat
> Und wart vrou Saelde gelîche gevar
> Über al schoene unde clâr,
> Dar zuo disiu schar gemein
> Jenhalp unde hie dissît
> Begunden singen widerstrît
> Ein lop ir wol schône
> Mit vil süezem dône,
> Und begunden alle nîgen.   (lines 15,870–80)

(When Gawein entered Fortuna's hall, her wheel stood still and Lady Fortuna became uniformly beautiful and radiant. The whole host of people on her wheel, those aloft and those below, competed in a sweet song of praise to an exquisite melody and all began to bow.)

Saelde's assurance of perpetual good fortune to Gawein and his king seems the less convincing when in the following *Wunderkette* involving strange meteorological eruptions, Gawein is almost trapped by a storm of volcanic ash. Clearly, despite being described as riding 'in vrou Saelden pflege' (line 15,928). Gawein still has to watch his every step against disaster, and Saelde is obliged to send an emissary to warn him not to become involved in the various virtuous causes which beckon to him.[40] She has indeed to depute her burgrave, Aanzim, to advise on how to make his escape from the dangerous environs of Ordohorht: Fortuna cannot apparently guarantee that her writ will hold good even as far as the perimeter of her own kingdom. When she tells him that the whole Arthurian Court would collapse if he were to accept any of the challenges offered by the host of deserving supplicants, this not

---

got an in geleit', and Karin R. Gürttler, *'Künec Artûs der Guote'. Das Artusbild der höfischen Epik des 12. Und 13. Jahrhunderts*, Studien zur Germanistik, Anglistik und Komparatistik 52 (Bonn: Bouvier, 1976), pp. 213–16 for further examples.

40 To be in Fortune's favour is apparently to renounce free will and become a 'Marionette der Glücksgöttin' (Keller, *Diu Crône*, pp. 268 and 275, note 40).

only seems to make a mockery of the very boon Gawein had just won from her but also to undermine his independent *raison d'être* as a knight errant.

There is a distinct 'lack of transcendence' (Wyss) about a Fortuna who does not exert her power supernaturally but rather through delegated intermediaries like any other secular *châtelaine*. The Arthurian courtiers at any rate later seem little impressed by Gawein's report of his triumph at Ordohorht, and by their very attempts to dissuade him from the rigours of the Grail quest would seem to discount the material and symbolic efficacy of Fortuna's ring given them as a token of her good will towards the Arthurian Court. Their undiminished fears would seem to express a scepticism about the possibility of winning the goddess's favours (or even conceivably about the phenomenological credibility of Gawein's interview with the goddess as reported by him). With the exception of those few passages where it is asserted (not demonstrated) that it was possible for Gawein to win Fortuna's perpetual support, there seems to be widespread accord amongst a number of characters (these including Gawein himself) about the fickleness and uncontrollability of Fortuna. This is demonstrated most clearly in the lengthy Colloquy on Fortune between Gawein and Riwalin, Gawein's ally against the giant Assiles. The latter opines that Fortune is 'circular' and therefore untrustworthy (lines 5965–7), an opinion amply supported by his interlocutor in a long and bitter speech in which he agrees that Fortuna is constant only in her inconstancy: 'Niender ist ez staet/Wan an unstaete aleine' (lines 6033–4).

Hence Fortuna in *Diu Crône* still retains essential aspects of the *fortuna anceps* of Antiquity, remaining immutable only in her mutability. Common experience apparently made it difficult to deny the place of mutability in human affairs, however injurious this might have been to the doctrine of Providence[41] and the differences between Heinrich's depiction and the standard iconography of his day are representational rather than conceptual. That is, instead of depicting his Fortuna as Janus-headed, Heinrich, using his common device of 'splitting' characters,[42] represents her benign and malign aspects in two separate persons. The presence of Saelde's sister, Giramphiel, a functional *fortuna adversa* ever ready to thwart Gawein's ambitions, annuls the possibility of unalloyed 'good fortune', an idea which is also implicit in

---

[41] Amurfina, when labouring under the misapprehension that her husband is dead, complains that God, Fortuna and Love personified ('Got, Saelde und vrou Minne', line 17,213) are at fault for her loss. On hearing the same false report of Gawein's death Kei too denounces God (lines 16,967–95).

[42] In the Didot *Perceval* the Grail quester is guided by Merlin. In *Diu Crône* the Merlin role is split (rather like Heinrich's Saelde and her son, Heil) into Gansguoter and his sister, Manbur, who *both* help Gawein on his way to the Grail. Heinrich also 'splits' the Grail adventure into two by having Kei have a separate adventure from Gawein in which he encounters what appears to be an effigy of the *roi maihaignié* (wounded through the knees) as opposed to the *altherre*. The device was of course not uncommon: cf. Wolfram's Anfortas and Titurel, or Pelles and Bron in *Perlesvaus*.

Heinrich's topography where Ordohorht, the land of Fortuna, lies perilously close to the land of the malign sister (cf. lines 22,855–56, 23,090–91).[43]

Saelde's family relationship with Giramphiel goes some way towards clarifying the ontological status of this rather powerless Fortuna figure. The term *gotinne* (a term widely used in *Diu Crône* and applied both to Manbur, Gansguoter's sister, and even to Arthur's aunt, Enfeidas) has sometimes been erroneously glossed as the equivalent in meaning of modern German *Göttin*. To follow that reading, however, leads to such a manifest absurdity as accepting Gansguoter as a 'god' because his sister, Manbur, is referred to as a *gotinne*. However if, as seems considerably more likely, gotinne means *fée* (as elsewhere in Middle High German literature, where the terms *fei* and *gotinne* are used interchangeably),[44] then Fortuna herself might be more appropriately understood as a *fée* (in the sense of a woman of power, of course, rather than in the sense of one of Shakespeare's gossamer-winged diminutives). This would seem all the more probable if, as I suspect, Fortuna is a split from Giramphiel rather than the other way round. For Giramphiel, probably based on certain aspects of Morgan le Fay, is introduced first in the work and plays by far the larger role and is therefore the most likely stem from which the shoot might have been removed.

Whilst in the hands of another writer the struggle between Saelde and her sister might have been developed as a cosmic battle over a mortal knight, in Heinrich's version any such story of the 'immortals' must count as (at best) 'fragmentary and unfinished'[45] since Saelde, sister to a *fée*, is clearly assimilated to the status of other *fées*, particularly Levenet (who supposedly gives Gawein the gift of eternal youth and is in that sense a double of Fortuna herself, lines 17,333ff). Gawein himself must be quite literally the *faber fortunae suae*. This is confirmed by an observation of the ways in which the concept of 'fortune' is regularly used in a metonymic relationship with 'valour'.[46] Fortuna's favours (assuming they can be won at all) can only be gained by the brave. Uther's flawless military record is seen to be implicit evidence of Fortuna's favour; there is no mention of his having had a

---

43 Francis Edward Keefe, 'Landschaft und Raum in der *Crône* Heinrichs von dem Türlin', unpublished dissertation, University of Kentucky, 1982, pp. 31–37; Annegret Wagner-Harken, *Märchenelemente und ihre Funktion in der 'Crône'*, pp. 183–88.

44 Famurgan is called *gotinne* in Hartmann's *Erec* (line 5161). On this point see Rosemary Wallbank, 'Irish fairy', p. 286, and Eberhard W. Funcke, 'Morgain und ihre Schwestern. Zur Herkunft und Verwendung der Feenmotivik in der mittelhochdeutschen Epik', *Acta Germanica* 18 (1985), pp. 1–64, especially 25.

45 Wallbank, 'Irish fairy', p. 293.

46 Cf. Karin Gürttler, *Künec Artus der Guote*, p. 213: 'Die *saelde* [. . .] ist keineswegs gratuitiv. Sie setzt ritterliche Tüchtigkeit und unerschrockenen *mannes muot* voraus, kluges und überlegtes Handeln, Beständigkeit in allen Dingen und Einhalten des rechten Maßes, Gerechtigkeit und soziales Verhalten, kurz, den Kanon ritterlich-sittlicher Werte, wie ihn der höfische Artusroman postuliert'.

personal audience with the goddess and her support must be inferred from his victories themselves:

> Daz er sô gar überreit
> Des breiten meres übervanc
> Daz ime nie misselanc
> dâ was saelden helfe schîn.   (lines 382–83)
>
> (The fact that Uther never failed in his excursions across many oceans bore witness to Fortuna's constant support of him.)

So far is 'fortune' a military virtue in Heinrich's usage that it is the imperialist military leader Uther and Gawein, the latter famed for having had the courage to filch Fortune's talisman and flowers (lines 6104–07) who stand out as Fortune's favourites. When Arthur and Gasozein engage in verbal fencing over Guinevere it is clearly a point of honour for both of them to claim that fortune is on their side, invoking the name of the deity as a badge of honour, their flyting underlining the notion that fortune is synonymous with valour (lines 4769–888). For Riwalin in his colloquy with Gawein it is axiomatic that, since luck invariably favours the brave, Gawein will win Fortune's favours (lines 6089–94). They both agree that her ways are unpredictable, but Riwalin mentions the strength and bravery for which Gawein is proverbial as the qualities most likely to incline Fortune in a knight's favour. In short, the various terms for fortune used in *Diu Crône* are subject to the strong semantic pull of 'Verritterlichung' and coloured by the chivalric scheme of values.

The striking interview between a knight of King Arthur and the goddess of the Ancients has no analogue in European literature but the dream of winning Fortune's favour is universal and it seems improbable that there was no older tradition underlying this part of the romance. It is possible that Arthur's loss of Fortune's favour on the eve of the final battle in a pre-literary version of the Lancelot–Grail tradition inspired a continuation in which Gawein retrieved Fortune's blessing for his beleaguered liege lord and so snatched Arthur back from the jaws of death.[47] However, the briefness of the Fortuna scene in *Diu Crône* indicates that Heinrich had no extensive narrative model of this sort to follow. It is perhaps more probable that Heinrich used the Fortuna scene opportunistically as a *coup de foudre* which, although it has no instrumental value for Gawein, is nevertheless symbolically important in distinguishing him from the irredeemably unfortunate Parzival, Heinrich's equivalent of the *chevalier mescheant* (whom Kei casts as an eternal unfortunate never destined to reach the Grail (lines 25,920–43). Losses caused by the cowardice of this German equivalent of Balain are made good by the offices

---

[47] For a similar conjecture see Helmut de Boor, *Geschichte der deutschen Literatur von den Anfängen bis zur Gegenwart*, ed. de Boor and Richard Newald, vol. 2, Die höfische Literatur (Munich: Beck, 1953), p. 198.

of his antipode, the supremely valorous Gawein. Gawein's association with Fortuna might then be understood rhetorically as a harbinger of his future 'good fortune' (although of course these successes will be all his own due to the circular logic of the Terentian *fortes fortuna adiuvat* informing *Diu Crône*).[48] In *Diu Crône* Christian and pre-Christian mythological conceptions[49] are frequently syncretised in locutions expressing faith in the joint sovereignty of Fortuna and the Christian God.[50] However, Heinrich's interest lay ultimately neither in 'magic', Fortuna's boons nor in Christian soteriology but in the strength of the chivalric order embodied in a knight who finally triumphs through 'kein zouber wan des mannes kraft' (line 27,787). Despite the occurrence of numerous magical and supernatural motifs there is little evidence of 'magical thinking' in *Diu Crône*.

48 F.-P. Knapp, 'Virtus und Fortuna in der *Krone*: Zur Herkunft der ethischen Grundthese Heinrichs von dem Türlin', *ZfdA* 106 (1977), pp. 253–65.

49 The Vienna manuscript even tells that the Arthurian knights 'swuoren bi ir goten' (line 1186). To be sure, MS P has 'bi irem gote' but this form gives a poorer rhyme with 'boten' at the end of the previous line.

50 Gawein is described as feeling confident in battle because he is being guarded over by God and Lady Fortuna alike (lines 7111–12; 7285–89). He professes himself to be unafraid of the possibility of a magical horn betraying his whereabouts to his enemy since, he reasons, 'If God wishes to go on protecting me he doubtless has the means to do so' (lines 7111–12) On the other hand, he hopes for 'Fortune's power' (line 7185) and Fortune's help (line 7200), fearing no danger 'because Lady Fortune was with him' (line 7289). His host Blandukors too can refer to God (lines 7257; 7268) and yet at the same time use the term 'Fortune's commandment' (line 7252).

5

The Grail Quest

I am by profession a scholar, sir, and not some magician or mountebank. Whose opinion was it but my own that the court sought for, relating to the great comet of 1577, after the judgement of certain so-called astronomers had unduly bred great fear and doubt? And who was it that prepared for our trades and voyages to Cathay and Muscovy with true charts and tables for our navigators? And who was it again that gave Euclid's propositions to the mechanics of this realm, from which they have derived inestimable benefit? I alone have achieved these things. Is it the work of a mountebank?

(Peter Ackroyd, *The House of Dr Dee*)

Before Gawein and his three companions set out on the Grail quest, Arthur's mother advises them to seek support from her second husband, Gansguoter, whom she had married after the death of Uther. That the Grail party should seek assistance from this magician-priest may seem anomalous from a post-Reformation perspective, however good his family connections; but it is likely to have seemed less so to Heinrich's original audiences for whom the interpenetration of magical and Christian practices would have seemed considerably less problematical.[1] Stephen Maksymiuk has recently made the case for a new understanding of this figure:

> In order to understand Gansguoter in his historical setting, we must reverse our rationalistic view of magicians. Here too, as in many other areas of medieval culture, our judgement of its mainstream values has been formed and distorted by the viewpoint of orthodox Christianity.[2]

---

[1] One of the Lollard Conclusions of 1395 was 'That exorcisms and hallowings, made in the Church, of wine, bread, and wax, water, salt and oil and incense [...] be the very practice of necromancy, rather than of the holy theology'. Cited by Keith Thomas, *Religion and the Decline of Magic* (New York: Scribner's, 1971), p. 51.

[2] Stephen Maksymiuk, 'Knowledge, politics and magic: the magician Gansguoter in Heinrich von dem Turlin's *Crône*', *The German Quarterly* 67 (1994), pp. 470–83, citation 470. See also Maksymiuk's *The Court Magician in Medieval German Romance*, Mikrokosmos 44 (Frankfurt: Lang, 1996), and Richard Kiekhefer, *Magic in the Middle Ages* (Cambridge: Cambridge U.P., 1990).

Gansguoter has been assigned to a group of 'dark' or 'liminal' characters inhabiting 'the borderland between good and evil, between light and dark [. . .] between everyday life and an Other World of magic and sorcery'.[3] Such figures inhabit neither that space expropriated by Christian allegory nor entirely that inhabited by denizens of the old Celtic pantheon and Gansguoter corresponds to a class of 'beings from the other side who can seem, confusingly, both enemy and friend'.[4] In his administration of the Beheading Test, he seems as enigmatic as Sir Bertilak de Hautdesert in the Middle English *Sir Gawain and the Green Knight* around whom too there hovers 'an irreconcilable variety of signs'.[5] Our first intimation of him is as the invisible presence behind the testing sword suspended over his niece's bed in the *Chevalier à L'Épée* episode. Unlike the voyeuristic, sexually abusive[6] old father of the French poem however, Heinrich's rehabilitated figure becomes a profane *cordis speculator* closer to the figure of Sir Bertilak than to the sadistic roué of the French fabliau-romance. This rehabilitation coheres with a general narrative strategy of making him into a godfather to the Arthurian order who supplies the Grail company with special intelligence and weaponry to aid their quest.

A magician figure is common to both of Heinrich's major sources yet whilst Wolfram's Clinschor is a practitioner of the black arts hostile to the courtly world, Heinrich's equivalent is granted the benign appellation Gansguoter von Micholde.[7] This signals his role as a dispenser of 'white' magic serviceable to the Arthurian world. The difference in portraiture between Heinrich and Wolfram could have a genetic origin stemming from Heinrich's partiality to French sources over their German adaptations. In that case Gansguoter would represent a reversion to the benign 'clers sages d'astronomie' of Chrétien's *Conte du Graal*. Yet such a passive reaction to source seems unlikely since Chrétien's magician plays a merely 'cameo' role whereas 'the whole *chastel marveil* episode has been fitted by Heinrich into his own scheme'.[8] That is, Gansguoter is introduced in the Rival Sisters story as

3   Edward R. Haymes, Preface to *The Dark Figure in Medieval German and Germanic Literature*, ed. Haymes and Stephanie Cain van D'Elden, GAG 448 (Göppingen: Kümmerle, 1986), p. iii.

4   Alan T. Gaylord, 'Arthur and the green world', in *Approaches to Teaching the Arthurian Tradition*, ed. Maureen Fries and Jeanie Watson (New York: Modern Language Association of America Publications, 1992), pp. 56–60, citation 56.

5   Helen Cooper, 'The supernatural', in *A Companion to the Gawain Poet*, ed. Derek Brewer and Jonathan Gibson (Cambridge: D. S. Brewer, 1997), pp. 277–91, citation 288.

6   In the German version the sexual initiative comes from Amurfina who is therefore not simply the pawn in her father's game as she appears to be in the French version.

7   For a discussion of the etymology of this name see Arno Mentzel-Reuters, *Vröude*, pp. 179–80.

8   M. O'C. Walshe, 'Heinrich von dem Türlin, Chrétien and Wolfram', in *Medieval Studies Presented to Frederick Norman* (London: Publications of the German Institute, 1965), pp. 204–18, citation 214.

an elegant, if somewhat Puckish knight – in contradistinction to the *vilain* of the French source.

Where in the French poem we are left with a disquieting impression, humiliating to the protagonist, 'that Gauvain has been put to a deal of trouble to find the missing piece of the harness, considering it was in the safe-keeping of its owner's sister all the time',[9] and that this charade might have been a gratuitous family joke, Heinrich's Gawein is assured by Gansguoter that he had in fact covered himself in glory and in so doing achieved the main object of the exercise, and Gawein's ostensibly fatuous exertions receive an important ulterior justification. Amurfina's tempting of Gawein to forsake the Assiles campaign reveals itself in retrospect to have been the initial step in a premeditated narratorial plan to bring the hero to the point where he can give incontrovertible proof of his worth in Gansguoter's chivalric academy. For as Arthur's step-father and an uncle by marriage to Gawein, Gansguoter is well placed to put a family cadet through his paces, and his influence and that of his family extends from this initial testing role to that of supporting the Arthurian knights in the Grail quest.[10]

'White' magic used for benign ends was not denounced at thirteenth-century German courts. Whatever the precise content(s) of the term might have been – and there is evidence of much suspension of disbelief with people choosing to believe in 'magical' causes for phenomena rather than mechanical ones[11] – considerable strategic importance was imputed to court magicians whose supposed magical powers were seen as an important part of a total arsenal of arts pertaining to the conduct of statecraft and warfare.[12] Rulers such as Charlemagne and even Frederick II (often condemned in his own lifetime for his proto-rationalist leanings) accorded the occult arts great respect and employed magical advisors at their courts. Although the Church's demonisation of magic ultimately drove the magical advisors from court, that event lay in the future and when Heinrich wrote, the supernatural had by no means yet become the discredited cultural legacy which was to be its fate in later centuries. Indeed, Christianity itself could be viewed as a form of magic and the two categories of religion and magic could effectively be

---

[9]   R. C. Johnston and D .D. R. Owen, *Two Old French Gauvain Romances*, Introduction, p. 5.

[10] Gawein receives a magic hauberk from the magician at his castle of Madarp and instructions how to counter the sorcery of Giramphiel and her champion, Fimbeus (lines 27,340ff); whilst Gansguoter's sister, Manbur, gives Gawein important advice on how to bring the quest to a successful conclusion, even officiating as Grail bearer in order to be able to prompt him to ask the correct question at the appropriate time (lines 29,396ff).

[11] 'No matter how well known these mechanisms (sc. mechanical automata) became, writers of fiction persisted in teasing their readers with the suggestion that such things were done by "necromancy" ' (Kiekhefer, *Magic in the Middle Ages*, p. 101.)

[12] A fictional expression of this is seen in Gawein's combat with the magician-knight, Laamorz of Janfrüege, against whom Gawein uses the magic coat given him by Siamerac of Lembil (lines 15,248ff) He also receives magic equipment from Salamide, the 'fairy' sister of Gasozein (lines 10,496ff) and from Gener of Kartis (lines 14,471ff).

collapsed. Hence independent healing properties were ascribed to the Host (used profanely in agriculture to cure sick animals) and to the Bible, sometimes used as a divinatory tool which, opened at random, might supply the kind of 'information' about human fate nowadays held out by horoscopes. In general, excepting the conceptions of the more progressive theological thinkers of the twelfth and thirteenth centuries, there are few enough continuities between the heavily 'demythologised' Christianity which was to emerge in the centuries following the Reformation and that form of the religion which was normally practised in the thirteenth century. It is perhaps particularly significant that magical powers were not uncommonly ascribed to the clergy (who, in officiating at the Mass, were thought to be superintending the most sublime form of magical transformation). It was this habit of thought which led to the rise of the most protean of all magicians in Arthurian legend, Merlin.[13]

From the early thirteenth-century French prose romances up to the present the figure of Merlin has seemed an indispensable part of the Arthurian legend. If such a warm reception is accorded him by our empirical age,[14] it would be surprising had not medieval audiences likewise been on the lookout for that supremely charismatic guru, a figure whom they may well have spied hiding behind Heinrich's generic appellation, 'Gansguoter' (considering the author's practice of methodically changing the names of characters of literary predecessors). This modus operandi can be seen clearly when he has a unitary source, such as 'the Chrétien–Wolfram adventures' (where the characters Obie, Obilot, Meliant and Tybalt are rechristened Flursensephin, Quebelplus, Fiers of Arramis and Leigamar respectively). The same is also the case for a number of other characters from Arthurian legend whose wonted features are thinly disguised by Heinrich's new nomenclature (such as Giramphiel/Morgan).[15]

The creation of such a 'second Merlin' (or, as Adelaide Weiss seemed to suggest, of a Merlin *avant la lettre*)[16] may also have been thought appropriate,

---

13 Merlin crops up in a variety of disguises including that of a shadow in the Didot *Perceval*, as a giant herdsman in the *Livre d'Artus* and as a forester in the Prose *Tristan*. In *Diu Crône* Gansguoter is said to be able to take any shape he wishes (lines 13,025–29).

14 In the course of a review in *Arthuriana* 6 (1996), p. 95, Lynn Ramey reported the following response of a Harvard University student to the film *First Knight*: 'What good is a story about Arthur without Merlin?'

15 The identification of Giramphiel with Morgan was made by R. S. Loomis, 'More Celtic elements in *Sir Gawain and the Green Knight*', *JEGP* 42 (1943), pp. 149–84, especially 154.

16 Noting the relative lateness of Merlin's formal appearance in German literature in Albrecht von Scharffenberg's rendition of Robert de Boron's *Merlin* (probably after 1250), Weiss contended: 'Nevertheless, it is not strange that there should be a lapse before Merlin enters into German literature; for heretofore other magicians, such as Aschmedai, Klinschor, Virgil, Gansguoter, Malduc and others claimed the popularity and had, as it were, preceded Merlin.' (*Merlin in German Literature. A Study of the Merlin Legend in German Literature from Medieval Beginnings to the End of Romanticism* (Washington: The Catholic University of America, Studies in German 3, 1933), repr. AMS (New York, 1970), p. 39). See

perhaps even de rigueur in the context of a story purporting to chart the rise to prominence of the Arthurian world. Merlin's magic arts as they had been deployed in Geoffrey of Monmouth's *Historia Regum Britanniae* and its French successor poems had provided the cradle for the Arthurian world when those arts were used to pander between Uther and Ygerne and so bring about Arthur's birth. Furthermore, there was a precedent for Gansguoter advising the four questers on the best way to achieve the Grail in the guidance provided by Merlin to the hero in the Didot *Perceval*. By his extensive use of Gansguoter as a kind of magical godfather to the Arthurians, Heinrich adheres to the spirit of that legendary tradition which depicted Merlin as an early magical adviser to Arthur's father and as one who had been instrumental in the conception and later prosperity of the early Arthurian kingdom.

In the numerous French romances deriving from Geoffrey's *Historia* and *Vita Merlini* Merlin continued to play a role in the advancement of the Arthurian kingdom. Robert de Boron's account of the Galfridian mage survives only in fragmentary form but the Prose Vulgate *Merlin*[17] contains a redaction of Robert's poem – with Merlin's responsibility for the construction of the Round Table, and a repeat of the Galfridian tradition of his procuring the birth of Arthur by magical means – and a long sequel. This account, in which Arthur fights to stamp his authority on British chieftains and invading Saxons with the aid of Gauvain's chivalry and Merlin's military prescience is contained in what is conventionally termed the 'historical' sequel. These historical echoes are no longer represented in the second notable extension of the Merlin legend on French soil, the *Suite du Merlin* of the Huth manuscript (the so-called 'romantic' sequel).[18]

This work, which was to have a considerable influence on the early phases of Malory's Arthuriad and on other notable European recreations of the legend, does away with the Britons and Saxons as Arthur's enemies and replaces them with more fabulous adversaries in the shape of the malign *fée*, Morgan, and her lover and champion, Accolon. The enmity between the couple and the Arthurian courtiers arises in this romantic account because Guinevere once intervened to break up Morgan's affair with a previous lover.

also Klaus M. Schmidt, 'Der verschmähte Merlin. Mögliche Gründe für die mangelnde Merlin-Rezeption in Deutschland', in *Die deutsche Literatur des Mittelalters im europäischen Kontext*, ed. Rolf Bräuer, GAG 651 (Göppingen: Kümmerle, 1995), pp. 61–83.

17 For the texts see H. Oskar Sommer, *The Vulgate Version of the Arthurian Romances*, 7 vols, repr. (New York: AMS, 1973). A thorough account of the interrelations between the different parts of the French cycle is given in the Preface and Introduction (by E. Jane Burns) to *Lancelot-Grail. The Old French Arthurian Vulgate and Post Vulgate in translation*, 5 vols, ed. Norris J. Lacy (New York and London: Garland, 1993).

18 Alexandre Micha, 'The Vulgate Merlin', in *Arthurian Literature in the Middle Ages. A Collaborative History*, ed. R. S. Loomis (Oxford: Clarendon, 1959), pp. 319–24, Fanni Bogdanow, 'Merlin's role in the thirteenth century prose romances', *Medium Aevum* 38 (1969), pp. 123–33.

This led to calculated acts of malice by Morgan against a Queen made vulnerable to Morgan's attacks on account of her proverbially easy virtue. These include Morgan's dispatching to Arthur's court of a magic drinking horn having the power to test the fidelity of the female courtiers by spilling tell-tale drops of wine (Prose *Tristan*); or the dispatching of the Green Knight with his beheading test in order to 'reave the wits of the courtiers and cause Guinevere to die of terror at that man who, like a phantom, stood talking before the high table with his head in his hand' (*Sir Gawain and the Green Knight*).

It was this 'romantic' sequel to the Merlin story in particular which seems to have influenced Heinrich. The intriguing against the Arthurians in the German version was probably a theme deriving from the tradition in which Morgan the Fay, having learned magic arts from Merlin, deployed them maliciously against Arthur and Guinevere. The second, 'glove' test (lines 23,058ff) which shames all the courtiers bar Arthur and Gawein, is expressly the result of the machinations of Giramphiel. Even Priure's first 'goblet' test has been claimed as bearing a family likeness with the kind of malign trick played by Morgan.[19] Meanwhile, the magical sheath of Escalibor which confers invulnerability on the bearer of the sword and which Morgan and Accolon contest with Arthur has its counterpart in the magic belt fought over by Gawein and Fimbeus.

In romance it is conventional for a hero's birth to be superintended by magical circumstances, but the adult hero typically 'outgrows' such early influences. According to that convention Arthur must lose the services of Merlin early in the great French cycle. There is therefore no supernatural balm available when, after the Grail quest, Lancelot falls back into his old adulterous ways with Guinevere and precipitates the schism which will lead to the final battle. Heinrich on the other hand, in order to preserve his Arthurian fellowship from a like disaster, clears up the adultery problem early in his romance and lifts the stone under which the magician had been prematurely interred, letting Merlin emerge again in the shape of the 'wholly good' magical advisor. By having Gansguoter as an active helper from the time of Gawein's marriage to Amurfina up to the Grail quest Heinrich gives a larger place to Gansguoter than does the Lancelot–Grail cycle to Merlin. Although both the romantic and the historical continuations of Robert de Boron's story of Merlin stress the interdependence of Gauvain's chivalry and Merlin's magic, they cause that partnership to come to an unfortunate end when

---

19 Marshall S. Grant argues a link between the pride (*surquidré*) of the courtiers being tested in the English poem and Gawein's sexual boasting (*sich vermëzzen*) in the German, concluding that 'as deflators of Gawein's pride, Morgan and Priure certainly have a lot in common': '*Sir Gawain and the Green Knight* and the quest for the Grail: Chrétien de Troyes' *Perceval, the First Continuation, Diu Krone* and the *Perlesvaus*', unpublished dissertation, Yale University, 1991, pp. 100 and 99, note 154.

Merlin is put under a disappearing spell by Viviane so that he exists only in the form of a spectral voice.[20] Heinrich on the other hand opposes that strand of tradition by giving Merlin an encore under a transparent disguise.

The fictional 'tricks' played by Morgan/Giramphiel may contain reflexes of intrigues played out at historical courts. The growing process of administrative centralisation in Western Europe starting in the Middle Ages culminated in extremely large court entourages. Such companies contained, in addition to official administrators such as chancellors and chamberlains, a group holding no formal office but whose members could nevertheless exert considerable personal power. Such people included entertainers, physicians, astrologers, ladies and men in waiting, lovers, illegitimate offspring, holy men and clerics, all of whom aimed to impress by some form of personal charisma. Members of both official and unofficial groups could see their popularity with the ruler wax or wane and in these circumstances rivalries became rife and murder not uncommon. Exploiting a widespread fear of malevolent powers, many intriguers sought either to channel magical forces for their own ends (sometimes enlisting a person with supposed magical powers to help) or else tried to denounce enemies thought to be using such allegedly occult practices.

This pragmatic use of 'magic' may be most readily understood in modern terms as a form of 'psychological warfare'. Giramphiel's theft of the magic requisites – which are not functionally essential to the Grail quest but only *said* to be necessary by her emissary, *der rittter mit dem boc* – is in effect a psychological ploy to undermine the morale of the Court.[21] Meanwhile Gansguoter, more proto-engineer[22] than magician, stresses the importance of intellectual power (*list*) coupled with *force majeure* to his schemes (rather than *zouber*). He claims that a combination of such resources are necessary for the successful transportation of the Grail party to the land of Sardin:

> Ez enmöhte ouch niemen hân getân
> Wan der den list künde
> Und dem sîn dar zuo günde
> Ouch sîn manheit und sîn kraft.   (lines 27,647–50).

(It could not have been accomplished by anybody without the proper skills or by one who was not endowed with bravery and strength.)

---

[20] Malory not unreasonably glosses this ghost-like condition as death in the passage where we are told 'how Merlin was assotted and doted on one of the Ladies of the Lake, and how he was shut in a rock under a stone and there died' (*Morte Darthur*, Book Four, chapter one).

[21] Her ploy certainly works in these terms and Gawein is obliged to 'counsel' the distraught Arthur against despair (lines 25,594–624).

[22] Mentzel-Reuters, *Vröude*, notes that a 'Verwissenschaftlichung des Zauberwesens, das ohne Dämonen und Teufel, rein in der Auseinandersetzung mit der *natûre* auskommt, muß auffallen' (p. 252).

That supernatural boons are little more than desirable auxiliaries in the generation of morale confirms the circular wisdom of the ancient adage 'Fortune favours the brave' cited at numerous points.[23] Fortuna's boons are assimilated to the more practical qualities of human resourcefulness, daring and strength,[24] and, curiously, nowhere are such down-to-earth qualities required more than in the pragmatically described Grail quest where Gawein supplies the requisite *mannes muot* and Gansguoter the *list* and *kunst* necessary to further the ambitions of the Grail party. Gansguoter's arts are frequently termed magical but in the event appear more as skills of the sort deriving from this prolific architect's extensive knowledge of the minutiae of castle architecture (lines 27,595–96).[25] The fundamental irrelevance of magical accessories to the Grail quest is especially apparent in the treatment of the magic girdle motif. Although Fortune's girdle fulfils an important integrative function in unifying a number of narrative strands,[26] it is not as necessary to the questers as we might have supposed from the hostile testimony of Giramphiel.

In the final tussle between Giramphiel and the Arthurians over the belt, a second messenger dispatched by Giramphiel, falsely purporting to represent the wishes of Giramphiel's sister, Fortuna, persuades the company that it needs a pair of magic gloves to complement the stone from Fortuna's belt already in its possession. The messenger tricks Gawein into parting with the stone from the belt by purporting to show him how to use it to best effect. Despite warnings from a young girl and from Kei against this threadbare

---

23 The thought is articulated by Gawein himself when he asserts that 'Manheit gert Saelden pflege' (line 22,619).

24   Kunst und gelücke
        Getürstekeit und mannes muot
        Ditz sint dem manne gewisse huot.   (lines 20,512–14)

25 In *Diu Crône* Gansguoter knows about the *mechanics* of lifting the portcullis of the flooded bridge leading over to the land of Giramphiel and Fimbeus and in this way ferries the Arthurian party into the forbidden kingdom of Sardin. By contrast, in the similar incident in *Wigalois* where the eponymous hero gains the land of Roaz at Glois, he is helped by a divine miracle to navigate the similarly treacherous waters (*Wigalois*, ed. Kapteyn, lines 6714–926). Where Wigalois is aided by the resources of *le merveilleux chrétien*, only the martial virtues of strength, skill and good tactics are shown to be of avail in *Diu Crône*.

26 Heinrich identifies the girdle as one which Frou Saelde originally fashioned for her sister, Giramphiel, and which the latter gave to her beloved, Fimbeus, so that he might acquire immunity from the wounds of knightly combat (lines 14,990ff). Fimbeus had subsequently come to Camelot and offered the magic belt to Guinevere provided she should become his lover (lines 23,291–98). Guinevere, keenly desiring the belt but not wishing to accept it on Fimbeus's terms, asks Gawein to win it for her in knightly combat. Reluctantly Gawein agrees (lines 14,956ff) and succeeds by dint of a lucky blow in dislodging the encrusted jewel giving the belt its power. Having received the belt from Gawein, Guinevere supposedly passes it to her lover, Gasozein. In an undisclosed way the belt must later have returned to Gawein's charge since Fimbeus and Giramphiel accuse Gawein of having purloined it from them (lines 25,406ff), and this dispute motivates the final combat the successful accomplishment of which permits Gawein and his fellows to proceed to the Grail.

ruse, Gawein is duped, whereupon the emissary, having tricked his foe into surrendering all the talismans, makes his escape over the castle walls. Gawein, however, is undeterred by his loss of the magic requisites since he remains confident of success without them. So little does he believe in their functional efficacy that, on later hearing that Giramphiel's tool, Gigamec, is once again giving out false news of his death, the Grail party return the gloves and Fortuna's ring (won back from Fimbeus as being supposedly indispensable to the Grail expedition) to Arthur as tokens that Gawein is still alive and in order to forestall a collapse of morale. When Gawein receives from Gansguoter equipment said to neutralise (hostile) magic, this compounds the impression that the magic appurtenances are something of a red herring, and Gawein's defeat of Fimbeus is appropriately described as being a fair one in which no magic is involved and in which Fortune's favours are distributed equally over both combatants.

Hence *Diu Crône*, in this one aspect resembling *Sir Gawain and the Green Knight*, presents some fine examples of 'magic that fails to work magically but that does work for the poem.'[27] The magical requisites, although they have no functional utility, become symbolic counters in the psychological warfare between Giramphiel and the Arthurians. That there is little sense of their practical efficacy becomes particularly striking if we compare some of Heinrich's magical machinery with Wirnt von Gravenberg's treatment of near-identical material in *Wigalois*. In Wirnt's romance magic undoubtedly affects outcomes. The magic girdle possessed by Joram has such overwhelming power that it cannot be wrested from him in combat by any of the Round Table knights. The power of the belt allows him to capture Gawein, the narrator keen to establish that Gawein had not been the inferior in arms but simply handicapped by not possessing the magic object (*Wigalois*, lines 562–70). Gawein, the hero's father, is given Fortuna's belt by King Joram together with the hand of his niece, Florie. When he later leaves Florie in order to return to Camelot, he forgets the belt and for that reason alone is unable to re-enter her enclosed domain. When Wigalois, called the Knight of Fortune's Wheel ('der rîter mit dem rade', line 5132) acquires the belt but then loses it to a fisherman, the loss is described as an all-too-real one which requires the help of God to indemnify him against future disasters (lines 5995–6005).

Hence the loss of the belt bears an important programmatic significance in Wigalois's spiritual biography. It announces a new phase in the hero's career where he leaves behind the championship of purely knightly ideals under the

---

[27] Helen Cooper, 'Magic that does not work', *Medievalia et Humanistica* 7 (1976), 131–46, citation 134 . With reference to a number of English examples such as Chaucer's *Squire's Tale* and *Richard Coeur de Lion* Cooper points out that 'there is frequently – indeed normally – a lack of excitement in the treatment of such talismans, and this is often reinforced by the minimal part they play in the plot itself' (p. 131).

tutelage of the goddess of the Ancients and espouses the Christian mission of redeeming the soul of the murdered King Lar. Wirnt indicates that lucky talismans have their place in the early life of a knight but that the mature hero should ultimately be directed by a greater power than that of Fortuna, in short, that 'Fortuna zwar das Glücksrad dreht, sie selbst aber vom Zügel der Providentia gelenkt wird.'[28] Such theodicean subtleties are absent from *Diu Crône* where there are 'few occurrences of divine intervention which directly affect the outcome of an adventure'.[29]

On only two occasions does God play anything but a conventional role[30] whilst invocations of the divine tend to be either pro forma or sometimes even faintly irreverent. There are on the one hand conventional invocations of God and the Trinity (lines 2391–93; 17233) and of the Virgin (lines 2385–90 and 2395–6). Arthur attends Mass before his projected combat with Gasozein (lines 10,458–65) and Gawein is portrayed as a knight for whom devotions before battle are a natural part of his knightly existence (lines 14,652–54; 1765–75). Other passages however appear to challenge the complacency of conventional pieties and direct complaints at God's providential arrangements. When Kei hears the false report of Gawein's death he reproaches God in an extended cry of dereliction (lines 16,967–95) whose intensity approaches the ploughman's plaint for his wife's demise in the *Ackermann aus Böhmen* two centuries later. Meanwhile, Gasozein is made to express openly anti-clerical sentiments when he complains about the unfairness of canon law and demands that the decision whether he or Arthur should have Guinevere be left to the goddess of love, Venus (lines 10,802–31).

Since neither profane magic nor Christian miracle play a determinative role in Gawein's quest, the Grail adventure might seem (even taking into account the medieval preference for representing spiritual struggle through martial terminology)[31] more a military than a spiritual challenge. In the light of the Continental evolution of Arthurian tradition this collective, quasi-military expedition to the Grail kingdom of Illes wears an archaic aspect, the pursuit of a communal goal being more reminiscent of the chronicle stage of Arthurian tradition than that of the romances of Chrétien, Hartmann and

---

[28] Peter Kern, 'Die Auseinandersetzung mit der Gattungstradition im *Wigalois* Wirnts von Gravenberg', in *Artusroman und Intertextualität*, ed. Friedrich Wolfzettel (Giessen: Wilhelm Schmitz, 1990), pp. 73–83, citation p. 80; for a similar judgement see Christoph Cormeau, 'Fortuna und andere Mächte im Artusroman' in *Fortuna* (=*Fortuna Vitrea. Arbeiten zur literarischen Tradition zwischen dem 13. und 16. Jahrhundert*), ed. Walter Haug and Burghart Wachinger (Tübingen: Niemeyer, 1995), pp. 23–33, esp. p. 31.

[29] Harding, 'Tradition and creativity', p. 185.

[30] These are in the incident where Gawein redeems a group of suffering women from a divine curse (lines 18,939–19,341) and in the final Grail scene where he performs the same function for the Grail retinue.

[31] Cf. Hans-Dieter Mauritz, *Der Ritter im magischen Reich. Märchenelemente im französischen Abenteuerroman des 12. und. 13. Jahrhunderts*, Europäische Hochschulschriften, series 13, vol. 23 (Berne: Lang, 1974).

Wolfram, whose heroes typically face challenges springing not from military exigencies but from tensions arising from competing moral commitments.

Following this shift of focus, the Arthur of the 'classical' romances becomes a largely symbolic figurehead whose tradition, detached from its insular origins, is borne along by moral concerns unrelated to his putative historical identity as an embattled British chieftain threatened by Saxons and other indigenous Britons. This stage of legendary evolution introduced the tradition of an individual knight detaching himself from the Arthurian fellowship and fighting in defence of an abstract principle. Outside the tourneying circuit the questing knight was not the reflection of historical circumstances but a literary invention, developed as a vehicle for the psychological exploration of character. It was in the context of that new literary milieu that the 'Grail' – unknown to the chronicle stage – first made its appearance. Because most modern readers have thought that 'to be able to doubt oneself, to grope one's lonely way, step by uncertain step, appears to represent a higher achievement of consciousness than naively to follow collective ideals,[32] the Middle English *Sir Gawain and the Green Knight* (even though it does not contain the motif of the Grail), has commonly been credited with recreating the spirit of the Continental Grail romances better than does *Diu Crône*. The English Gawain's mid-winter journey from geographically identifiable terrain into spiritually disorientating 'contrayez straunge' has for instance been favourably compared with Parzival's snow-bound itinerary to the hermit counsellor.[33] In both the Middle English romance and *Parzival* the familiar footprints of the courtly world are erased, the underlying motif of a knight's setting out to offer military satisfaction to a challenger being in each case transformed into a moral quest in which the protagonists must draw on their own spiritual resources rather than on the armed support of their peers.

In this more 'modern' context Morgan's intrigues against Arthur and Guinevere stand out as remnants of a tradition unrelated to the new themes which the *Gawain* poet wished to develop. His interests so far transcended the theme of a courtly intrigue against a feudal monarch and his wife that the very inclusion of the figure of the enemy to their lineage casts up a number of narrative contradictions. When we learn that the Green Knight had been sent by Morgan the Fay to drive Guinevere mad, this has struck many readers as if 'Gawain's moral pilgrimage is revealed finally to be no more than a small part of a sordid personal vendetta [. . .] we have virtually forgotten the original challenge and have come to accept that the purpose of the whole adven-

---

[32] Emma Jung and Marie-Louise von Franz, *The Grail Legend*, trans. Andrea Dykes (Boston: Sigo, 1986), p. 215. Cf. the verdict of Wallbank that 'the aspiration to contemplate the sublime mysteries of the Christian faith, the dignity of noble endeavour even, or perhaps especially, in failure – these evidently were themes that made little appeal to Heinrich's earth-bound and sceptical turn of mind' ('Irish fairy', p. 285).

[33] Alain Renoir, 'Gawain and Parzival', *Studia Neophilologica* 31 (1958), pp. 155–58.

ture was to test Gawain's loyalty and faith.'[34] Hence we are obliged to 'make allowances for' the *Gawain* poet who was attempting to forge a new sense out of recalcitrant material.[35] With his royal couple securely enthroned, their power taken for granted as the background for Gawain's quest rather than problematised, the last-minute inclusion of the threat by the renegade Morgan distracts from the essential theme of the protagonist's individual knightly integrity (*trawthe*) pitted against our common mortality and how Gawain deals with the knowledge of it. Where the *Gawain* poet points up the importance of the individual conscience in a work which sets out to 'problematize the moral laws we live by',[36] Heinrich symbolically opposes the convention of a lone hero when he has his Gawein absorb the roles of a number of other heroes of the Arthurian cycle such as Erec, Yvain, Tristan and Wolfram's Parzival, making of him 'an eclectic summation of previous courtly heroes'.[37] *Diu Crône* clearly does not belong within the same tradition as *Sir Gawain*, and even its title as a Grail romance in the tradition of Wolfram's *Parzival* has been disputed on the grounds that Heinrich's Grail is simply 'un objet de conte, dépourvu de tout symbolisme mystique et religieux'.[38]

Accepting this verdict, a closer analogy might be with a work which possesses various appurtenances of the Grail quest yet lacks the Grail motif itself: *Les Merveilles de Rigomer*. This post-Chrétien verse romance penned by the otherwise unknown Jehan (possibly a collective *nom de plume* for a number of scribes) has a triple quest in which Lancelot (unsuccessfully) and Gauvain (successfully) set out to lift the curse of the mysterious castle of Rigomer, followed by the torso of an account in which King Arthur himself takes up the challenge. Lancelot's encounters with a sick host who can stay alive only if visited by a succession of stranger knights recalls Chrétien's maimed Fisher King, whilst the presence of two main protagonists may also be an echo of Chrétien's *Conte du Graal*, the difference being that, as the restorer of a land blighted by a curse, Gauvain takes on something of the messianic character of Perceval and Galahad. The *mise-en-scène* in Ireland may well be a bluff, but perhaps the poet's biggest bluff is the impression given that successive questers are going to face a spiritual challenge whereas

---

34 J. Eadie, 'Morgan la fée and the conclusion of *Sir Gawain and the Green Knight*', *Neophilologus* 52 (1968), pp. 299–303, citation 299.

35 Otherwise we might go on asking such unproductive questions as 'Why should Sir Bertilak wish to cuckold himself in order to decapitate Gawain? Why need he decapitate Gawain at all, since the ostensible object of the whole action had been to frighten Guinevere to death, and that had failed a year before?' (Derek Brewer, *English Gothic Literature* (London: MacMillan, 1983), p. 164.)

36 Ad Putter, *Sir Gawain and the Green Knight and French Arthurian Romance* (Oxford: Clarendon, 1995), p. 5.

37 Lewis Jillings, *Diu Crône*, p. 234.

38 Danielle Buschinger, 'Un roman arthurien post-classique: *La Couronne* de Heinrich von dem Türlin', *Le Moyen Âge* 89 (1983), pp. 381–95, citation 393.

in fact the challenge is merely to the questers' sexual self-control. The teasing references to the 'merveilles' of Rigomer, a term used in *Diu Crône* to describe the baleful enchantments of the Grail (*wunder*), turn out to be mere sexual entanglements. Lancelot succumbs to the wiles of a sexual siren and Gauvain releases him through the exercise of conventional knightly *pröece* (line 13,878). It is Gauvain (who has a happily monogamous relationship with the *fée*, Lorie) who endorses the virtues of *service d'amour* and resists the ignominy of an understairs *val sans retour* in the siren's castle and so triumphs in his secular quest.

By choosing Gauvain to be his successful quester, Jehan brought the tradition of the knightly quest down from its esoteric heights to a more pragmatic level, appropriating the glamour of the quest tradition but demystifying it and making it a more appropriate vehicle for the knight of proverbially great *raisun*. Similarly Heinrich rejects notions of a *chevalerie celestiel* deriving from the *Queste del Saint Graal* tradition. He too sought instead a literary niche for Gawein, a knight who, in the First Continuation falls asleep before the Grail but who in *Diu Crône* remains vigilant to the imperatives awaiting him at Illes. However, whilst *Les Merveilles de Rigomer* provides a somewhat reductionist or possibly parodic *lectio facilior* of the Grail story,[39] *Diu Crône* is more complex and possesses levels of coherence not present in the French work.

On the one hand the German romance is concerned with the freeing of the old Grail king from the curse, a theme which is interlaced with the issue of possession of Fortune's trophies, but on the other, an additional moral dimension for Gawein resides in the unresolved issue of his knightly homicide and the consequential summons transferred to him by Angaras to seek 'daz sper und den rîchen gral' (line 18,921). As in Chrétien, this sequence is in large part concerned with 'the diplomatic solution of a judicial conflict'[40] over the issue of Gawein's slaying of Dahamorht's brother. Heinrich relates the homicide incident twice (lines 18,839–460 and 22,640–96), the second occasion being when Gawein himself reports on the incident to the assembled Arthurian Court in an extended flashback. Here he claims that he had been instrumental in the death of the brother whom he had encountered on a field in the Orient, protesting that the incident had been essentially a case of an unlucky blow:

> Ze dem selben turnoi was
> Von Karamphî Angeras
> Und sîn bruoder Dahamorht,

39 See Neil Thomas, 'The secularisation of myth: *Les Merveilles de Rigomer* as a *contrafactura* of the French Grail romances', in *Myth and its Legacy in European Literature*, ed. N. Thomas and F. Le Saux (Durham: Durham Modern Language Series, 1996), pp. 159–69.
40 Erdmuthe Döffinger-Lange, *Der Gauvain-Teil in Chrétiens Conte du Graal; Forschungsbericht und Episodenkommentar*, Studia Romanica 95 (Heidelberg: Winter, 1998), p. 42.

Den ich mit ritters tât entworht.
Leider dâ mir missegie,
Wan ich ime die coife nider hie
Undern wâfenroc ze tal:
Daz wart unser beider val,
Daz ich gote klagen wil:
Ez wart sînes lîbes zil,
E denne sich schiet daz spil.
Sunder schult was ich dar an:
Vil lützel ich mich versan:
Wan die rede geschach,
E ich rehte versach,
Daz er sich übel hât bewart;
Sîn tôt mich harter beswârt
Danne er ieman an in.
Umbe den ritter ich nu bin
Komen in michele nôt;
Alsô gilte ich sînen tôt,
Dêswar, ân mîn schulde gar.   (lines 22,652–69)

(Angeras of Karamphi and his brother Dahamorht had come to the same tournament where I offered a knightly challenge. Unfortunately things went badly since I knocked his coif down under his surcoat. This was a misfortune for both of us, which I shall always lament to God, for his life was gone before the tourneying ended. I bear no guilt for this event since I was not aware of what was happening since the incident had occurred before I noticed how poorly he was defending himself. His death saddened me more than anyone bar Dahamorht himself. Now I am in deep trouble over this knight and must atone for his death although I am innocent.)

According to Gawein's self-report his action had been unpremeditated and therefore venial. In the terms of canon law it was a *malecidium casu, non volens*, and not a *malecidium sponte*,[41] although whether the homicide would have been adjudged entirely venial is made problematical by the fairly close analogy with Parzival's unwitting killing of Ither in *Parzival* for which Wolfram's protagonist is denounced by the Grail messenger (*Parzival*, section 314, line 19 – 315, line 15). Furthermore, whilst there is nothing to confute Gawein's self-exculpatory testimony directly, there is the indirect testimony of the implacable anger shown against him by Dahamorht's brother and his peers. These otherwise chivalrous opponents so far let their feelings override their breeding as to transgress their laws of hospitality to a stranger knight by attacking Gawein, a guest. There is also some further circumstantial testi-

---

41 D. H. Green, 'Homicide and Parzival', in *Approaches to Wolfram von Eschenbach*, ed. D. H. Green and L. P. Johnson (Berne: Lang, 1978), pp. 11–82.

mony furnished by Keii to the effect that Gawein's oaths are not invariably to be trusted.[42]

Furthermore, Dahamorht is only one of a number of victims who had met their deaths either at the hands of Gawein or at those of his kin in what is portrayed as being the kind of casual violence which was frequently denounced in Church edicts such as those of the Fourth Lateran Council of 1179 in its invectives against tournaments. Inter-baronial feuding and vendettas, being an ineradicable feature of medieval aristocratic life, would inevitably have been a contentious and challenging contemporary theme. With regard to Chrétien's text 'the cumulative impression of bloodshed created in the course of the romance is disturbing, and Gauvain does not entirely disprove the various accusations levelled at him'.[43] Indeed, Gauvain's being implicated in the fatal effects of unchecked combat places a very large moral question mark over his head in Chrétien's *Conte du Graal*. Wolfram, by choosing to create from the incidental data of Chrétien's account an alternative story by-passing its original terms of reference, was in an incurious minority in not having been tempted to 'answer' that implied query; for, to judge from the number of echoes in subsequent literature, the charge of murder levelled at Gauvain must have been found disquieting by Chrétien's literary successors.

In the First Continuation the original charge of murder as narrated in the *Conte du Graal* is made to appear the more serious when Gauvain is challenged to a duel by a second knight, Disnaderet, for having allegedly committed a second murder against the plaintiff's father. The tension remains unresolved because Gauvain gives satisfaction to neither challenger (the issue being fudged when Arthur appeases Gauvain's accusers by offering them his two granddaughters as sexual bribes). Meanwhile, the theme of Gauvain-as-homicide spawned a further accusation of murder in the Pucele de Lis episode of the same romance. After Gauvain despoils that maiden of her virginity, her father, Norré, accuses him not only of the sexual offence against his daughter but also of having killed his brother (lines 1743–47). Gauvain's dwindling reputation takes a further blow when he takes over the Grail quest from a knight who mysteriously falls dead in front of him – an action which creates the impression that Gauvain is here presented as being second best for the task. This seems to be confirmed when the inhabitants of the Grail castle are cast down when the knight who comes before them is not

---

[42] Kei contends to the last, and even against the contrary evidence of the second, 'glove' test, that Gawein had used improper means to divest Fimbeus of his magic belt (even with the extenuating circumstance that he was committing the deed at Guinevere's behest). Notably, Keii counters Gawein's shifty words of mitigation and denial (lines 24,349–56) with the uncomfortable point that Gawein's action (even on behalf of his queen) constituted 'strâzenroub' (line 24,362).

[43] Keith Busby, *Perceval (Le Conte du Graal)*, Critical Guides to French Texts, 98 (London: Grant and Cutler, 1993), p. 83.

the mysteriously stricken knight but Gauvain who had taken over the quest by default. They give voice to their misgivings when their first, unfavourable impressions are confirmed when Gauvain is unable to mend the symbolic fissure in the Grail sword, (he having fallen asleep before he can experience full knowledge of all the attendant mysteries of the Grail).

In *Les Merveilles de Rigomer* Gauvain is imprisoned for a time by the knight Gaudionet whose brother he had slain, whilst further charges of murder are brought against him in *Escanor* and in Wolfram's *Parzival*. In *Escanor*, although we are told finally that Gauvain was innocent of murder, his initial reaction to the indictment is so suspicious that many bystanders are led to doubt his protestations of innocence.[44] Similarly ambiguous is the account of the accusation in *Parzival*. Whereas in Chrétien's version Guigambresil accuses Gauvain of having killed his lord without the proper preliminary challenge (lines 4759–61), there is an additional implication in *Parzival* that Gawan unchivalrously feigned friendship with a 'Judas kiss' in order to take his victim, Kingrisin, off guard (section 321, lines 10–15). Gawan's rather hesitant response to this charge (his brother, Beacurs and Arthur intervene to rebut the charge before Gawan speaks a word (section 322, line 15–section 323, line 12) does little to dispel the suspicion of guilt. Although Wolfram eventually blinded the homicide motif by making another knight (Ekhunat) responsible for the murder, this narratorial evasion does little to address earlier doubts about Gawan.[45]

From the number of charges cited in numerous romances it can be observed that 'those intent on criticising Gauvain in subsequent romances make good use of the theme'.[46] We may infer that literary posterity must have accounted this charge as much a part of Gauvain's legendary reputation as his more benign attributes since, in the absence of an influential literary defence advocate, the case for the prosecution succeeded by default. The literary fall-out of the suspiciously unanswered charge can be followed in an uninterrupted sequence from the Lancelot–Grail cycle through to Malory and Tennyson. Only Heinrich chose an effective defence strategy to rehabilitate the accused knight: that of having him confront the accusation straightforwardly. That is, Gawein accepts the charge but pleads extenuating circum-

---

44 *Girart d'Amiens, Escanor. Roman Arthurien en Vers de la Fin du XIII Siècle*, ed. Richard Trachsler, 2 vols (Geneva: Droz, 1994), vol. 1, lines 6958–7860.

45 On this point see see Bonnie Büttner, 'Gawan in Wolfram's *Parzival*', pp. 32–35.

46 Keith Busby, 'Diverging traditions of Gauvain in some of the later Old French verse romances', in *The Legacy of Chrétien de Troyes*, ed. Noris J. Lacy, Douglas Kelly and Keith Busby, 2 vols (Amsterdam: Rodopi (Faux Titre 37), 1988), vol. 2, pp. 93–109, citation 107. The Pucele de Lis episode of sexual misconduct also made its way to German soil in *Wigalois* and in the fourteenth-century *Nüwe Parzifal* of Wisse and Colin (which contain references to sexual harassment and rape respectively). See Ute Schiessl, 'Die Gawangestalt im *Wigalois* des Wirnt von Gravenberc', unpublished dissertation, University of Munich, 1968, pp. 156–74.

stances over the unlucky blow and agrees to the quest as a means of atonement for what he sees as the lesser charge.

The narrative scheme of sin-and-rehabilitation brings the structure of this strand of Gawein's career into an apposition with the 'classical', bipartite scheme established by Chrétien in his *Erec* and *Yvain*. The erstwhile homicide's quest for peace and reconciliation may also have been meant as a riposte to the homicidal Gauvain of the Lancelot–Grail trilogy. In the *Queste*, Gauvain is reproached by a hermit for killing his enemies (whereas Galahad only overpowers them), whilst in the *Mort Artu* Gauvain, unable to forgive Lancelot for the killing of his two brothers, persuades Arthur to redouble his military efforts against the queen's lover. The final result of Gauvain's *desmesure* is the fall of the Round Table through the ensuing polarisation of the Court into pro-Arthur and pro-Lancelot factions. In *Diu Crône*, on the other hand, the mature Gawein is strongly dissociated from that French tradition when, as an exponent of diplomacy and *mâze*, he is able to save the Court from destruction.[47]

Chrétien's indications, albeit brief, were enough to suggest that Gauvain's challenge, had the French author been given the opportunity to depict it, was to be of a different type than that of Perceval, and Heinrich clearly endeavoured to respect Chretien's clues as to the nature of the exploit. Where Wolfram had whitewashed Gawan by pronouncing him innocent of the murder of Kingrisin, Heinrich remains vigilant to the presumption of guilt left by Chrétien. Hence Gawein's quest for the Grail, functioning as a means of expiating his guilt,[48] provides a bona fide continuation and resolution of the French torso. Heinrich, who repeatedly uses the proverb 'Alt schult lît und rostet niht',[49] gives Gawein the opportunity to rehabilitate himself for his past misdemeanour through a compact with the brother of the deceased. In terms of the phenomenological realities perceptible to Gawein, the 'Grail' represents largely a penitential obligation imposed upon him by Angaras and the assembled soldiery of Karamphi Castle. It is an option he chooses in order to avoid having to duel with Angaras. Gawein's choice of punishment appears to be functionally similar to the Solemn Penance that the Church reserved for those usually aristocratic malefactors who had committed particularly evil crimes such as murder.[50] Having suffered his penance pragmati-

---

[47] The malign words of Giramphiel's emissary that Gawein was responsible for the downfall of Camelot (lines 25,482–84) may contain a cryptic allusion to the *Mort* tradition. Possibly Heinrich's desire to 'prevent' such a catastrophe caused him to tell a story about Gawein as the redeemer of the Arthurian order against the tradition of one who contributed to its destruction.

[48] Cf. Werner Schröder, 'Literaturverarbeitung', p. 170: 'Heinrichs Gral ist Symbol einer ungesühnten Schuld'.

[49] See lines 18,837ff and also lines 25,436–37: 'Wan diu schult diu ist niuwe/ Alle wege, diu ungerochen ist'.

[50] The father of William the Conqueror, Duke Robert of Normandy, obtained his inheritance

cally and without complaint, Gawein successfully makes up his rift with Angaras and inducts him into the Arthurian fellowship, this compromise being presented as a prerequisite for the continued peace and prosperity of the Court.

Gawein's exploits are in one sense personal (bearing on his self- rehabilitation for his albeit unwitting slaying of Angaras's brother); but they also take on wider messianic dimensions when he is obliged to evidence sufficient moral resources to lift a curse weighing upon whole kin groups. He is, we are told by the old Grail king, obliged to bear responsibility both for the sins of his own kin and for that of Parzival and so, in an extended metaphorical sense, we may infer, for the sins of the whole order of knighthood for its frequent re-enactments of the sin of Cain (lines 29,462–554). Heinrich prepares this messianic dimension of the quest in the scene where his sources feature the interview of Perceval/Parzival with the hermit uncle (lines 18,934–19,345). This scene clearly had to be omitted since the discredited Parzival is rejected as the protagonist for *Diu Crône* and his confession scene is therefore of no account. Heinrich replaces it with Gawein's encounter with a group of women who appeal for his aid against a divine curse. Other knights had attempted to save them from the visitation but had failed; only a knight predestined by God could lift the curse and Gawein is informed that he is the elect knight. Foreshadowing the circumstances of Gawein's final redemption at the Grail castle, one of the women explains that her family receives the baleful attentions of a black knight acting as a *flagellum dei* ('vrônebote', line 19,268; 'wîzenaere', line 19,269) on account of the hubris ('hôchvart', line 19,257) which had characterised the past actions of some members of their kin. She then offers up thanks that Gawein's long-prophesied intervention against the Black Knight has taken place and cleansed them of their sins and the consequential torments:

> Ez was lange gewîsseit,
> Daz ditze wernde leit
> Sô lange wern solde,
> Ob daz got iemer wolde,
> Daz Gâwein kæme in ditz lant:
> So würde ez von sîner hant
> Erlôst ane allen strît.   (lines 19,295–301)

by poisoning his brother and was instructed to undertake the pilgrimage to Jerusalem barefoot (on which journey he died), whilst in 1172 Pope Alexander III absolved Henry II for the murder of Thomas Becket by getting him to submit to a public flogging and to lead a three years' crusade to the Holy Land. See Andrea Hopkins, *The Sinful Knights. A Study of Middle English Penitential Romance* (Oxford: Clarendon, 1990), p. 45 and Jonathan Sumption, *Pilgrimage. An Image of Medieval Religion* (London: Faber and Faber, 1975), especially chapter five.

(It was long since prophesied that this terrible affliction would last as long as it was God's will but that, should Gawein come to this land, then he would stop it with great ease.)

Heinrich, clearly well versed in the Gauvain adventures of Chrétien, all manuscripts of which present the Perceval/hermit uncle scene as an interpolation within the thematically distinct Gauvain sequence, uses the encounter with the mourning women to promote Gawein from the merely 'secular' sphere toward a considerably more spiritual mission. Viewed against the Gauvain/Gawein figure of Chrétien and Hartmann, this new image of Heinrich's Gawein as a knight shouldering onerous spiritual (as opposed to merely chivalric) burdens might seem 'out of character'. It seems, however, that Heinrich might have been taking over not so much the 'classical' image of the Gawein of the romances of Chrétien and Hartmann as advancing further an image of him which had first been articulated in *Wigalois*.

Wirnt had set an important precedent in the direction of giving Gawein a greater responsibility within the spiritual sphere by letting him join his son in the campaign against Lion (a supporter of the pagan Roaz), a venture in which Gawein marries secular and spiritual duties. Similarly, in the Assiles sequence of *Diu Crône*, Heinrich's Gawein must encounter devilish adversaries of the sort faced by his legendary son. These include such scions of the race of Cain as 'ein wilder wazzerman' (line 9237) whose demonic companions, like the giant Assiles himself, are capable of uprooting trees to use as weapons. This terrible crew is later augmented by a female of their species, a wild woman dubbed 'des tiuvels prût' (line 9347), the latter almost certainly based on Ruel in *Wigalois*, the demonic hag whom Wirnt calls 'des tievels trût'.

Heinrich adapted for his Grail sequence a similar metaphysical logic as that found in the principal redemptive act of Wirnt's eponymous hero.[51] In *Wigalois* the good king Lar is murdered by the necromancer Roaz, and Lar and his murdered men languish in a purgatory (hence the King's appellative denoting his spectral condition – his other name is Jorel). Wigalois is warned that the journey to his castle at Korntin will constitute a *descensus* in which he will have to brave the realm of death (the challenge being 'gelîch dem tode gar', line 1764). Lar's surviving subjects pray that Wigalois will redeem him, typologically linking the hoped-for redemption with the act of the universal saviour, 'der mange sêle erlôste/ûz der helle mit sîner kraft' (lines 3990–92), that is, with Christ's Harrowing of Hell where he rescues Adam, Eve and the Patriarchs from limbo before his ascension. Lar, like Hamlet's father, is a ghost to whom God grants a periodic respite from purgatorial torments as a

---

51 This was pointed out by Irma Klarmann, 'Heinrich von dem Türlin: *Diu Krône*, Untersuchungen der Quellen', unpublished dissertation, University of Tübingen, 1944, p. 62.

recompense for his charitable acts when he was alive (lines 4663–88); yet he and his spectral troupe of knights still languish in purgatorial flames, as is shown when Lar breathes fire and when the shaft of Wigalois's lance ignites when it makes contact with Lar's ghostly retinue. Similarly, the *altherre*, the old Grail king of *Diu Crône* whom Gawein must redeem, is a spectre, like Lar; and the same motif of purgatorial fire recurs in the *Wunderketten* where Gawein witnesses sights such as the slain army which catches fire and causes night to become as bright as day and the burning inhabitants of a castle attacked by a giant – all events which had been 'caused' by the Grail, according to the testimony of the *altherre* (lines 29,549–29,551).

The contention that Gawein in *Diu Crône* represents merely the 'secular' wing of chivalry must be revised by reference to the redemptive purpose of his final challenge at the Grail castle. Although the term 'Integrationsfigur' has often been used to describe Gawein's role in *Diu Crône* (since he appears in broad terms to amalgamate the spiritual role of Wolfram's Parzival and the secular one of Gawan),[52] the term is not entirely accurate because his final redemptive act is based on that of Wirnt's hero and not on that of the marginalised Parzival. To be sure, Heinrich, unlike Wirnt von Gravenberg, was not a Christian moralist representing 'the many faces of medieval piety with a sincerity which is pronounced even when the expression itself is a commonplace'.[53] Yet despite a lack of profound Christian inspiration, he 'never rejects the employment of spiritual elements unequivocally (and) relishes the stereotyped analogies to the saviour myth',[54] being rhetorically skilled enough to make such analogies enhance the mythic meaning of his work.

[52] On the parellelism of the two worlds see Winder McConnell, 'Otherworlds, alchemy, Pythagoras and Jung. Symbols of transformation in *Parzival*', in *A Companion to Wolfram's 'Parzival'*, ed. Will Hasty (New York: Camden House, 1999), pp. 203–22.

[53] J. W. Thomas (trans.), *Wigalois. The Knight of Fortune's Wheel* (Lincoln: University of Nebraska Press, 1977), p. 50.

[54] Ernst Dick, 'Tradition and emancipation: the generic aspect of Heinrich's *Crône*', p. 78. Other mythological elements include elixirs of youth, numerous representations of the mythology of death and even one apparent reminiscence of Gawein in his aspect of solar hero safeguarding solar power from the depredations of a giant who 'slew the sun near the sea' (lines 9031–33). On the appropriation of mythic story patterns see further Neil Thomas, 'Heinrich von dem Türlin's *Diu Crône*: An Arthurian Fantasy?', *ABäG* 36 (1992), pp. 169–79, esp. 175–78.

6

The Arthurian Crown

'Artûs, du bist ein krône
Und ein spiegel aller êren.'   (*Diu Crône*, lines 3110–11)

The French Lancelot–Grail cycle quickly achieved the status of what in a related context Gottfried von Strassburg termed received imaginative truth (*wârheit*). This at first makes it difficult to imagine any other development of the Arthurian legend than that in which a noble fellowship, beginning in high hope, eventually succumbs to the forces of political and sexual betrayal. By Malory's century the sequence of the Arthurian tragedy was familiar enough to be described by Caxton in proverbial terms as 'the byrth, lyf, and actes of the sayd Kyng Arthur, of his noble knyghtes of the Round Table, theyr mervayllous enquestes and adventures, th'achyeving of the Sangreal, and in th'ende the dolorous deth and departyng out of thys world of them al'.[1] The *Lancelot* proper, *Queste del Saint Graal*, and *Mort Artu*, even if not originally planned as a trilogy, clearly came to be perceived as such by dint of Lancelot's unifying role as the flower of Arthurian chivalry, father of the predestined Grail-hero, and contributing cause of Arthur's downfall.

The originators of this best-known rendition of the Arthurian story in world literature are anonymous, but many aspects of the *Queste* point towards a Cistercian inspiration, including the emergence of the virginal Galahad as the warrior saint figure riding at the head of the *Chevalerie Jhesucrist* and the demotion of Gauvain and Arthur to the other ranks of the *chevalerie terriene*. Since the Cistercians viewed virginity as a correlative of spiritual purity, the adultery motif would have gained its particularly negative resonance from misogynist notions of tragic causality according to which female infidelity led to disunity amongst male ranks.[2] Homicide committed

---

1   See Sir Thomas Malory, *Le Morte D'Arthur*, ed. Janet Cowan with an Introduction by John Lawlor, 2 vols (Harmondsworth: Penguin, 1969), vol. 1, Introduction, p. xxix for discussion of this point.

2   On this point see Fritz Peter Knapp, 'Das Ideal des *chevalier errant* im französischen Prosa-Lancelot und in der *Krone* Heinrichs von dem Türlin', in *Artusrittertum im späten Mittelalter. Ethos und Ideologie*, ed. Friedrich Wolfzettel, Beiträge zur Deutschen Philologie 57 (Giessen: Wilhelm Schmidt, 1984), pp. 138–45, especially 145.

against co-religionists was also proscribed by the order and special ire was directed against the round of often fatal combats which formed the substance of many a knightly existence. Gauvain's tally of eighteen knightly homicides and Arthur's threat of the stake to his adulterous wife would have been viewed as particularly grave transgressions in a work in which neither Arthur himself nor any one of his habitual entourage can lay claim to the status of a role model.[3]

Although this negative interpretation of the Arthurian legends succeeded in influencing most European literatures, it failed to achieve canonical status on German soil where the process of canon-formation took a different turn. Heinrich, indebted to French tradition for much of his material, nevertheless exploited a freedom of expression not shared by the writers of the French prose cycle for whom 'invention becomes a matter of grouping together the elements bequeathed by earlier writers and supplying the missing links in a way that would ensure the emergence of a structure at once more spacious and more coherent'.[4] As an outsider to the French *atelier*, the German author would not have had to adhere to this ancillary role and would have enjoyed the freedom both to create his own Arthurian proto-history and to move the story on to later stages of the reign at will. By the exercise of this freedom he was able to produce an alternative Arthuriad according to his own imaginative conceptions, rewriting Arthurian (hi)story in a positive and pragmatic spirit in defiance of the misanthropic tone set by the *Queste* and the pessimistic tenor of the *Mort Artu*.

In the attempt to draw the sting of the French prose tradition, the German narrator at first dilates freely on the woes of the Arthurian first age only to shift his focus from this initial nadir to the high standard lauded as the norm of the Court in the works of Heinrich's 'classical' predecessors. Initially we are introduced to images of a queen out of sympathy with her spouse, of a king so powerless to cope with the crisis that he contemplates executing her and of their ménage held together less by its own internal strength than by the courage and diplomacy of the king's second-in-command. The presence of Parzival as a scapegoat however absolves the royal family from ultimate responsibility. It is insinuated that their troubles, though real enough, are not wholly self-inflicted because there are extenuating circumstances. The curse on Parzival and his kin implies an *external* origin for the Court's spiritual malaise for, where Arthurian and Grail realms remain separate categories in Wolfram, the two spheres are welded in *Diu Crône* so that the curse from the one dynastic branch is able to 'spread' from Parzival's immediate kin to Arthur and his peers. That curse, by analogy with the far-reaching effects of

---

3 Hence the invention of Galahad, a figure with no compromising prototypes in earlier tradition.
4 Eugène Vinaver, 'The Dolorous Stroke', *Medium Aevum* 25 (1956), pp. 175–80, citation 180.

Balain's Dolorous Stroke, is the canker responsible for reducing the Arthurian Court to its initial state of a moral wasteland.

In order to counter the effects of the curse and to forestall the Arthurian Armageddon towards which his material might be thought to be tending, Heinrich rearranges the chronology established in the French tradition so that the adultery – the traditional prelude to the downfall – is positioned early in his romance. Gawein is at the same time allowed to progress from his early status of somewhat feckless renegade to a niche at the moral centre of the Court's affairs. From that position of centrality he is able to resolve the crisis over the queen and to rise to the position of successful Grail quester, banishing the curse for which Wolfram's protagonist is held responsible and fulfilling the unrealised ethical potential of the Gauvain figure of the First Continuation.[5] A diplomatic solution to the Guinevere affair is then brought about by marrying the would-be usurper of her favours to a third party in the person of the elder of the sibling rivals, Sgoidamur. This does away with the traditional precondition for the civil war and provides a trenchant corrective to the story of treason and death by implying that the king's life had fallen blamelessly to the caprice of the three Fates whom all must ultimately encounter rather than ignominiously at the point of a treasonably brandished sword. By lifting the scandal from the traditional legend of Arthur's death in internecine conflict Heinrich makes *his* Arthurian story not a merely negative exemplum (however sublime) but a positive mirror for princes, saving Arthur's good name from obloquy through its immemorialisation in his literary 'crown'.

More than any other thirteenth-century German work – with the possible exceptions of Stricker's *Daniel von dem blühenden Tal* and Pleier's *Tandareis und Flordibel* [6] – *Diu Crône* foregrounds the person of the king and makes him a fallible, eminently human figure beset by both sexual and political difficulties. The depiction of an intense and passionate Guinevere conjures up the image of a young king's rule being complicated by some hectic sexual competition for the young beauty with the mysterious 'past'. Guinevere, unlike Wirnt's heroine of the same name, is not a prudent matron who at Gawein's behest obediently returns the magic belt to its fairy owner but rather one

---

5   Whereas in the First Continuation Gauvain himself falls asleep before the Grail, it is only Gawein's companions who do so in *Diu Crône*.

6   The romance *Tandareis und Flordibel* (ed. F. Khull) problematises the common motif of the King's rash boon when the Indian princess Flordibel gains from Arthur the undertaking that he will execute anybody who should sue for her favours. When the young and blameless Tandareis does so with the maiden's approval, Arthur still refuses to go back on his original word. Tandareis is supported by Gawan as his legal advocate and by Kei who places the blame on the king for his intransigence ('diu schult ist von rehte sîn', line 2513). It is finally Arthur, rather than Tandareis, who has to yield by acknowledging the futility of trying to legislate in affairs of the heart, so resolving a tension which the king had failed to resolve in many previous romances, namely, how to strike a proper balance between stern absolutism and regal magnanimity.

whose stubborn determination to retain the girdle prevails *against* Gawein's good counsel (*Crône*, lines 23,412–16). She is, moreover, swathed in the additional mystique of her presumed mythological ancestry. We are never told unambiguously what her relationship with the Other Worldly pretender/saviour Gasozein had been but are given sufficiently obvious clues to accept Gasozein's version of events against Guinevere's furious rebuttals. Those rebuttals, we must infer from her fears of Arthur's possible reprisals, suggest a state of traumatic denial[7] springing from her attempt to repress memories of a more colourful and gratifying sexual past in the 'fairy' domain.

After the triumphalism of his elaborately planned Court celebration is subverted by Priure's test and Gasozein's challenge, Arthur shows himself to possess a blend of aggression and weakness reminiscent of the traditional character of Kei. His psychological rationalisations that the rumoured sexual challenger might be a mere phantasm come close to the irresolute conduct of Gottfried's King Marke when faced with clear evidence of adultery between his nephew and his wife. Arthur's nadir comes when he tries to shift the burden of his torment through brittle humour at the expense of the three knights who had not deserted him – their justifiable anger at his inappropriate remarks threatening the dissolution of even the rump of his Court. His decision to reveal to Kei, Aumagwin and Gales his suspicions concerning the possibility of Guinevere's prior betrothal would have been regarded as profoundly discrediting by audiences believing that a wife's sexual dishonour would compromise the political security of her spouse. Meanwhile, Arthur's fears about not being able to live up to his father's example are perhaps an echo of a more general contemporary fear that the recent French cultural import of chivalry, however splendid, might have sapped the strength of the recent generation compared with the rougher warriors of the pre-chivalric age,[8] for on the lips of some Churchmen and other moral fundamentalists, 'courtliness' was often condemned for its decadence and effeminacy.[9]

Unlike Wirnt von Gravenberg, who is content to accept Arthur's own generation as an unquestioned byword for chivalric excellence,[10] Heinrich

---

7   Cf. lines 10,965–11,036 when Guinevere, brought into the judicial ring, is intimidated by the crush of her husband's knights to declare herself for Arthur and to renounce any sentimental attachments to the pretender.

8   This can be observed in the portraiture of Gunther relative to Siegfried in the *Nibelungenlied* or in that of the 'courtly' King Marke in Gottfried's version of *Tristan* who, unlike the 'pre-courtly' tyrant of Eilhart's *Tristrant*, is portrayed as a prevaricator (*zwîvelaere*) unable to cope emotionally with the lovers' intrigues.

9   See Ad Putter, 'Arthurian literature and the rhetoric of effeminacy', in *Arthurian Romance and Gender*, ed. Wolfzettel, pp. 34–49, and C. Stephen Jaeger, 'The Nibelungen poet and the clerical rebellion against courtesy', in *Spectrum Medii Aevi. Festschrift for G. F. Jones* (Göppingen: Kümmerle, 1983), pp. 177–205.

10 Wirnt's frequent use of the *laudatio temporis acti* trope indicates that he too sees the past as a locus of chivalric value, but in his frequent role as moralist he is content to use the age of

appears to have taken full account of the *Artuskritik* of his classical predecessors where the king, despite formal plaudits, often appears as a figure in the tradition of the *rex inutilis* and his knights as failing to come to terms with some aspect of their knightly avocation. Against such symptoms of contemporary decadence Heinrich invokes new strength from past example, making symbolic attempts to reinvigorate Arthur's reign in the Castle of Wonders sequence by retrieving for it some of the prestige of Uther's heroic age.

In Chrétien's version, that castle is a mythic abode of the dead complete with a ferryman corresponding to Charon and a hostile club-footed guard acting as a Cerberus.[11] In *Diu Crône*, Sâlie is the location of a mysterious Arthurian diaspora[12] into which different generations of Gawein's own kin and that of Arthur had disappeared, and the hero's triumph over this land *d'ou nul ne retorne* supplies a typological echo of Christ's Harrowing of Hell, only here it is the elect of the Arthurian nobility who are restored to their proper estate. Part of Gawein's liberation takes the form of retrieving rejuvenating flowers for Arthur's mother, suggesting a symbolic resuscitation from her mortal state. The resurrection theme is further strengthened by the emergence of a second father-by-marriage for Arthur to compensate him for the loss of his natural father. As Igern's second husband, Gansguoter represents a second Uther able to supply something of the strength and skill whose disappearance Arthur lamented in the early death of his natural father. This rehabilitation of Wolfram's hostile Clinschor figure confers on Gansguoter considerable patriarchal authority. Gawein as a younger scion of a branch of the Arthurian family is placed in the position of cadet to his senior. This provides a motive for Gawein's prolonged testing by a figure with the authority to establish the younger kinsman's competence according to customary standards. Gawein's relative youthfulness in the chronological scheme of *Diu Crône* is further pointed up by Heinrich's inclusion of a version of the Gauvain/Proud Lady sequence.

Although Heinrich's feckless Mancipelle, the all-too malleable dupe of the villainous Lohenis and Ansgü, is not as impressive a tester as Chrétien's Haughty Lady and Wolfram's Orgeluse, the sequence from which she derives was commonly associated with the proving of a *youthful* knight. This is indicated by Wirnt's adaptation of a similar narrative pattern for the portrayal of the testing of Gawein's son by the haughty messenger, Nereja, in *Wigalois*.[13] If

Arthur himself as the remote standard with which to berate his contemporaries and makes no mention of Uther. See *Wigalois* (ed. Kapteyn), lines 2349–95; 2146–58.

[11] Chrétien's name for the castle is Champguin meaning 'white or holy field' (Old Welsh *guin*) with its associations of ghostly presences (white being the colour of death in Celtic mythology). On mythic narrative structures in this sequence see Heinrich Zimmer, 'Gawan beim grünen Ritter', in *Der arturische Roman*, ed. Kurt Wais (Darmstadt: Wissenschaftliche Buchgesellschaft (Wege der Forschung 157), 1970), pp. 282–300.

[12] In the *Conte du Graal* Ygerne has been dead for sixty years (line 8738) and her daughter for twenty.

[13] This reflex of the proving tradition has Gawein's legendary son, Wigalois, being tested by

Mancipelle's moral flaws make her a somewhat dubious tester, Gansguoter (like the Merlin who can detect adulterous conduct beneath Ganieda's hypocritical façade in the *Vita Merlini* and its French adaptations) has ample resources for detecting hidden vice, and Gawein's prior betrothal to Flori and casually amorous conduct with Sgaipegaz show the magician's 'suspended sword' test in his niece's boudoir[14] to be an apt enough one for him. In these early characterisations of Gawein we are given rare (imagined) insights into the youthful excesses of a knight who in most previous romance traditions already appears (notwithstanding some stray hints about youthful sexual exuberance) in his mature phase as a knight of reason and sensibility.

Meanwhile, the series of combats which Gawein performs under Gansguoter's direct supervision in the revolving castle are entirely probative since the magic bridle, together with the castle and all its occupants, were already Gawein's property through his marriage to Amurfina. It was hardly necessary for him to fight to claim what was already his own other than to impress Gansguoter. Only after the series of probations culminating in the Castle of Wonders sequence do Gawein's combats gain an instrumental purpose in the quest for the Grail (at the revolving castle and at *Chastel mervillôs* he is obliged to turn down the guerdon prepared for the successful liberator since in the first case he was already married to the sister of the intended prize and in the second, had he accepted the standard sexual reward, this would have led to incest either with his sister or his mother). Heinrich's phased characterisation of Gawein shows how his youthfully transgressive conduct yields to a standard of conduct more consistent with the role which he plays as Grail quester. We are permitted to follow his moral ascent first to the stage of responsible married knight and thence to redeemer, the status conspicuously denied him by Wolfram von Eschenbach. Heinrich's modus operandi amounts to a narrative strategy of prefixing accounts of characters' 'earlier' deeds to their later, more wonted biographical profiles so as to simulate a diachronic process of progression.[15]

Despite the long proving of Gawein, however, *Diu Crône* is not primarily concerned with the independent exploits of an individual(ist) knight but with the purpose to which that knight dedicates himself: the safeguarding of

his censorious guide, Nereja (until he should show unequivocal proof of being up to the mature standard of his father), this scenario suggesting 'a reminiscence of the Gawain-Proud-Lady story, having been transferred from father to son' (Jessie L. Weston, *The Legend of Sir Gawain* (London: Nutt, 1897), p. 56, note 2).

14 Through hints that the magic bed at Amurfina's castle and the *lit marveil* in the Castle of Wonders were both constructed by Gansguoter (lines 8202–16), Heinrich firmly links the magician with the sexual Sword of Damocles suspended above his niece's bed.

15 Such is even to some extent the case with Arthur, who undergoes a rudimentary form of development from the role of harassed sexual competitor to that of his more usual, sedentary role, debarred by his followers at this later stage from submitting himself to the kind of life-endangering escapades which he had contemplated in his early quarrel with Gasozein (lines 25,777–868).

Camelot as a collective institution. In one of the more remarkable speeches in the work, Kei even floats the notion of a co-regency shared by Arthur and Gawein when he pleads that Gawein should have the (moral) right to be king of the Arthurian order. This impassioned motion occurs in the context of the 'second Gawein' episode where Aamanz, a physical double of Gawein, is slain by the knights Gigamec and Zadoech and his head borne to the Court (lines 16,497–17,313). That event precipitates a crisis of faith in Kei (who takes the head to be that of Gawein). His imagined loss so devastates him that from the extremity of his grief he calls upon Arthur retrospectively to memorialise Gawein's moral leadership through what would be a truly remarkable self-denying ordinance:

> Künec Artûs, ir sült ûf seln
> Daz rîche und die krône,
> Und gebet ime daz ze lône,
> Daz iuwer vröude an ime stuont,
> Alsô vriunden vriunde tuont.
> Waz touc uns vröude âne in?   (lines 17,026–31).

> (King Arthur, you must renounce your land and crown and give them as a reward to him on whom your joy depended, just as one friend is wont to do for his fellow. What joy is left to us without him (sc. Gawein)?)

Gawein is not however permitted to eclipse Arthur in importance, as has been claimed,[16] for Arthur's second-in-command invariably acts in a representative capacity on behalf of his lord. Where in *Iwein* the creation of a second source of authority in the shape of Laudine's realm has often been thought to be a formal herald of the Grail realm[17] and the consequential demotion of Camelot, Heinrich defends his Arthurian 'crown' from these depredations. Even after achieving the Grail quest, Gawein returns to Arthur's Court and sets up no independent kingdom of his own. In one sense Heinrich's title lends itself to a metonymic reading as being about the perpetuation of Arthur's crown.[18]

The pursuit of a collective goal distinguishes Heinrich's romance from the tradition of the individualistic hero represented in the 'classical' tradition where narrative focus is typically trained on the moral development of single protagonists rather than on the king himself. Where Wolfram goes so far as to alter the traditional premises for a successful Grail quest to allow his hero to receive *tuition* for a task which the previous 'rules' had stipulated should be

---

16 Ebenbauer, 'Gawein als Gatte', pp. 53–54.

17 Hildegard Emmel, *Formprobleme des Artusromans und der Graldichtung. Die Bedeutung des Artuskreises fur das Gefüge des Romans im 12 und 13 Jahrhundert in Frankreich, Deutschland und den Niederlanden* (Berne: Francke, 1951), p. 39.

18 The term crown is used metonymically to mean kingship and queenship respectively in lines 10,350, 11,330.

performed unbidden, Heinrich's negative reception of the character of Parzival evidences little sympathy with the educative processes involved in Parzival's spiritual maturation. Parzival is provocatively used as a negative foil to Gawein, rather than vice versa,[19] and the vituperative pyrotechnics launched against him might suggest that principled dissent from his predecessor's choice of hero provided the inspiration for a narrative for which Parzival's inexpiable sin of omission is the essential narratological precondition.

Hence, as observed above, *Diu Crône* wears a somewhat archaic aspect in comparison with *Erec*, *Parzival* or with *Sir Gawain and the Green Knight* with which it shares similar material. In *Parzival*, Cundrie's denunciation is first directed to the whole Court for bearing responsibility for Parzival's shame, but this wider accusation remains unproblematised and the onus finally comes to rest on Parzival to correct his *individual* sin. Similarly, the English *Gawain* poet does not problematise the question of the king's power and legitimacy in the face of the Green Knight's taunts, for these things are assumed. In this new moral context the fairy machinery of Morgan the Fay and her malevolent designs becomes anomalous, yet in *Diu Crône* Giramphiel's hostility remains integral to the plot because it remains a powerful symbol of the Court's vulnerability to psychological warfare. Whilst Giramphiel's material depredations are neglible, her effect on the morale of the Court is potentially catastrophic: by the standards of later, persecuting centuries, both she and her legendary prototype, Morgan, might have fallen victim to charges of witchcraft.[20]

The narrator's observations about not spoiling his 'well-wrought crown' with gratuitous additions provide indications of a desire to place a 'copyright' over his chosen form of closure. This would have prevented a continuator following the example of Wolfram or Wirnt and adding an account of an exotic form of kingship detrimental to the *Arthurian* Crown. Gawein's immediate return to Court after his visit to the Grail castle indicates that Heinrich was little drawn to the kind of utopian realm which Wolfram and Wirnt added to the conclusions of their narratives. The naturalistic details[21] which characterise the last four thousand verses of *Wigalois* and the

---

19 *Diu Crône* adapts the hero-plus-foil pattern of Keu/Gauvain in *La Mule sans Frein* (Keu fails before the revolving castle scene, Gauvain succeeds) or of Lancelot/Gauvain in the *Merveilles de Rigomer* (Lancelot succumbs to a *fée*'s evil charms, Gauvain resists them).

20 Cf. *Erec*, ed. Leitzmann lines 5240–42 where Morgan (Famurgan) is described as acting 'wider Kriste'.

21 Descriptions of time and place in the last 4000 lines are realistic and bear no relationship to the fantastic locations and supernaturally swift accomplishment of exploits found in earlier sections of the narrative. Whereas the hero is able to accomplish numerous feats in a single day when he fights to prove himself a knight errant, the campaign against Lion with its siege engines is a war of attrition lasting six weeks (*Wigalois*, line 11,047). On this point see Wolfgang Mitgau, 'Nachahmung und Selbständigkeit Wirnts von Gravenberc in seinem *Wigalois*', *ZfdPh* 82 (1963), pp. 321–37, especially 330–32.

non-Arthurian material used by Wolfram to articulate his vision of an Oriental utopia based on the Prester John legend are commonly seen as evidence of improvisation on the part of both authors. No written source or analogue exists for Wigalois's preaching to Roaz's pagan subjects or for his leading a crusade against Roaz's sympathiser, Lion, in the final 4000 verses of Wirnt's romance. Assuming a late date for *Wigalois*, Wirnt's depiction of a theocracy in which the values of the spirit king, Lar, are melded with those of Gawein and other Arthurian knights,[22] may have been influenced by Parzival's ecumenical form of Grail kingship under whose aegis the pagan half-brother, Feirefiz, is permitted to marry the Grail bearer, Repanse de Schoye. In *Diu Crône* on the other hand the Arthurian Court is not demoted to the status of a transitional stage of cultural development whose purpose is to point toward a higher realm. After the curse on the *altherre* is lifted there are no further moral/regal entailments and Gawein returns to Court to report the benefits of what from the point of view of himself and his peers is primarily a famous victory for the Round Table.

Unlike his legendary son in Wirnt's *Wigalois*, Gawein will have no truck with an independent crown since he labours exclusively for the Crown of Camelot.[23] His loyalty is particularly in evidence when, even though personally honour-bound by his oath to Angaras of Karamphi to search for the Grail, he nevertheless requests the permission of Arthur's courtiers before taking his leave (lines 22,772ff). This solicitous attitude is conspicuously different from his behaviour at an earlier stage of the narrative where he had casually and carelessly turned his back on the Court by going absent without leave. Heinrich chooses the knight on whom Hartmann had conferred the lapidary title of 'der höfschte man' (*Iwein*, line 3037) for his proverbial loyalty, rejecting Wolfram's Parzival, who forsakes Karidol for the Grail realm of Munsalvaesche and subsequently for the Oriental kingdom of 'Prester John'.

Rejecting the image of a mystical quester whose aspirations might draw him away from the Court, Heinrich bases his mature Gawein on the extant tradition of Gawein as foremost courtier of the Arthurian order. According to the tradition of Chrétien/Hartmann Gawein's values are grounded so securely in the Arthurian fellowship that he can scarcely conceive of the existence of competing values. Hence he is unable fully to comprehend the emotional pressures which keep Erec absent from Court or how Iwein's

---

22 See Claudia Brinker, ' "Hie ist diu âventiure geholt!". Die Jenseitsreise im *Wigalois* des Wirnt von Gravenberg: Kreuzugspropaganda und unterhaltsame Glaubenslehre?' in *Contemplata aliis tradere. Studien zum Verhältnis von Literatur und Spiritualität*, ed. Brinker (Berne: Lang, 1995), pp. 87–110.

23 Wolfram creates a future genealogy from the sons of Parzival (Loherangrin and Kardeiz) and from Feirefiz and the Grail bearer, Repanse (Prester John), and Wirnt creates an imagined future son for Wigalois in the shape of Lifort Gawanides, creating a family succession (Gawein-Wigalois-Lifort Gawanides) which permits the projection of Gawein's legacy into the future. There is nothing of this in *Diu Crône*.

desire to rejoin his wife could override his obligation to Arthur. His fateful advice to Iwein not to become (like Erec) a prisoner of his love precipitates the crisis in which Iwein loses Laudine's favour, for which Gawein is blamed by Hartmann's narrator (lines 3029–58). By contrast the telling apologia for Iwein in *Diu Crône* challenges the conception that there was anything incompatible with marital *triuwe* in Iwein's forsaking of his wife for the world of knights (lines 1354–60) and implicitly inculpates Laudine for deflecting her husband from the path of duty. In the light of this interpretation of *Iwein* it is significant that when in *Diu Crône* Gawein takes a wife, she comes to dwell with him at Court and that the potential threat to the Court from the lure of exogamy is contained.

Gawein's languishing at Amurfina's side, although it seems to last thirty years to him, in fact lasts only fifteen days, and he is soon able to escape even that degree of erotic thralldom once he comes to realize that his duty is to be at Arthur's side. Although Amurfina is in origin based on a similar fairy mistress model as Laudine, she is made to forfeit a good part of her 'fairy' nature when she marries a knight whose ceaseless knightly activities are little curtailed by his new estate of married man. Whilst Laudine remains a traditionally imperious figure to the last, when Amurfina is domiciled at Camelot she joins the ranks of courtly *vrouwen*. Rather like Brünhilde in the *Nibelungenlied* or the female inhabitants of the Castle of Wonders, she is finally 'erlöst vom Bann ihrer amazonenhaften Überlegenheit'[24] and her conduct adheres henceforth to courtly norms.[25]

Heinrich's rewritings of Arthurian legendary produce a gallery of characters whose names are familiar but whose characters have been fleshed out in line with the author's imaginative requirements. In the case of his protagonist, Heinrich's choice of Gawein as Grail quester is unique in European literature (unless one accepts Jessie L. Weston's old hypothesis that he was the 'first' Grail quester whose role was later usurped by Perceval and Galahad). The choice appears to have been determined by the ambition to show that the Grail quest could be achieved without benefit of an extraordinary spiritual grace or exotic pedigree. To be sure, Gawein reaches a tolerable standard of personal integrity before undertaking the quest in the scenes linking the father with his legendary son's more spiritual challenges in Wirnt's *Wigalois*. Despite these spiritual forays, however, Gawein never forsakes his role of the Arthurian knight par excellence. After his defeat of the sylvan demons in the Assiles episode (which has echoes of the legendary son's contests with various scions of the race of Cain such as Ruel and Marriën), he swiftly

24 Heinrich Zimmer, 'Gawan beim grünen Ritter', in *Der Arthurische Roman*, ed. Wais, pp. 282–300, citation 299.
25 Little is heard in the sequel of the dynamic woman who had once cheated her sister and compelled Gawein to her side (apart from the scene where she conforms to the passive role of grieving wife when lamenting the (false) news of Gawein's death).

applies himself to the task of rescuing a girl in distress, an action which 'leads Gawein back to the courtly world after his brush with the supernatural'.[26]

Despite Heinrich's vigorous polemics against Wolfram's Parzival, Gawein is not shown to be *morally* superior to Wolfram's protagonist. Just as the latter has guides and mentors in Sigune, Cundrie and Trevrizent, so Heinrich's Gawein receives assistance from a variety of sources including Gansguoter and his sister, Manbur, who prompts him to ask the Grail question. Heinrich did not labour to transform the traditional figure of Gawein into a person of superlative spiritual distinction since such a change would have been at odds with his portrayal of the Grail quester as the quintessential *Arthurian* knight. The only 'Grail premise' in *Diu Crône* is that a knight 'ervarn solte diese grôze âventiure' (line 29,517).[27] The verb 'ervarn' ('get to know about') might imply that the task is largely cognitive and that the hero must merely find out 'waz [. . .] daz wunder bediute' (lines 29,436–37). But since the cognitive task is rendered nugatory by Manbur's prior instructions about how and when to ask the question, this has not unfairly been taken to represent an *Erlösungsmechanismus* rather than an *Erlösungsproblematik*.[28]

The decisive issue, as the old Grail king confirms, is not the asking but the quality of courage shown by Gawein in having reached the Grail in the first place. Gawein does not succumb to existential despair either when facing the intimidations of flesh-and-blood opponents or when faced by the more infernal spectres of the *Wunderketten* whose presence before him in time and space would have been understood as 'a dangerously liminal time when the dead might seek to seize companions from the world of the living to accompany them into the abodes of the deceased'.[29] Rather does he show the courage to come to the abode of the dead, look Death full in the face and refuse pessimistic/ absurdist interpretations of his condition.[30] Courage was for the generality of men at arms a more fundamental quality with a far more important survival value than the ability to achieve profound spiritual insights. Since cowardice was 'an accusation which struck at the core of chivalry and undermined the whole military and social basis of a knight's

---

[26] Harding, 'Tradition and creativity', p. 142.

[27] Cf. Schröder, 'Zur Literaturverarbeitung': 'Den Gral und seine Geheimnisse hat er nicht ergründet, er hat ihn liquidiert; er wollte niemals *des grales herre wesen*' (p. 171).

[28] Schmid, *Familiengeschichten und Heilsmythologie*, p. 206.

[29] *The Place of the Dead. Death and Remembrance in Late Medieval and Early Modern Europe*, ed. Bruce Gordon and Peter Marshall (Cambridge: Cambridge U.P., 2000), Editorial Introduction, p. 7. Often the dead themselves were seen as malign, as in the recurrent theme of the perilous graveyard tradition (*âtre périlleux*) whose hostile spirits are on the lookout for innocent souls.

[30] Cf. Hans-Dietrich Altendorf, 'Die Entstehung des theologischen Höllenbildes in der alten Kirche', in *Himmel, Hölle, Fegefeuer. Das Jenseits im Mittelalter*, Exhibition of the Swiss National Museum (Verlag Neue Zürcher Zeitung: Zurich, 1994), pp. 27–31: 'Ist die Höllenvorstellung gar ein Pendant zum neuzeitlichen Nihilismus und ein Bekenntnis zur Absurdität?' (p. 31).

existence';[31] it was of the greatest moment in a work endorsing the value of feudal solidarity that the prime champion of the Arthurian order should possess courage above any of the gentler virtues.

There is in fact little attempt in *Diu Crône* to disguise the ethos of force lying at the heart of the chivalric enterprise and the romance does not lend itself easily to the kind of anachronistic reading which has been criticised for presenting in other romances of this period a 'gleichsam verklärend-sittliche Version von Ritterlichkeit, die ihren Ursprung in der Ideologie des 19 Jahrhunderts hat'.[32] Kei's charge that Gawein procured the magic belt of Fortuna by force,[33] although it remains judicially unexplored, is never rebutted because it so self-evidently represents Gawein's habitual modus operandi. The same stricture applies to his theft of Giremelanz's 'flowers of Fortune' (line 6107), for here this action makes clear that the amoral Fortuna grants her boons only to the bold. Indeed, Gawein's courage in making off with such grandiose boons is announced as constituting the very core of his chivalric repute in Riwalin's praise of these thefts:

> Sîn manheit ist bekant
> Der Finbeus, dem wîgant,
> Die gürtel nam und genas,
> Dâ diu Saelde mit gegürtet was,
> Und Leigormon der meide
> Ze Colurment an der heide
> Der Saelden bluomen abe brach,
> Da was vrou Saelde wider in.   (lines 6101–09)

(His courage is proverbial. He took from the warrior Finbeus the belt formerly worn by Fortuna herself and against that goddess's wishes also plucked the flowers of the meadow Colurment for the maiden Leigormon.)

For Gawein the end invariably justifies the means and there is a certain moral roughness in his use of Sgoidamur as a bribe/bride to integrate Gasozein into the Arthurian world. Meanwhile, by warding off dangers through tactical treaties such as the final reconciliation with Angaras, Gawein practises a peaceful form of Arthurian imperialism. Even the quest for the Grail is for the most part more a military struggle for Camelot than a spiritual pilgrimage. *Diu Crône* presents an apologia for Gawein as an example of the old, unregenerate romance hero (in contradistinction to Perceval or Galahad).

---

31 Jillings, '*Diu Crône*', p. 112.
32 Hubertus Fischer, *Ehre, Hof und Abenteuer. Vorarbeiten zu einer historischen Poetik des höfischen Epos* (Munich: Fink, 1983), p. 31.
33 The charge is repeated by the *ritter mit dem boc* who adds the further reproach that he (Gawein) would have been prepared to kill Fimbeus without the proper declaration of a feud (lines 25,405–43).

Accepting those ethical limitations, we can see on the other hand that the narrator's ambition was to provide an imaginative hypothesis as to the moral route taken by the 'early' unreconstructed knight-homicide on his long journey to the Grail, and to show how he redeems himself from the image of 'hardened sinner, whose misfortune is symbolised by his involuntary slaying of his best friends'[34] which prevails in the French prose tradition. It might be thought that there can be little talk of a moral struggle when the irresistible external forces which compel Gawein's fidelity to his wife include a love potion and a menacing sword bearing all too great a functional similarity to the modern shotgun. However, the text shows clearly that he had decided to join Amurfina *before* he consumed the magic draught or been threatened by a sword, leading us to conclude that an erotic charge must have been present before Gawein drank the potion. In the sexual sphere as elsewhere in *Diu Crône*, magic requisites play a symbolic role, and, despite the plethora of supernatural elements, the causal chain depends on human agency.

The notion of character change has been invoked to describe Keii's shift from malicious sniper to fine-feeling elegist on his hearing the (false) rumour of Gawein's death, to sage guardian of the Court,[35] and finally to a knight who has a separate challenge to face in the Grail land of Illes for which he is ultimately given a hero's welcome at Court (lines 29,897–998); but the same notion has not previously been thought appropriate to describe other figures in *Diu Crône*. Yet this concept applies *a fortiori* to Gawein, whose initial, uncommitted hovering about the periphery of the Arthurian world yields to his gradual repositioning at the moral centre of the Court's affairs. In the *Conte du Graal* and in the First Continuation Gauvain gives the impression of a knight 'going round in circles'.[36] Heinrich's strategy appears to have been to remove the sense of disorientation and make it yield to a more purposeful characterisation in which Gawein's quest for the Grail is firmly linked to the one moral isue which clouds his reputation in many other romances.[37] The origins and moral pedigree of the 'classical' conception of Gawein as an eirenic 'Katalysator der Menschlichkeit'[38] become clearer once we accept Heinrich's account of Gawein's successfully negotiated ethical apprentice-

---

[34] Fanni Bogdanow, 'The Character of Gauvain in the thirteenth century prose romances', p. 155.

[35] Only he and the little unnamed Cassandra figure have the wit to warn against the trickery of Giramphiel's henchman, the Knight on the Goat (lines 25,135ff).

[36] For a discussion of this point see Keith Busby, *Gauvain in Old French Literature* (Amsterdam: Rodopi, 1980), pp. 162–79. (In the *Conte du Graal* he sets off on a circular journey which, after numberless peregrinations, terminates where it had begun in company with the the knight Greoreas.)

[37] Ralph Read suggested that it was 'inept' of Heinrich not to have made Gawein into a Grail quester until line 18,685 ('Heinrich von dem Türlin's *Diu Krône* and Wolfram's *Parzival*', p. 130). This view however overlooks the way in which Gawein must be groomed for a task of which at first he has little understanding.

[38] Wolfgang Mohr, 'Parzival und Gawan', *Euphorion* 52 (1958), pp. 1–22, citation 14.

ship on a quest whose purpose is in large part to avert the unnecessary blood-shed of a continuing feud.

Both Wolfram and Heinrich in their different ways realised the potential for romances taking Gawein as a romance hero, but Wolfram achieved this by blinding the motif of Gawan as homicide and forestalling the need for his rehabilitation. He created instead a semi-independent romance for his deuteragonist unrelated to the Grail theme. His image of Gawan as the sexual saviour of Obie, Orgeluse and the immured youths and maidens of *schastel marveile* is essentially a new story superimposed upon a narrative which contemporaries might have expected to deal with the charge of murder made by Kingrimursel. They would have had only Wolfram's assurance for his hero's innocence and for the guilt of the obscure 'Ekhunat'. Heinrich, on the other hand, confronts Gawein's problematical past directly and, not allowing him evasive peregrinations, makes him do penance for his misdeed through a precisely focused Grail action.

Diu *Crône*, opposing a monastic appropriation of the Arthurian genre, finds a literary niche for a knight whose ambiguous performance in the *Conte du Graal* and its First Continuation left him ripe for rehabilitation in the hands of a writer keen to stress the value of 'Arthurian' virtues. Gawein's Grail expedition adheres to the spirit of Chrétien by making the journey not an open-ended journey of self-discovery but a specific penitential obligation imposed by the brother of the knight whom Gawein had killed. Heinrich engages here with the same theme in the Arthurian milieu that Wolfram treats in the sectarian context of *Willehalm*: the inbuilt destructive aggression which impels the world of 'chivalry' and which Wolfram bluntly decons-tructs as *mort*.[39]

Not all medieval writers were as direct in their denunciation of homicide as Wolfram in *Willehalm* but the frequency and bitterness with which charges of homicide are brought in medieval romances indicates a strong awareness of a moral aporia in the knightly code. Systematic attempts to address the unregulated excesses of knightly feuding in Germany were made in the form of the various peace movements arising during the late twelfth and the thir-teenth centuries, these being part of a 'long process whereby ecclesiastical and lay authorities tried to contain warrior activity, to subject warfare to Christian, ethical notions, and to extend peace in a society in which the feud was still regarded, by the lay aristocracy, as a proper legal process and an inborn right.'[40] In literature the disquiet often finds expression in the image of a killing which so rends the fabric of the courtly moral universe as to bring

---

39 *Willehalm*, ed. Werner Schröder with modern German translation by Dieter Kartschoke (Berlin: de Gruyter, 1989), section 10, lines 18–20.
40 W. H. Jackson, *Chivalry in Twelfth-Century Germany. The Works of Hartmann von Aue* (Wood-bridge: Boydell & Brewer, 1994), p. 85. For an analytical discussion of the various *Landfrieden* in the light of recent historiographical debate see Jackson, pp. 84–96.

divine wrath upon that whole world. Medieval Grail romances are typically based on the conception that a murder, heinous in itself, can have further repercussions when it brings sickness to the bereaved kin and a blight upon its land. These misfortunes will endure until the curse is overcome, either through the exercise of some spiritual power or by revenge upon the perpetrator. In many versions the Grail tradition is linked to the theme of a succession to kingship in which the heir presumptive must avenge his predecessor and restore his blighted realm. Such is the case in *Peredur, Sir Percyvell of Galles* and in Manessier's Continuation where Perceval uses the reforged Grail sword to slay the Lord of the Red Tower who had slain the brother of the Fisher King. The two methods of redeeming a harried land are combined in Wirnt von Gravenberg's *Wigalois* (which, though not a Grail romance, advances a similar range of themes as *Parzival*). Here the hero triumphs over the homicidal Roaz by his faith in a Christian God more powerful than Roaz's pagan deities and also exacts revenge for the dead Lar by slaying Roaz and taking over the crown which Roaz had usurped from Lar. Heinrich on the other hand ignores the twin entailments of revenge and succession. In *Diu Crône* there is no attempt to develop the narrative along the lines of punishing the original malefactor in Parzival's kin (who remains unnamed), nor does Gawein attempt to make any particularist territorial claims of his own.

Despite taking over much of the metaphysical logic of the Wirntian account, Heinrich ignores the revenge motif because such a conception would not have harmonised with his non-belligerent solution to the problem of the curse or with the peaceful resolution of the Dahamorht issue. Gawein's vision of the six hundred knights mown down by invisible foes is a telling image of anonymous, mechanical killing rather like the *mêlée* in which he himself unwittingly killed Dahamorht. The synchronisation of his own penance for homicide with his deliverance of Parzival's kin from the after-effects of a past murder lends a harmony to his personal and public roles comparable to the *locus classicus* for such a fusion where Erec, by freeing Mabonagrin from his uxorious thrall, symbolically overcomes his own sexual thrall to Enite. Whilst it may be the case that Gawein's lack of an arduous spiritual trial make his spiritual qualities appear modest, he is at least granted the grace both to honour his obligation to the bereaved party and also to shoulder the messianic role imposed upon him by the shortcomings of his peers.

The result of his endeavours is that it relieves him of the necessity of having to endanger his life at the hands of the hostile knights of Karamphi Castle and so possibly deprive the Arthurian Court of its champion. Heinrich provides a pragmatic solution to narrative problems implicit in the work of Chrétien but makes little attempt to advance millenarian nostrums for his age. Even after Gawein's restoration of the polite fiction of marital harmony, Guinevere's sexual conflict is left as an unresolved tension not addressed within the narrative sequel, and the same goes for Gawein's other redemptive

acts. Giramphiel, even though ultimately defeated by the protagonist, nevertheless remains alive (hence with the potential for further mischief). Even the
conquest of the 'Grail' gives a less than completely satisfying sense of security
to Arthur's Court. For Gawein, having achieved the Grail quest and thus
granted satisfaction to Angaras over the *immediate* homicide which had alienated the two knights, simply returns to Camelot and therefore, it may be
inferred from the lack of any further details, to the *status quo ante*, which
would have meant the same old round of life-endangering combats which
had obtained hitherto. Although Heinrich shows a maturation of Gawein's
character, he gives few hints of a capacity to deconstruct and transcend
'Arthurian' values. His formation and development, although more sugges-
tively delineated than has commonly been acknowledged, certainly does not
involve the kind of *metanoia* which could have led him to a whole-hearted
espousal of eirenic values. The Arthurian tragedy is deferred rather than
averted (as the narrator's proleptic reference to the future, unstayable attentions of Atropos concedes).

The narrator's faith is placed finally not in metaphysical notions of
enduring good fortune nor in the 'Grail' and its resources of Christian miracle
but rather in its protagonist's chivalric prowess together with that skill in
Realpolitik which prompts Gawein to borrow what might nowadays be
termed technical support from the magician/military tactician, Gansguoter.
The seemingly omnipresent and omnipotent figure of Gansguoter is, in the
absence of any strong sense of a controlling God, the *de facto* 'director of the
action'[41] for most of the romance. A quite ingenious explanation has recently
been put forward to explain the name Gansguoter[42] but perhaps the most apt
one might be (by the figure of anotonomasia) the *summum bonum* – a witty
play on the medieval periphrasis for God.[43] In Gawein's pact with
Gansguoter lies an implicit plea for a restoration of the ancient partnership of
the Arthurians and Merlin in which chivalrous prowess allied itself with the
kind of elemental knowledge which was later eclipsed by what Jessie L.
Weston once called the 'ecclesiasticisation' of the Grail legend. Such a

---

41 The phrase 'Regisseur der Handlung' is that of Mentzel-Reuters, *Vröude*, p. 179.

42 By Keller, *Wunderketten, Gral und Tod*, which I give here in full: 'Es ist vielleicht kein Zufall,
    daß der Name Gansguoter anagrammatisch den Namen Artus enthält. Die Verwand-
    schaft zu Artus entsteht durch Gansguoters Verbindung mit Îgerne, die der Zauberer mit
    "videlen" (v. 23708) und, akzeptiert man ein weiteres Anagramm, mit "gutem Gesang"
    ("guoter sanc") bezirzt hat' (p. 411, note 309). For a more cautious derivation see
    Mentel-Reuters, *Vröude*, pp. 179–80.

43 Although in many versions of Arthurian story the half-evil origins of Merlin express
    themselves as an innocuous Puckishness, an example of a 'wholly bad' magician appears
    in the shape of Eliavres in the Caradoc section of the First Continuation (cf. Appendix ii,
    below). Heinrich's conferring upon his magician figure the sobriquet of The Wholly
    Good/Highest Good indicates the German's selective perception of a legendary figure
    whose descent from an incubus and a nun meant that he often appeared as a union of
    opposites. On this point see P. E. Schiprowski, *Merlin in der deutschen Dichtung* (Breslau:
    Antonius Verlag, 1933), pp. 24–25.

partnership, reminiscent of the early period of the Court as Robert de Boron's continuators had envisioned it, is shown to be the best way of achieving the 'Grail' in the profane sense of the acme of the chivalric estate. The way to Heinrich's lower-case Grail comes not so much from progressive spiritual revelation as from the ability to manipulate the correct military/magical levers.

Although it has been generally contended that Heinrich's attempt to write an account of Arthur's early years 'does not amount to much' (Jillings, '*Diu Crône*', p. 195), this conclusion is justified only if we judge the author solely by the anachronistic criterion of being able to find or invent entirely unheard-of material (or else if we interpret the term *kinttage* by the misleadingly restrictive semantic analogy of modern German *Kind* and its cognates), for Heinrich's romance undoubtedly contains some notable rewrites of Arthurian tradition.[44] Whereas Hartmann von Aue, Wolfram von Eschenbach and Wirnt von Gravenberg depict Arthur as an 'unmoved mover' whose foibles (though evident) go largely unchallenged, Heinrich problematises the king's regal status, confronting him with reverses and challenges as he attempts to establish his authority with peers and external challengers. By depicting his Camelot as vulnerable to internal and external challenge Heinrich arguably does more to simulate credible impressions of the problems of a young king's early reign than does the *Historia Regum Britanniae* and its Continental successors. Geoffrey advanced Arthur by way of some soaring hyperbole beyond any putative role of Celtic guerrilla leader to the status of a battle-hardened imperialist conquering the kingdoms of Ireland, Norway, Gaul, France, even threatening Rome itself. Of a man (in any verisimilitudinous sense) there is little. Heinrich, by contrast, enhances his claim to be telling the progress of a fledgeling regime where he depicts the initial vulnerability of the Arthurian order, proceeding from tremulous beginnings to chart the Court's ascent to the Grail as the zenith of his narrative teleology. Where Chrétien and Hartmann narrate stories from an apparently timeless heyday of Arthur's reign, Heinrich develops the story of how Arthur struggles to gain that peerless authority which 'later' becomes his secure possession.

Whereas an earlier generation of scholars was apt to suppose that the Arthurian romances of the Middle Ages derived from more ancient archetypes which better reflected the 'authentic' terms of the pristine legend, it is now widely recognised that the Arthurian legend was more the product of

---

[44] On creative re-writing see Elspeth Kennedy, 'The re-writing and re-reading of a text. The evolution of the Prose *Lancelot*', in *The Changing Face of Arthurian Romance. Essays on Arthurian Prose Romances in Honour of Cedric Pickford*, ed. Alison Adams (Woodbridge: Boydell & Brewer, 1986), pp. 1–9; Elisabeth Schmid, 'Texte über Texte. Zur *Crône* des Heinrich von dem Türlin', *GRM* 44 (1994), pp. 266–87; and Peter Kern, 'Bewußtmachen von Artusromankonventionen in der *Crône* Heinrichs von dem Türlin' in *Erzählstrukturen der Artusliteratur. Forschungsgeschichte und neue Ansätze*, ed. Friedrich Wolfzettel (Tübingen: Niemeyer, 1999), pp. 199–218.

writers of the High Middle Ages than of Celtic antiquity. Heinrich's artfully couched claim to have found out new things about 'the origins of Arthurian chivalry' (line 170) answers to a similar craving amongst his own contemporaries for authority and the support of ancient testimony. Although Heinrich presents his would-be chronicle romance with pseudo-historical affidavits, he provides no newly discovered tradition but rather an artfully woven confection of (mainly French) traditions in a new sequence and hence with a new sense. Yet since Heinrich's unequalled knowledge of Arthurian tradition provides substantial grounds for believing his claim that he was part of a primary reception of French themes and their adaptation for German audiences, it is unlikely that a majority of that intended audience would have been acquainted with all the material in its original French contexts. Such an audience might then the more readily have responded to it at face value in the novel configuration bestowed upon it by the German adapter.

Modern readers already acquainted with the French traditions in their original contexts may then need to exert some determined suspension of disbelief to appreciate the romance in the same way as a medieval public. Indeed, it is perhaps because modern readers have been unable to respond to the text in the same, straightforward way as Heinrich's first audiences that the work has remained something of a literary-historical enigma. *Diu Crône* must even for us today exert some appeal as a bravura performance of narrative legerdemain whose decanting of new wine into old bottles conjures up a compelling foundation myth, namely, the story of the redemption of Camelot from an initial condition of factionalism, sexual betrayal and diminished morale under an inexperienced king to one of law, order and security under the aegis of one supremely resourceful knight in the unflinching service of his liege lord. Neither in its narrative nor ethical structure is *Diu Crône* a symbol of the decline of courtly literary tradition. The contention that 'it is intended to offer on one level a lively chivalric romance culminating in a quasi-religious act of liberation by Gawein, and at a deeper level which stands in inherent contradiction to this, to undermine chivalry from within by its satirical treatment of courtly figures and values' (Jillings, *'Diu Crône'*, p. 12)[45] is opposed by the analysis offered above.[46] Rather by its construction of a new

---

[45] For other criticism of Jillings see also Ebenbauer, 'Gawein als Gatte', esp. pp. 37–43 and p. 48, note 76.

[46] *Diu Crône* did not stand alone in opposing the spiritualising tendencies unleashed by the Lancelot–Grail tradition. See Bart Besamusca, *'Walewein*: A Middle Dutch antidote to the Prose *Lancelot'*, *BBIAS* 47 (1995), pp. 301–10. See also Elizabeth Andersen, 'Diu Crône and the Prose Lancelot', and for an analysis of the attempts by other near-contemporary German writers (Der Pleier; Albrecht, author of *Der Jüngere Titurel*; Wisse and Colin, authors of the Rappoltstein *Parzifal*, and Ulrich Füeterer) to promote a 'muscular' form of knightly/ Christian ethics see Neil Thomas, *The Defence of Camelot. Ideology and Intertextuality in the 'Post-Classical' German Romances of the Matter of Britain Cycle* (Berne: Lang, 1992), esp. pp. 213–20.

moral genealogy for the Arthurian world does the romance give a more secure imaginative foundation to an Arthurian ideal which clearly maintained its appeal in Germany well beyond the 'classical' period of the first decade of the thirteenth century.

Appendix: Summaries of Analogues

I *Der Mantel*[1]

The narrator begins his short narrative by expressing surprise that his peers do not lament the death of King Arthur more loudly. Kei is introduced as an uncouth figure shunned for his venomous tongue ('eitermeilige(n) zunge'). Arthur refuses to eat until some adventure has taken place, whereupon a youth enters the Court of whom we are told that anybody who can emulate him shall have the Sword of Fortune ('der Saelden swert'). The stranger says he has been sent as an emissary by his queen from a distant land to bring for the womenfolk a magical cloak designed to discover whether any have betrayed their husbands in thought or deed. Guinevere puts on the cloak which fits her very badly – greatly to her shame and to Arthur's displeasure. Kei bids his *amie* don the cloak, whereupon she stands bare underneath the line of her belt. Since the other courtiers are cowed by Kei's sarcastic tongue, nobody dares inform Kei of this event except for Bruns Senpite who, as his name suggests, shows as great a capacity to gloat as Kei himself. Gawein's *amie* also fails the test as does Enite, although only on account of a minor character blemish. The narrator concludes with some animadversions on the incorrigibly malicious conduct of Kei.

II The *First Continuation*[2]

The final scene of Chrétien's *Conte du Graal* had left Arthur and his courtiers in Orkney where the king fainted through worry about the missing Gauvain's well-being. The continuator picks up the thread of this story when a young messenger (already mentioned by Chrétien) arrives to tell Arthur that Gauvain is alive and well. This news fills all the courtiers with great relief,

---

1   *Das Ambraser Mantel Fragment*, ed. Werner Schröder (Stuttgart: Franz Steiner, 1995). This short romance of just under 1000 verses was once thought to have been by Heinrich von dem Türlin but is probably a later work influenced by *Diu Crône*.

2   *Première Continuation de Perceval (Continuation-Gauvain)*, ed. William Roach, trans. Anne Van Coolput-Storms (Paris: Librairie Generale Française, 1993). Like *Diu Crône*, this romance contains the motifs of the missing Gauvain, Gauvain accused of murder, and a Castle of Maidens to which Arthur's mother has resorted. It also takes Gauvain rather than Perceval as its Grail quester, although the latter does not enjoy the unequivocal success in the quest of Heinrich's Gawein.

particularly Arthur and Keu (and the narrator praises Keu for being a discerning knight despite his sharp tongue). Gauvain through the page requests Arthur's aid in seeing fair play in his impending duel against Guiromelant (the beloved of Gauvain's sister, Clarissant). Arthur accordingly sets off with 30,000 knights and 15,000 ladies to the castle of Ygerne, Arthur's mother, where Gauvain presently resides. There Arthur is reconciled with the mother he had not seen for 50 years (being informed by Gauvain that, upon the death of Arthur's father, Uther Pendragon, Ygerne had fled with great treasure, seeking an isolated retreat). Gauvain's own mother had also come to the same retreat after the death of her husband, King Lot of Orkney.

Gauvain readies himself for his combat with Guiromelant by taking confession with a bishop, but Gauvain's sister pleads for the duel to be halted. Gauvain says he will agree to a cessation of hostilities only if Guiromelant withdraw his accusation of murder against him. In that case, he says, he would also agree to his sister becoming Guiromelant's wife. But Guiromelant and Clarissant wed before any such formal withdrawal of the accusation has been made, and Gauvain rides off angrily. All the courtiers are distraught, fearing Gauvain's permanent alienation. Meanwhile Gauvain continues his quest for the lance (begun in Chrétien's *Conte du Graal*) and presently comes across a maimed king at the Grail castle. Here he witnesses the lance 'bleeding' from its tip and a beautiful young woman bearing the Grail aloft. As she processes, tears can be seen in her eyes, but Gauvain remains ignorant of why she cries and of the import of what she is carrying. Then four servants enter carrying a body on a bier covered with royal silk on which a broken sword rests. The procession circulates three times but nobody says a word to Gauvain who, suspecting that he has seen the Grail and the lance which were the objects of his quest, now asks the maimed king the meaning of the wondrous events. At this point the king asks for the broken sword to be brought to him and tells Gauvain that, if he can mend it, he will be told the full truth about the mysteries which he has observed. Gauvain fails to be able to perform this task, with the result that the old king (whilst informing Gauvain that he might yet at some future time come to know the full truth) tells him that now only the man who can join the sword perfectly can be inducted into the secrets of the procession. While the old man is speaking, Gauvain falls asleep, waking the next day to find himself lying on marshland with his horse tethered to a tree on a heath nearby.

Now Gauvain remembers his pledge to Guigambresil to return to the Castle of Escavalon (Heinrich's Karamphi) to face the combat to which he had agreed were he not successful in his mission to the Grail. At this point Gauvain comes across a second accuser – the knight Disnaderet, who wishes to avenge himself on Gauvain for his allegedly having murdered *his* father. After some preliminary skirmishing they both agree to defer their combat to a later date, and Gauvain continues his journey to Escavalon. Coming before the king of that land, he confesses that, despite his best efforts, he has not been able to find the Grail and the lance and that he will therefore prepare himself to give satisfaction in armed combat. His old opponent, Guigambresil, is just about to ready himself for the encounter when the second accuser, Disnaderet, enters the arena, demanding that Gauvain fight him too. Gauvain consents to fight the two simultaneously but when King Arthur hears of this dangerously unequal battle, he repairs quickly to Escavalon in order to negotiate peace terms, essentially placating the two belligerents through sexual bribes: he gives two of his granddaughters in marriage to Guigambresil and Disnaderet respectively. The two knights then become Arthur's liegemen and Gauvain is released from his original oath to give satisfaction to Guigambresil for the alleged killing of his father.

The next section (lines 2054–12,690) forms a semi-independent narrative devoted to the knight Caradoc (Carados). Caradoc senior comes to Court to ask Arthur to grant him a wife. The king bestows upon him his niece, Ysave of Carahes, but she is also loved by the magician, Eliavres, who tricks her by magic into surrendering her body to him, using similar magic to trick Caradoc into sleeping with animals. Caradoc is born of the union of the magician with Ysave. Years later Eliavres comes to the Arthurian Court to play the Beheading Game with Caradoc junior, his natural son. Caradoc, given the first blow, cuts off the magician's head but Eliavres, having miraculously retrieved his head, vows to return the blow in a year's time (in the event sparing the young man whom he knows to be his son). Shamed and outraged when told the news of his true paternity, the young man informs Caradoc senior, and they both immure Ysave in a stone tower to prevent any repetition of the shameful act; but Eliavres manages through magical means to gain access to the tower and enjoy Ysave's embraces once again. As a punishment for this transgression the younger Caradoc makes Eliavres lie with animals just as Caradoc senior had once been made to do. In retaliation, Eliavres with the full consent of Caradoc's mother hatches a plan to make a viper coil itself around the son's arm, to the horror of Arthur and of Caradoc's *amie*, Guinier. The only remedy for this curse turns out to be a piece of magic of Eliavres which Caradoc's friend, Cador, manages to get Ysave to tell him about, namely, that the sight of a maiden's breast would induce the serpent to leave Caradoc's arm. Guinier cooperates in this cure by exposing her breast and Cador is duly able to slay the serpent once it releases its grip. Then the young Caradoc becomes reconciled with his mother and he and Guinier are married, this section of the narrative ending with a 'testing goblet' story in which Caradoc and Guinier alone are able to prove their absolute purity and fidelity.

Rejoining Gauvain as protagonist we find him in the strange circumstance of taking over the mission of a knight who has just dropped down dead in front of him before Guinevere's pavilion. (Neither the identity of the corpse nor the circumstances of his terminal injuries are explained – although Keu is strongly suspected of having a hand in the matter.) Trusting that the dead man's horse will know the right way, Gauvain rides off into thunder and lashing rain, presently arriving at a chapel where a terrible black hand emerges from behind the altar to snuff out a candle. Gauvain's horse rears up and Gauvain crosses himself (after which the torrential rain and thunder cease). At this point the narrator informs us that nobody should tell of the wonders that Gauvain encountered. Anyone who did so would regret his disclosures and suffer great woe, for the 'wonders' were all part of the 'Grail'.

The dead man's horse then takes Gauvain to a causeway planted with overhanging trees lashed by storms from the sea. Not brooking any halt the horse gallops across the long causeway until its rider finds himself in a large hall, where the populace seem to know that Gauvain is not the knight whom they were expecting. Gauvain sees a corpse on a bier and two halves of a broken sword, one half lying on the dead man's chest. Then a white-haired king emerges, and all sit down at table where they are fed by a 'Grail' which moves back and forth dispensing its victuals without human agency. When the tables are cleared, Gauvain witnesses a bleeding lance dripping blood into a vase. Then the lord appears bearing the sword that had belonged to the dead knight whose mission Gauvain had taken over and which Gauvain had brought with him to the castle. The lord laments the great misfortune which is causing the kingdom to perish and asks Gauvain to mend the sword and invites him to ask about any of the mysteries which he has observed. Gauvain asks about the nature of the sword and bleeding lance and also about the dead knight and how his death might be avenged. His host, who says that nobody before Gauvain had dared ask such questions, replies that the lance is that of Longinus (used by the Roman centurion to pierce Christ's side on the Cross and so halt his redeemer's suffering). The sword was that used to deliver a terrible blow to the Kingdom of Logres but before the host is able to reveal the identity of the corpse Gauvain falls asleep. The next thing Gauvain knows is that he is on a high promontory overlooking the sea, his horse beside him, and no habitation of whatever kind in the vicinity: it grieves the knight that he did not learn the full story. But at least the kingdom has been restored to fecundity from the state of a wasteland because Gauvain had at least asked the question about the bleeding lance. Gauvain has had partial success – although bystanders still reproach him for not having found out the whole truth about the mysteries surrounding the Grail. The final verses (lines 13,603–15,322) turn to the exploits of Gauvain's son and brother.

III De Ortu Walwanii, Nepotis Arturi[3]

Arthur's father, Uther Pendragon, holds Lot, King of Norway, under his sway. Lot becomes the lover of Anna, Uther's daughter. She becomes pregnant with Lot's child but in order to conceal her baby she entrusts him to the care of some wealthy merchants together with a ring, a valuable cloak (*pallium*) and a document attesting his birth. These proofs of identity are however lost when the young boy is abducted by Viamundus, a man poor in possessions but noble by birth and bearing. Viamundus wins favour with the Roman emperor and when he feels close to death begs the emperor together with Pope Sulpicius to take charge of Arthur's nephew, now twelve years old. He also recommends that the boy should be kept ignorant of his identity until a later date and be called simply 'puer sine nomine' for the present. The emperor brings him up with his other children, giving him military instruction so that he is later able to join the prestigious Equestrian Order, achieving the rank of centurion and permitted to wear the crimson tunic of that order. From this point he is known as 'miles cum tunica armature'. He becomes a valiant defender of the cause of Rome and the Christian faith in a number of wars, for which he is fêted by the emperor and the Senate. Presently the young unknown gets to hear of the valour of Arthur and his knights and, disdaining a life of sloth, asks permission of the emperor to depart for Demetia where Arthur holds court at Caerleon-on-Usk. The emperor, judging this to be the proper moment for his charge to be informed of his ancestry (and hoping he might play a role in regaining Britannia for the empire), grants permission for his departure. Just as Walwanius approaches Caerleon, Guendoloena has a vision that a knight even stronger than her husband is approaching their court, prophesying that the newcomer will furnish her with rich gifts the next morning. When the queen falls asleep, Arthur goes off in the middle of the night with Kay to search for the mysterious stranger. When they come across the Knight of the Surcoat, Arthur asks him whether he is an exile, bandit or spy – insulting words which unleash a battle in which both Arthur and Kay are unhorsed. Arthur subsequently creeps back through the cold, wet night to Guendoloena, giving a fictitious reason for his sodden state. His deception is however revealed the next day when Walwanius brings up the horses of Arthur and Kay. Arthur, though shamefaced, feels

---

3 *The Rise of Gawain, Nephew of Arthur/ De Ortu Walwanii, Nepotis Arturi*, ed. and trans. Mildred Leake Day (New York: Garland, 1984). This Latin romance is preserved in only one manuscript (British Museum Cotton Faustina B vi, 23r–38r) of the first half of the fourteenth century but the date of original composition is probably c. 1175–1200. It contains a version of the challenging of Arthur (of which Guinevere has some foreknowledge) in which the challenger is not a stranger who makes sexual claims upon the queen like Heinrich's Gasozein but rather Arthur's own nephew. The combat between Arthur and Walwanius is therefore closer here to the fight-between-friends motif familiar to us from the bloodless combats between Parzival and Gawan and Feirefiz in Wolfram's *Parzival*.

considerably better when written documents which Walwanius had brought with him from Rome prove that he is his own nephew. After a further campaign in which Walwanius stands at Arthur's side to relieve a pagan siege of a Christian castle, Arthur reveals his identity to Walwanius amongst general celebrations.

IV The Vulgate Lancelot-Grail cycle (including Prose *Lancelot*)[4]

This extensive sequence consists of five narratives drawn together to form a cycle (*L'Estoire del saint Graal, l'Estoire de Merlin, the Lancelot proper, Queste del saint Graal, Mort Artu*). The first represents a pious proto-history of the Grail written as a retrospective sequel detailing the history of the dish used by Christ at the Last Supper in apostolic times up to the time when Joseph of Arimathea committed the holy vessel (token of God's covenant with the faithful) to Alain. The castle of Corbenic is build for the Grail, the succession of Fisher Kings is inaugurated, and the coming of the Good Knight awaited. The next part of the sequence begins with the Merlin story initiated by Geoffrey of Monmouth and developed by Robert de Boron, in which we hear of Merlin's incubus father (from whom the magician derives his prophetic gifts), his basing of the Round Table on those of the Grail and of the Last Supper, his use of magic to allow Uther Pendragon to lie with Ygerne, the Cornish duke's wife, to beget Arthur, and the sword-in-the-stone motif which establishes the young Arthur's pre-eminence amongst his barons. There follows a sequel to Robert's work, beginning with the story of how Merlin offers his aid to Arthur and Gauvain in their combats against the rebellious barons (the sequel was itself developed in the *Suite du Merlin*, see below, section VI). The trilogy representing the main story, probably completed by c. 1225, presents the following material:

The *Lancelot* proper introduces the eponymous hero as the son of Ban of Benoic. Ban perishes when he is attacked by Claudas. Lancelot is snatched from his mother's care by the Lady of the Lake and is brought up in her palace together with his cousins, Lionel and Bors. At the age of eighteen Lancelot is taken by his foster-mother to Arthur's court and is knighted at her request. At Camelot he falls in love with Guinevere. Lancelot becomes the firm friend of Galehaut, an enemy of Arthur who, becoming impressed by Lancelot's valour, drops his opposition to Arthur. It is through the offices of Galehaut that Lancelot and the queen are able to start a series of trysts. Lance-

---

4   *The Vulgate Version of the Arthurian Romances*, ed. H. O. Sommer, 7 vols, repr. (Washington: Carnegie Institution, 1909–16, repr. New York: AMS, 1973); *Lancelot-Grail. The Old French Arthurian Vulgate and Post Vulgate in Translation* ed. Norris J. Lacy, 8 vols (New York and London: Garland, 1993). This work contains an account of the rise and fall of Camelot accepted as standard by posterity.

lot's loss of virginity leads to predictions that he will in future lose his customary title of best knight in the world. When unable to reach a tomb because of encroaching flames, a voice announces that his failure to do so is due to lechery and that only a pure knight of his kindred will eventually complete the Grail quest. The allusion here is to Lancelot's future son, Galahad (Galaad) whom, with the connivance of the Grail King Pelles, he begets with Pelles' daughter under the impression that he is lying with Guinevere. Guinevere sees that Lancelot's sin will prevent his achieving the Grail quest, and she condemns herself for contributing to his failure. Lancelot, however, is loath to face this fact.

In the *Queste* section a maiden takes Lancelot to a nunnery where Galahad has been raised to young manhood. Galahad, being the son of the Grail king's daughter and of Lancelot, the previous 'best knight in the world', passes the tests of the Siege Perilous and the sword-in-the-stone and Arthur salutes him as the knight who will bring to a close the adventures of the Grail and heal the Maimed King. The hermit Nascien announces that the Grail will soon appear at Court. It appears in an intense flash of light, feeds each knight according to his requirements and then disappears. Following this epiphany the knights vow to quest for the Grail but meet varying standards of success, faring essentially according to their personal standard of purity. The knights Lionel, Hector and Gauvain do not get very far in their quest. A hermit reprimands Gauvain for not having been shriven for four years and only when Lancelot confesses his guilt is he permitted a brief experience of the Grail. Of all the knights Galahad is the supreme in virtue, although Perceval and Bohort and others are also allowed temporary visions of the Grail. These few knights enter Corbenic, the Grail castle, into which the maimed king is brought on a couch. Bishop Josephe, son of Joseph of Arimathea, descends from heaven to join them, and angels bring in the bleeding lance and set it before the Grail. Josephe performs Mass, and the crucified Christ issues from the Grail and administers the sacrament to those present. Galahad heals the maimed king with blood from the lance. Eventually, having witnessed the supreme mystery, Galahad expires in the city of Sarras, to be followed shortly by Perceval, leaving Bors alone to report their experiences; a hand removes both Grail and lance to heaven.

In the *Mort Artu* Bors returns to Court to tell of the knights' experiences at the Grail castle and Gauvain confesses that he had killed eighteen knights out of his own sinfulness. Lancelot, forgetting the vows of chastity he had made on the Grail quest, resumes his relationship with Guinevere, breaking the heart of the maid of Escalot through his obsession. Arthur learns of the adultery when Morgan the Fay lures him to her palace on whose walls pictures of the love affair had been painted by Lancelot when once imprisoned by Morgan. At the suggestion of Agravain, Gauvain's brother, a trap is set for the lovers and Lancelot is caught in the queen's bedchamber. In the course of skirmishes there, Gauvain's other brother, Gahariet, is killed by Lancelot. Arthur condemns Guinevere to be burned but she is saved by Lancelot, after which ensues a civil war when Arthur lays siege to Lancelot's castle at Joyeuse Garde. The pope intercedes to demand that Arthur become reconciled with his wife, but Gauvain vows war until he can avenge the death of his brother at Lancelot's hands. At Gauvain's instigation Arthur crosses to Lancelot's territory in Gaul and continues the feud, leaving the queen in what he takes to be the safe hands of Mordred (here represented as the king's own son from an incestuous union). Gauvain insists on fighting Lancelot even against the general condemnation of his friends, who deem his actions excessive. Only on his deathbed does he repent of his exaggerated hostility toward Lancelot and advise Arthur to enlist Lancelot as an ally against the treacherous Mordred who had meanwhile seized his wife and lands. Arthur returns to Logres but before the final battle on Salisbury Plain has a sinister vision of being dashed from Fortune's wheel. Later on a rock are found inscriptions of Merlin foretelling a battle which will orphan Arthur's land. In the battle Mordred is killed and Arthur is mortally wounded. At his end Arthur commands the knight Giflet to throw his sword into a lake, whereupon a hand from the water receives the blade. Guinevere takes the veil and Lancelot, who survives the battle, slays Mordred's sons (who had made themselves masters of Arthur's kingdom), after which Lancelot ends his life as a hermit. At his death, Lancelot's soul is borne aloft by angels.

V *Wigalois*[5]

Beginning with an account of Wigalois's parents, Gawein and Florie, and of the hero's youth, the romance tells how, in early manhood, Wigalois sets out in search of his father (who had by misadventure become separated from him in his infancy). Arriving at the Arthurian Court his outstanding prowess is quickly acknowledged and Gawein (whom he does not recognise) is appointed his tutor. Despite his youth, Wigalois gains Arthur's permission to go on a mercy mission with Nereja, the messenger of Princess Larie, whose kingdom is threatened by the assaults of the heathen Roaz. Nereja is at first

5   Wirnt von Gravenberg, *Wigalois, Der Ritter mit dem Rade,* ed. J. M. N. Kapteyn, Rheinische Beiträge und Hülfsbücher zur germanischen Philologie und Volkskunde, 9 (Bonn: Klopp, 1926). *Wigalois, The Knight of Fortune's Wheel,* trans. J. W. Thomas (Lincoln and London: University of Nebraska Press, 1978). Written c. 1210/15 or later by the otherwise unknown Wirnt from the East Franconian town of Gravenberg (present-day Gräfenberg), the romance had a large circulation in the Middle Ages and is referred to in *Diu Crône* lines 2938–49. With the latter romance it shares most notably the motif of a redemptive hero elected to bring peace to a troupe of lost souls (although it does not link this theme with the Grail topos).

sceptical about the young knight's ability to help but at length Wigalois demonstrates his abilities to her and Nereja permits him to proceed to the major challenge of saving Larie's land of Korntin and of redeeming the unquiet souls of Larie's father, the murdered King Lar, and his retinue, who languish in a purgatory until the injustice can be righted and their souls can be redeemed to eternal rest. The pious hero, relying on God's aid to help him against his devilish opponents, defeats Roaz and his troupe. He thereby wins the right to take Larie's hand in marriage and become king in Korntin. In the ensuing celebrations he is joined by Gawein, whom he now comes to recognise as his father, and Gawein and other Arthurian knights support him in his final combat against an ally of Roaz, Lion. Then Wigalois visits Nantes to swear allegiance to Arthur, after which he returns to the kingdom he has won, where his rule conforms to the highest standards of courtly and Christian conduct.

VI *Perlesvaus*[6]

One day Arthur finds Guinevere in tears because their Court, which had begun well, had fallen into decline. Previously there had been brave knights at their Court but their number had dwindled and she feels that God has abandoned them. Arthur acknowledges that he is to blame and agrees to Guinevere's admonition that he repair to St Austin's chapel to pray that he might be reformed. Before the chapel a hermit exhorts him to renew Christ's Law on earth and tells him of Perceval's misadventure at the castle of the Fisher King (where he had omitted to ask about the lance and Grail). A maiden tells Arthur that Perceval has since redeemed himself to become 'the best knight in the world', but she denounces Arthur (whose identity she does not know). She reports that all his knights have deserted him because he has fallen so far from his previous high standard. A voice now speaks to Arthur admonishing him to hold Court once again and the king is filled with a new determination to do so, sending out letters to his knights (who had also fallen into inaction) to order them to convene again. Three maidens arrive at Court and report on the Fisher King's descending into languor because of Perceval's omission and of his kingdom descending into strife. Gauvain vows to quest for the Grail but becomes lost in a rêverie about God and the angelic host, and

6 *Perlesvaus, Le Haut Livre du Graal*, ed. William A. Nitze and T. A. Jenkins, 2 vols (Illinois: University of Chicago Press, 1932–7); N. Bryant, *The High Book of the Grail. A Translation of the Thirteenth-Century Romance 'Perlesvaus'* (Cambridge: D. S. Brewer, 1978). Like *Diu Crône, Perlesvaus* traces the malaise of the Arthurian world to Arthur's slothful inactivity and to Perceval's omission in not having asked the requisite question on his visit to the Grail. Unlike the German work, it allows Perceval to rehabilitate himself, in this case as a defender of the Church militant who is able to return the Grail to within the ken of humanity.

so fails to pose the critical question. Exhausted after seeking the Grail for so long, he falls asleep. Lancelot too fails in the quest because, as a young girl tells him, his amorous relationship with Guinevere forbids him success in the quest.

Perceval now learns that that the Fisher King has died and that the wicked king of Castle Mortal has seized the Grail castle. Perceval lays siege to the castle and the king of Castle Mortal commits suicide when he sees that he has lost the battle. The knights and ladies of the Fisher King are now free to return to the abode from which they had been ousted. The Grail and lance now reappear and Perceval as a defender of the Church militant initiates an internal crusade to rout out those who refuse to subscribe to the New Law. There follow a number of adventures undertaken by Arthur, Gauvain and Lancelot before a ship appears destined to take Perceval out of human sight to the mystic Ille Plentereuse. A voice enjoins Arthur to go on a pilgrimage to the reconquered Grail castle in order to increase his faith and that of his people. The romance ends with various attempts mounted by recalcitrants to subvert the implementation of the New Law, all of which are quelled.

VII *Les Merveilles de Rigomer*[7]

An emissary of the châtelaine of Rigomer, Dionise, challenges the Arthurian knights to remove a spell from her mistress's castle. Lancelot volunteers and sets out for her fastness in Ireland . He witnesses there a number of strange sights including an eerie house haunted by a corpse on a bier and a sick host who, because of a spell, can remain alive only if visited periodically by a number of stranger knights. On his way to Rigomer he is informed by various interlocutors that the castle contains many dangers and sexual temptations. On gaining Rigomer he succumbs to the wiles of an enchantress and inadvisedly accepts a magic spear from a maiden which paralyses him, whereupon a ring is placed on his finger which robs him of his wits. Helpless to defend himself he is consigned to an understairs *val sanz retour* in the kitchens of the castle. The sequel concerns the liberation of Lancelot by Gauvain. Gauvain faces the same challenges as his peer, but, inspired by his fairy consort, Lorie de la Roche Florie, he is granted immunity from the enchantress's arts. The latter's loss of power allows Gauvain to proceed unmolested to a liberation of Lancelot. On finding the witless Lancelot he

---

[7] *Les Merveilles de Rigomer*, ed. Wendelin Foerster and Hermann Breuer, 2 vols (Dresden: Niemeyer, 1908), 1915; trans. as *The Wonders of Rigomer* by Thomas Vesce (New York: Garland, 1988). This composite romance, in which a number of scribal hands are discernible, is similar to *Diu Crône* in that the supreme challenge awaiting the hero (Lancelot) at the ostensibly enchanted castle of Rigomer is essentially a secular one requiring prowess at arms (and sexual self-control) rather than spiritual distinction.

breaks the ring on his finger and with it the spell which detains him. Dionise, who had long awaited the superlative knight who could break the enchantments of her realm, is disappointed when Gauvain declines her hand because of his liaison with Lorie. However, Gauvain chivalrously agrees to procure for Dionise a worthy husband whom he finds in the person of the young prince, Midomidas.

VIII The *Suite du Merlin* (Huth *Merlin*)[8]

Shortly after Arthur's coronation the queen of Orkney (wife of King Lot) comes to Court with her son, Gauvain. Arthur, not knowing that the queen is his sister, makes her pregnant with the future Mordred. Arthur thereafter has frightening visions, interpreted by Merlin to mean that a child yet unborn will one day destroy the kingdom. Merlin furnishes Arthur with an unbreakable sword held aloft from a lake by a mysterious hand. Arthur gives his sister, Morgain, to Urien in marriage, of which union Yvain is born. When the time approaches for the birth of the 'evil child' prophesied by Merlin, Arthur tries to do away with all the children born in that month of May, but Mordred manages to escape when his boat is shipwrecked and he gains the shore. A poor Northumbrian knight, Balain, comes to Court and excels in the battle in which Gauvain's father, Lot, is killed by Pellinor (for which Gauvain swears vengeance). Merlin falls in love with Morgain who exploits his love for her to extract from him his magical secrets and to gain from him the magical scabbard of his sword, Escalibor.

Balain, after many misadventures, comes to the good King Pellean's castle where he strikes the Dolorous Stroke, maiming Pellean and precipitating the baleful 'marvels of Britain' which lead to much death and destruction. After suffering further misfortunes, Balain is forced to do battle with his own brother, neither recognising the other until both are on the point of death. Some time after the marriage of Arthur and Guinevere, Merlin falls in love with Viviane who, like Morgain before her, makes him reveal his magic secrets, after which she entombs him. Morgain, wishing for Arthur's death and the consequential exaltation of herself and her lover, Accolon, sends the latter armed with Escalibor and its magical scabbard to kill her brother, Arthur. Arthur is saved from death only by Viviane's magic. Now Morgain

---

8   *Merlin*, ed. Gaston Paris and Jacob Ulrich, 2 vols (Paris: Firmin Didot, 1888). A thirteenth-century continuation of the prose redaction of Robert de Boron's *Merlin*, often termed the 'romantic' continuation to distinguish it from the pseudo-historical Vulgate continuation. The accounts of Balain's Dolorous Stroke and the Enchantments of Britain consequentially unleashed by Balain's action resemble Parzival's irrevocable sin of omission in *Diu Crône*. The Enchantments also bear some likeness to the succession of accursed 'living dead' encountered in the *Wunderketten* sequences in *Diu Crône* (which Heinrich's old Grail king claims to be related to Parzival's original sin).

tries to murder her husband, Urien, in his sleep but is prevented from doing so by their son, Yvain. Banished from Court by Arthur, she nevertheless manages to steal the magic scabbard and casts it into a lake before Arthur can apprehend her. A final attempt made by Morgain to murder Arthur is thwarted when Viviane forewarns Arthur of the impending danger.

IX The Livre d'Artus[9]

Despite the young Arthur's ability to draw the sword from the stone, many British warriors (including Gauvain's father, Lot of Orkney and Urien) refuse to do him homage since they disbelieve Merlin's claim that Arthur is the son of Uther. On Merlin's advice Arthur sends to Brittany for Ban and Bohort and with their help quells the rebellious barons. Thereafter Arthur and Merlin help King Leodegan in his batles and Arthur marries Leodegan's daughter, Guinevere. The still defiant Lot is wounded in battle by his son, Gauvain. Now Arthur forgives his wounded adversary, who in turn consents to swear allegiance to Arthur. Eventually Arthur becomes reconciled with most of his indigenous adversaries (Urien being a notable exception) and they make common cause against the Saxon invaders.

Alain of Escavalon comes to the Court together with Guiromelant, Guingambresil and Greoreas, who are all related to the Gosangos who loves Guinevere. Merlin praises Alain but not his companions who harbour envious feelings towards the Arthurian knights. A more immediate source of conflict erupts when Arthur takes the side of his seneschall, Keu, in an argument against Gauvain's brother, Gahariet. Gauvain and his brothers angrily depart from the Round Table (and Guinevere asks to be taken with them), the imbroglio being glossed by Sagremors (one of the defectors) as the noble fellowship being destroyed by Keu's sharp tongue. News of the rift reaches Arthur's enemies, Urien and Aminaduf, leader of the Saxons. Disaster is averted from this quarter only when Gauvain, accepting the apologies of Arthur and of Keu's father, Antor, for his son's insult, agrees to be reconciled and to help once again in the Saxon wars.

Gauvain saves Guinevere from her abduction by Urien and later fathers a child by Floree, the daughter of Alain of Escavalon. The narrative now turns to how Merlin relinquished his magic secrets to Viviane and to an account of the affair between Morgan and Guinevere's cousin, Guiomar. The queen puts a stop to the couple's intimacies so that the affair should not anger Arthur.

---

9   The Vulgate Version of the Arthurian Romances, ed. H. O. Sommer, vol. 7. This, together with the Vulgate sequel and the Suite du Merlin of the Huth manuscript, is a continuation of Robert de Boron's Merlin, and was probably composed as a link between the Merlin and Lancelot sections. Like the initial sections of Diu Crône, this work deals with the early days of Arthur's reign and his attempts to stamp his authority on opposition parties.

Morgan, embittered by the prohibition, withdraws to a forest, begging God to send her Merlin as an advisor. The omniscient Merlin,who already knows her grief, consoles her by teaching her his magic arts. Armed with magic skills, and wanting Guiomar by her side and also to detain knights whom *Guinevere* desires, Morgan builds a tower in a valley into which to entice her lover and to imprison knights and ladies who are faithless in love – the place being called the *val sanz retour* or *val des faux amants*.

In the final part of the incomplete work knights come across a Grail procession but do not understand its import until it is revealed to them by Nascien the hermit. The romance concludes with further adventures of Sagremor, Gauvain and Arthur.

X The Didot *Perceval*[10]

The romance begins with an account of Arthur's coronation after the nobles have witnessed his drawing the sword from the stone. Merlin tells them that Arthur is the son of Uther Pendragon and Ygerne. The nobles inform Arthur that Merlin had been Uther's Court seer and the architect of the Round Table. Merlin predicts Arthur's future greatness and tells of the sick Fisher King who awaits a knight who will pose the question which will allow him an easeful death and put an end to the Enchantments of Britain. Alain Le Gros, father of Perceval, hearing of Arthur's fame, sends his son to Court. Alain receives a divine message that his son will be successful in the future Grail quest. In the meantime, however, Perceval's hubris is punished when he decides to take his place prematurely on the Siege Perilous. For the seat splits, darkness envelops the Court and a voice reproves Perceval for his temerity, warning that the seat will not become intact again nor the Enchantments of Britain be dissipated until the adventure of the Grail is accomplished. Perceval resolves to undertake the quest at which a hermit uncle (brother of Perceval's father) enjoins Perceval to avoid sin and the killing of knights on his quest. Not long afterwards, however, he is forced to kill in self-defence a knight abducting his sister. Merlin appears in the shape of a shadow to Perceval in order to warn him not to go back on his Grail vows. Having attained the castle of the Fisher King (who is Perceval's grandfather) he fails to pose the appropriate question since he does not wish to trouble his host and because his mother had warned him not to ask too many questions. A

10 *The Didot Perceval According to the Manuscripts of Modena and Paris*, ed. William Roach (Philadelphia: Philadelphia U.P., 1941); *The Romance of 'Perceval' in Prose*, trans. Dell Skeels (Seattle: University of Washington Press, 1961). Written c. 1190–1215, the romance is contained in two manuscripts (Paris Didot and Modena E) which relate intertextually to the Merlin, Grail and *Mort Artu* traditions. This romance contains another version of the Enchantments of Britain theme in which Merlin gives advice to Perceval in his quest for the Grail as does Gansguoter to the Grail party in *Diu Crône*.

maiden reproves him for his failure but tells him he must return to try again. It takes Perceval seven years of aimless wandering before he can return again. At length he confesses his sins to the hermit uncle and encounters Merlin who puts him back on the right way to the Grail. The work concludes with an abbreviated version of material familiar from the *Mort Artu*, detailing the last days of the Arthurian reign.

Bibliography

EDITIONS AND TRANSLATIONS

Diu Crône

Diu Crône von Heinrich von dem Türlin, ed. G. H. F. Scholl (Stuttgart: Bibliothek des Litterarischen Vereins 27, 1852, repr. Amsterdam: Rodopi, 1966).

Schröder, Werner, *Herstellungsversuche an dem Text der 'Crône' Heinrichs von dem Türlin*, 2 vols (Mainz: Franz Steiner, 1996).

Zatloukal, Klaus, *Heinrich von dem Türlin: Diu Crône. Ausgewählte Abbildungen zur gesamten handschriftlichen Überlieferung*, Litterae, 95 (Göppingen: Kümmerle, 1982).

Die Krone (Verse 1–12281) nach der Handschrift 2779 der Österreichischen Nationalbibliothek (Altdeutsche Textbibliothek 112), ed. Fritz Peter Knapp and Manuela Niesner, ATB 112 (Tübingen: Niemeyer, 2000).

The Crown, trans. J. W. Thomas (Lincoln and London: University of Nebraska Press, 1989).

Other works

German

Hartmann von Aue, *Iwein*, ed. G. F. Benecke with modern German translation by Thomas Cramer, 2nd edn (Berlin: de Gruyter, 1974).

——, *Erec*, ed. Albert Leitzmann and Ludwig Wolff, ATB 39 (Tübingen: Niemeyer, 1972).

——, *Erec*, trans. Thomas Cramer (Stuttgart: Fischer, 1972).

Konrad von Stoffeln, *Gauriel von Muntabel: eine höfische Erzählung aus dem 13. Jahrhundert*, ed. Ferdinand Khull (Graz: Leuschner und Lubensky, 1885).

Der Ritter mit dem Bock. Konrads von Stoffeln 'Gauriel von Muntabel', ed. Wolfgang Achnitz (Tübingen: Niemeyer, 1997).

Der Mantel. Brüchstück eines Lanzeletromans des Heinrich von dem Türlin nebst einer Abhandlung über die Sage vom Trinkhorn und Mantel und die Quelle der Krone, ed. Otto Warnatsch, Germanistische Abhandlungen, 2 (Breslau: Wilhelm Koebner, 1883).

Das Ambraser Mantel Fragment, ed. Werner Schröder (Stuttgart: Franz Steiner, 1995).

Der Pleier, *Tandareis und Flordibel*, ed. Ferdinand Khull (Graz: Buchhandlung Styria, 1885).

————, *The Arthurian Romances of Der Pleier*, trans. J. W. Thomas (New York: Garland, 1992).

Merlin und Seifried de Ardemont von Albrecht von Scharfenberg in der Bearbeitung Ulrich Füeterers, ed. Friedrich Panzer (Tübingen: Bibliothek des Litterarischen Vereins, 1902).

Der Stricker, *Daniel von dem blühenden Tal*, ed. Michael Resler, ATB 92 (Tübingen, 1983).

————, *Daniel of the Blossoming Valley*, trans. Michael Resler, Garland Library of Medieval Literature Series B, vol. 58 (London and New York: Garland, 1990).

Ulrich von Zatzikhoven, *Lanzelet*, ed. K. A. Hahn with a 'Nachwort' and Bibliography by Frederick Norman (Berlin: de Gruyter, 1965).

————, *Lanzelet*, trans. K. G. T. Webster with an Introduction by R. S. Loomis (New York: Columbia U.P., 1951).

Wirnt von Gravenberg, *Wigalois, Der Ritter mit dem Rade*, ed. J. M. N. Kapteyn, Rheinische Beiträge und Hülfsbücher zur germanischen Philologie und Volkskunde 9 (Bonn: Klopp, 1926).

————, *Wigalois*, trans. J. W. Thomas (Lincoln and London: University of Nebraska Press, 1978).

Wisse, Claus, and Philipp Colin, *Parzifal. Eine Ergänzung der Dichtung Wolframs von Eschenbach*, ed. Karl Schorbach (Strassburg and London: Trübner, 1888).

Wolfram von Eschenbach, *Parzival*, ed. Karl Lachmann, 6th edn, with modern German translation by Dieter Kühn and Commentary by Eberhard Nellmann (Frankfurt am Main: Deutscher Klassiker Verlag, 1994).

————, *Parzival*, trans. A. T. Hatto (Harmondsworth: Penguin, 1980).

————, *Willehalm*, ed. Werner Schröder with modern German translation by Dieter Kartschoke (Berlin: de Gruyter, 1989).

French

Boron, Robert de, *Le Roman du Graal; Manuscrit de Modène*, ed. Bernard Cerquiglini (Paris: Union Générale d'Editions, 1981).

Chrétien de Troyes, *Le Roman de Perceval ou Le Conte du Graal*, ed. Keith Busby (Tübingen: Niemeyer, 1993).

Perceval, The Story of the Grail, trans. Burton Raffel with Afterword by Joseph J. Duggan (Yale: Yale University Press, 1999).

The Continuations of the Old French Perceval of Chrétien de Troyes, ed. William Roach, 5 vols (Philadelphia: University of Pennsylvania Press, American Philosophical Society, 1949–83).

Première Continuation de Perceval (Continuation-Gauvain), ed. William Roach, trans. Anne Van Coolput-Storms (Paris: Librairie Generale Française, 1993).

The Didot Perceval According to the Manuscripts of Modena and Paris, ed. William Roach (Philadelphia: Philadelphia U.P., 1941, repr. Geneva: Slatkine, 1977).

The Romance of 'Perceval' in Prose, trans. Dell Skeels (Seattle: University of Washington Press, 1961).

Le Roman des Eles and *L'Ordene de Chevalerie*, ed. Keith Busby (Amsterdam: Benjamins, 1983).

Two Old French Gauvain Romances, ed. R. C. Johnston and D. D. R. Owen (Edinburgh and London: Scottish Academic Press, 1972).

Meyer, Paul, ed., '*Les Enfances Gauvain*. Fragments d'un poème perdu', *Romania* 39 (1910), pp. 1–32.

Girart d'Amiens, *Escanor. Roman Arthurien en Vers de la Fin du XIII Siècle*, ed. Richard Trachsler, 2 vols (Geneva: Droz, 1994).

Gliglois. A French Arthurian Romance of the Thirteenth Century, ed. C. H. Livingstone (Cambridge (Massachusetts): Harvard U.P., 1932)

Wulff, F. A., 'Le Conte du Mantel', *Romania* 14 (1885), pp. 343–80.

Perlesvaus, Le Haut Livre du Graal, ed. William A. Nitze and T. A. Jenkins, 2 vols (Illinois: University of Chicago Press, 1932–37).

The High Book of the Grail. A Translation of the Thirteenth-Century Romance 'Perlesvaus' by Nigel Bryant (Cambridge: D. S. Brewer, 1978).

The Vulgate Version of the Arthurian Romances, ed. H. O. Sommer, 7 vols (Washington: Carnegie Institution, 1909–16, repr. New York: AMS Press, 1973).

Lancelot-Grail. The Old French Arthurian Vulgate and Post Vulgate in Translation, ed. Norris J. Lacy, 5 vols (New York and London: Garland, 1993).

The Lancelot-Grail Reader. Selections from the Medieval French Arthurian Cycle, ed. Norris J. Lacy (New York and London: Garland, 2000).

The Quest of the Holy Grail, trans. Pauline Matarasso (Harmondsworth: Penguin, 1969).

Marie de France, *Espurgatoire Saint Patrice*, ed. Michael J. Curley (Binghampton: University of Binghampton Press, 1993).

Merlin, ed. Gaston Paris and Jacob Ulrich, 2 vols (Paris: Firmin Didot, 1888).

Les Merveilles de Rigomer, ed. Wendelin Foerster and Hermann Breuer, 2 vols (Dresden: Niemeyer, 1908 and 1915).

The Marvels of Rigomer, trans. Thomas Vesce (New York: Garland, 1988)

La Mort le Roi Artu. Roman du XIIIe Siècle, ed. Jean Frappier, 3rd edn (Geneva: Droz, 1959).

Gaston Paris, ed., 'Le Lai de Tyolet', *Romania* 8 (1879), pp. 40–50.

English

Sir Gawain and the Green Knight, ed. J. R. R. Tolkien, E. V. Gordon and Norman Davis, 2nd edn (Oxford: Clarendon, 1967).

Sir Gawain and the Green Knight, ed. and trans. W. R. J. Barron (Manchester: Manchester U.P. and Barnes and Noble, 1974).

Brewer, Elizabeth, *Sources and Analogues of 'Sir Gawain and the Green Knight'* (Cambridge: D. S. Brewer, 1973).

Malory, Sir Thomas, *Le Morte D'Arthur*, ed. Janet Cowan with an Introduction by John Lawlor, 2 vols (Harmondsworth: Penguin, 1969).

Ywain and Gawain. Sir Percyvell of Gales. The Anturs of Arther, ed. Maldwyn Mills (London: Dent, 1992).

Latin

The Rise of Gawain, Nephew of Arthur / De Ortu Walwanii, Nepotis Arturi, ed. and trans. Mildred Leake Day (New York: Garland, 1984).

Geoffrey of Monmouth, *The Historia Regum Britanniae of Geoffrey of Monmouth*, ed. Neil Wright, 2 vols (Cambridge: D. S. Brewer, 1985, 1987).

————, *The History of the Kings of Britain*, trans. Lewis Thorpe (Harmondsworth: Penguin, 1966).

STUDIES

Altendorf, Hans-Dietrich, 'Die Entstehung des theologischen Höllenbildes in der alten Kirche', in *Himmel, Hölle, Fegefeuer. Das Jenseits im Mittelalter*, Exhibition of the Swiss National Museum (Zurich: Verlag Neue Zürcher Zeitung, 1994), pp. 27–31.

Andersen, Elizabeth, 'Heinrich von dem Türlin's *Diu Crône* and the Prose *Lancelot*; an intertextual study', *Arthurian Literature* 7 (1987), pp. 23–49.

Besamusca, Bart, '*Walewein*: A Middle Dutch antidote to the prose *Lancelot*', *BBIAS* 47 (1995), pp. 301–10.

————, 'Gawain', article translated from the Dutch by Tanis Guest in *A Dictionary of Literary Heroes. Characters in Medieval Narrative Traditions and their Afterlife in Literature, Theatre and the Visual Arts* (Woodbridge: Boydell & Brewer, 1998), pp. 113–20.

Bleumer, Hartmut, *Die 'Crône' Heinrichs von dem Türlin. Form-Erfahrung und Konzeption eines späten Artusromans*, MTU 112 (Tübingen: Niemeyer, 1997).

Bogdanow, Fanni, 'The character of Gauvain in the thirteenth century prose romances', *Medium Aevum* 27 (1958), pp. 154–61.

————, *The Romance of the Grail. A Study of the Structure and Genesis of a Thirteenth-Century Prose Romance* (Manchester and New York: Manchester U.P. and Barnes and Noble, 1966).

————, 'Morgan's role in the thirteenth century prose romances', *Medium Aevum* 38 (1969), pp. 123–33.

————, 'The evolution of the theme of the fall of Arthur's kingdom', in *King Arthur. A Casebook*, ed. Edward D. Kennedy (New York and London: Garland, 1996), pp. 92–103.

Boll, Lawrence Leo, *The Relation of 'Diu Krone' of Heinrich von dem Türlin to 'La Mule sanz Frain'. A Study in Sources*, Catholic University of America Studies in German 11 (New York: AMS Press, 1970).

Braches, Hulda H., *Jenseitsmotive und ihre Verritterlichung in der deutschen Dichtung des Hochmittelalters* (Assen: Van Gorcum, 1961).

Brewer, D. S., *English Gothic Literature* (London: MacMillan, 1983).

Brinker, Claudia, ' "Hie ist diu âventiure geholt!". Die Jenseitsreise im *Wigalois* des Wirnt von Gravenberg: Kreuzzugspropaganda und unterhaltsame Glaubenslehre?', in *Contemplata aliis tradere. Studien zum Verhältnis von Literatur und Spiritualität*, ed. Brinker (Berne: Lang, 1995), pp. 87–110.

Brown, A. C. L., 'The Knight of the Lion', *PMLA* 20 (1905), pp. 673–706.

————, 'The bleeding lance', *PMLA* 25 (1910), pp. 1–59.

Bumke, Joachim, *Courtly Culture. Literature and Society in the High Middle Ages*, trans. Thomas Dunlap (Berkeley, Los Angeles, Oxford: University of California Press, 1991).

Bumke, Joachim, *Wolfram von Eschenbach*, 7th edn, Sammlung Metzler 56 (Stuttgart: Metzler, 1997).

Burns, E. Jane, *Arthurian Fictions. Rereading the Vulgate Cycle* (Columbus: Ohio State University Press, 1985).

Burrow, J. A., *A Reading of Sir Gawain and the Green Knight* (London: Routledge and Kegan Paul, 1965).

Busby, Keith, *Gauvain in Old French Literature* (Amsterdam: Rodopi, 1980).

——, 'Diverging traditions of Gauvain in some of the later Old French verse romances', in *The Legacy of Chrétien de Troyes*, ed. Norris J. Lacy, Douglas Kelly and Keith Busby, 2 vols (Amsterdam: Rodopi, 1987), vol. 2, pp. 93–109.

——, 'Medieval French Arthurian literature: recent progress and critical trends', in *The Vitality of the Arthurian Legend. A Symposium*, ed. Mette Pors (Odense: Odense U.P., 1988), pp. 45–70.

——, *Perceval (Le Conte du Graal)*, Critical Guides to French Texts 98 (London: Grant and Cutler, 1993).

Buschinger, Danielle, 'Un roman arthurien post-classique: *La Couronne* de Heinrich von dem Türlin', *Le Moyen Âge* 89 (1983), pp. 381–95.

——, 'Burg Sâlie und Gral. Zwei Erlösungstaten in der *Crône* Heinrichs von dem Türlin', in *Die Mittelalterliche Literatur in Kärnten*, ed. A. Cella and P. Krämer, pp. 1–31.

Büttner, Bonnie, 'Gawan in Wolfram's *Parzival*', unpublished dissertation, Cornell University, 1984.

Cavendish, Richard, *King Arthur and the Grail. The Arthurian Legends and their Meaning* (London: Paladin, 1980).

Chandler, Frank W., *A Catalogue of Names in the German Court Epics. An Examination of the Literary Sources and Dissemination, together with Notes on the Etymologies of the More Important Names*, rev. Martin H. Jones, King's College London Centre for Late Antique and Medieval Studies Publications (London, 1992).

Cooper, Helen, 'Magic that does not work', *Medievalia et Humanistica* 7 (1976), pp. 131–46.

——, 'The supernatural', in *A Companion to the Gawain-Poet*, ed. Derek Brewer and Jonathan Gibson (Cambridge: D. S. Brewer, 1997), pp. 277–91.

Cormeau, Christoph. *'Wigalois'und 'Diu Crône'; Zwei Kapitel zur Gattungsgeschichte des nachklassischen Aventiureromans*, MTU 57 (Munich: Artemis, 1977)

——, 'Fortuna und andere Mächte im Artusroman', in *Fortuna Vitrea. Arbeiten zur literarischen Tradition zwischen dem 13. und 16. Jahrhundert*, ed. Walter Haug and Burghart Wachinger (Tübingen: Niemeyer, 1995), pp. 23–33.

Coulton, G. G., *The Plain Man's Religion in the Middle Ages* (London: Simpkin, Marshall, Hamilton and Kent, 1916).

De Boor, Helmut, *Geschichte der deutschen Literatur von den Anfängen bis zur Gegenwart*, ed. De Boor and Richard Newald, 8 vols, vol. 2, *Die höfische Literatur* (Munich: Beck, 1953).

——, 'Fortuna in mittelhochdeutscher Dichtung, insbesondere in der *Crône* Heinrichs vom dem Türlin', in *Verbum und Signum. Beiträge zur mediävistischen Bedeutungsforschung. Festschrift für Friedrich Ohly zum 60 Geburtstag*, ed. Hans Fromm, Wolfgang Harms and Uwe Ruberg, 2 vols (Munich: Fink, 1975), vol. 2, pp. 311–28.

Dick, Ernst, 'Katabasis and the Grail epic: Wolfram von Eschenbach's *Parzival*', *Res Publica Litterarum* 1 (1978), pp. 57–87.

——, 'Tradition and emancipation: the generic aspect of Heinrich's *Crône*', in

Genres in Medieval German Literature, ed. Hubert Heinen and Ingeborg Henderson, GAG 439 (Göppingen: Kümmerle, 1986), pp. 74–96.

————, 'The hero and the magician: on the proliferation of dark figures from *Li Contes del Graal* and *Parzival* to *Diu Crône*', in *The Dark Figure in Medieval German and Germanic Literature*, GAG 448 (Göppingen: Kümmerle, 1986), pp. 128–50.

Dinzelbacher, Peter, *Vision und Visionsliteratur im Mittelalter* (Stuttgart: Anton Hiesemann, 1981).

————, 'Mittelalterliche Vision und moderne Sterbeforschung', in *Psychologie in der Mediävistik*, ed. J. Kühnel, H.-D. Mück, Ursula and Ulrich Müller, GAG 431 (Göppingen: Kümmerle, 1985), pp. 9–45.

Döffinger-Lange, Erdmuthe, *Der Gauvain-Teil in Chrétiens 'Conte du Graal'. Forschungsbericht und Episodenkommentar*, Studia Romanica 95 (Heidelberg: Winter, 1998).

Duby, Georges, 'Dans la France du nord-ouest au XIIe siècle: les "jeunes" dans la société aristocratique', *Annales ESC* 19 (1964), pp. 835–46.

Eadie, John, 'Morgan la Fée and the conclusion of *Sir Gawain and the Green Knight*' *Neophilologus* 52 (1968), pp. 299–303.

Ebenbauer, Alfred, 'Fortuna und Artushof. Bemerkungen zum "Sinn" der *Krone* Heinrichs von dem Türlin', in *Österreichische Literatur zur Zeit der Babenberger*, ed. Ebenbauer, Fritz-Peter Knapp and Ingrid Strasser, WAGAPH 10 (Vienna: Halosar, 1977), pp. 25–49.

————, 'Gawein als Gatte', in *Die Mittelalterliche Literatur in Kärnten*, ed. A. Cella and P. Krämer, pp. 33–66.

Economou, G. D., *The Goddess Natura in Medieval Literature* (Cambridge, Massachusetts: Harvard U.P., 1972).

Emerson, Oliver F., 'Legends of Cain, especially in Old and Middle English', *PMLA* 21 (1906), pp. 831–929.

Emmel, Hildegard, *Formprobleme des Artusromans und der Graldichtung. Die Bedeutung des Artuskreises für das Gefüge des Romans im 12. und 13 Jahrhundert in Frankreich, Deutschland und den Niederlanden* (Berne: Francke, 1951).

Ferguson, Niall, *Virtual History, Alternatives and Counterfactuals* (London: Picador, 1997).

Fischer, Hubertus, *Ehre, Hof und Abenteuer. Vorarbeiten zu einer historischen Poetik des höfischen Epos* (Munich: Fink, 1983).

Frakes, J. C., *The Fate of Fortune in the Early Middle Ages. The Boethian Tradition* (Leiden: Brill, 1988).

Fries, Maureen, 'Women in Arthurian literature', in *Approaches to Teaching the Arthurian Tradition*, ed. Maureen Fries and Jeanie Watson (New York: Modern Language Association of America, 1992), pp. 155–58.

Freymond, E., 'Beiträge zur Kenntnis der altfranzösischen Artusromane in Prosa', *Zeitschrift für französische Sprache und Litteratur* 17 (1895), pp. 1–128.

Fromm, Hans, 'Komik und Humor in der deutschen Dichtung des Mittelalters', *DVLG* 36 (1962), pp. 321–39.

Fuchs, Stefan, *Hybride Helden: Gwigalois und Willehalm. Beiträge zum Heldenbild und zur Poetik des Romans im fruhen 13. Jahrhundert*, Frankfurter Beiträge zur Germanistik 31 (Heidelberg: Winter, 1997).

Funcke, Eberhard W., 'Morgain und ihre Schwestern. Zur Herkunft und

Verwendung der Feenmotivik in der mittelhochdeutschen Epik', *Acta Germanica* 18 (1985), pp. 1–64.

Gaylord, Alan T., 'Arthur and the green world', in *Approaches to Teaching the Arthurian Tradition*, ed. Maureen Fries and Jeanie Watson (New York: Modern Language Association of America, 1992), pp. 55–60.

Gerhardt, Christoph, 'Iwein-Schlüsse', *Literaturwissenschaftliches Jahrbuch der Görres Gesellschaft* 13 (1972), pp. 13–39.

Gerritsen, Willem P. and Anthony G. van Melle, trans. Tanis Guest, *A Dictionary of Medieval Heroes. Characters in Medieval Narrative Traditions and their Afterlife in Literature, Theatre and the Arts* (Woodbridge: Boydell & Brewer, 1998).

Gilson, Etienne, *Reason and Revelation in the Middle Ages* (New York and London: Scribners, 1939).

Glassner, Christine, 'Der Aufbau der *Crône* Heinrichs von dem Türlin: Handschriftengliederung und Werkstruktur', unpublished dissertation, University of Vienna, 1991.

Le Goff, Jacques, *The Birth of Purgatory*, trans. Arthur Goldhammer (Chicago: Chicago U.P., 1984).

Gordon, Bruce and Peter Marshall, eds, *The Place of the Dead. Death and Remembrance in Late Medieval and Early Modern Europe* (Cambridge: Cambridge U.P., 2000).

Gowans, Linda, *Cei and the Arthurian Legend* (Cambridge: D. S. Brewer, 1988).

Grant, Marshall Severy, '*Sir Gawain and the Green Knight* and the quest for the Grail: Chrétien de Troyes' *Perceval*, the *First Continuation, Diu Krone* and the *Perlesvaus*', unpublished dissertation, Yale University, 1991.

Green, D. H., 'Homicide and Parzival', in *Approaches to Wolfram von Eschenbach*, ed. D. H. Green and L. P. Johnson (Berne: Lang , 1978), pp. 11–82.

Gülzow, Erich, *Zur Stilkunde der 'Krone' Heinrichs von dem Türlin*, Teutonia 18 (Leipzig: H. Haeffel, 1914).

Grubmüller, Klaus, 'Der Artusroman und sein König. Beobachtungen zur Artusfigur am Beispiel von Ginovers Entführung', in *Positionen des Romans im späten mittelalter*, ed. Walter Haug and Burghart Wachinger, Fortuna Vitrea 1 (Tübingen: Niemeyer, 1991), pp. 1–21.

Grimm, Jacob, *Deutsche Mythologie*, 2 vols (Göttingen: Dieterische Buchhandlung, 1854).

Guerin, M. Victoria, *The Fall of Kings and Princes. Structure and Design in Arthurian Tragedy* (Stanford: Stanford U.P., 1995).

Gürttler, Karin R., '*Künec Artûs der Guote'. Das Artusbild der höfischen Epik des 12. Und 13. Jahrhunderts*, Studien zur Germanistik, Anglistik und Komparatistik 52 (Bonn: Bouvier, 1976).

Harding, George Edward, 'Tradition and creativity: narrative elements in Wirnt von Gravenberg's *Wigalois* and Heinrich von dem Turlin's *Diu Crône*', dissertation, Ann Arbor: University Microfilms International, 1985.

Hardman, Philippa, 'Scholars retelling romances', *Reading Medieval Studies* 18 (1992), pp. 81–101.

Haug, Walter, '*Das Land, von welchem niemand wiederkehrt'. Mythos, Fiktion und Wahrheit in Chrétiens 'Chevalier de la Charrete', im 'Lanzelet' Ulrichs von Zatzikhoven und im 'Lancelot'-Prosaroma* (Tübingen: Niemeyer, 1978).

———, 'O Fortuna. Eine historisch-semantische Skizze zur Einführung', in

Fortuna, ed. Walter Haug and Burghart Wachinger, Fortuna Vitrea 1 (Tübingen: Niemeyer, 1995), pp. 1–22.

Haupt, Jürgen, *Der Truchseß Keie im Artusroman. Untersuchungen zur Gesellschaftsstruktur im höfischen Roman*, Philologische Studien und Quellen 57 (Berlin: Erich Schmidt, 1971).

Haymes, Edward and Stephanie Cain van d'Elden, *The Dark Figure in Medieval German and Germanic Literatur*, GAG 448 (Göppingen: Kümmerle, 1986).

Heller, Edmund K., 'A vindication of Heinrich von dem Türlin based on a survey of his sources', *Modern Language Quarterly* 3 (1942), pp. 67–82.

Henderson, Ingeborg, 'Dark figures and Eschatological Imagery in Wirnt von Gravenberg's *Wigalois*', in *The Dark Figure*, ed. Edward R. Haymes, pp. 99–113.

Henderson, George, *Early Medieval* (Harmondsworth: Penguin, 1972).

———, *Gothic* (Harmondsworth: Penguin, 1967).

Höltgen, Karl Josef, 'King Arthur and Fortune', in *King Arthur. A Casebook*, ed. Edward Donald Kennedy (New York and London: Garland, 1996), pp. 121–37.

Homberger, Dietrich, 'Gawein. Untersuchungen zur mittelhochdeutschen Artusepik', dissertation, University of Bochum, 1969.

Hopkins, Andrea, *The Sinful Knights. A Study of Middle English Penitential Romance* (Oxford: Clarendon, 1990).

Hynes-Berry, Mary, 'A tale "breffly drawne oute of Freynshe" ', in *Aspects of Malory*, ed. Toshiyuki Takamiya and Derek Brewer (Cambridge: D. S. Brewer, 1981), pp. 93–106.

Jackson, W. H., *Chivalry in Twelfth-Century Germany. The Works of Hartmann von Aue* (Cambridge: D. S. Brewer, 1994).

Jackson, Timothy R., Nigel Palmer and Almut Suerbaum, eds., *Die Vermittlung geistlicher Inhalte im deutschen Mittelalter* (Tübingen: Niemeyer, 1996).

Jaeger, C. Stephen, 'The Nibelungen poet and the clerical rebellion against courtesy', in *Spectrum Medii Aevi, Festschrift for G. F. Jones* (Göppingen: Kümmerle, 1983), pp. 177–205.

Jillings, Lewis, 'Ordeal by combat and the rejection of chivalry in *Diu Crône*', *Speculum* 51 (1976), pp. 262–76.

———, '*Diu Crône' by Heinrich von dem Türlin. The Attempted Emancipation of Secular* Narrative, GAG 258 (Göppingen: Kümmerle, 1980).

———, 'The rival sisters dispute in *Diu Crône* and its French antecedents', in *An Arthurian Tapestry. Essays in Memory of Lewis Thorpe*, ed. Kenneth Varty (Glasgow: International Arthurian Society, 1981), pp. 248–59.

———, 'Heinrich von dem Türlein. Zum Problem der biographischen Forschung', in *Die Mittelalterliche Literatur in Kärnten*, ed. A. Cella and P. Krämer, pp. 87–102.

Jones, Martin H., 'Parzival's fighting and his election to the Grail', in *Wolfram Studien*, vol. 3, ed. Werner Schröder (Berlin: Erich Schmidt, 1975), pp. 52–71.

Jung, Emma and Marie-Louise von Franz, *The Grail Legend*, 2nd edn, trans. Andrea Dykes (Boston: Sigo, 1986).

Kasper, Christine, '*Von miesen Rittern und sündhaften Frauen und solchen, die besser waren': Tugend- und Keuschheitsproben in der mittelalterlichen Literatur vornehmlich des deutschen Sprachraums*, GAG 547 (Göppingen: Kümmerle, 1995).

Keefe, Francis Edward, 'Landschaft und Raum in der *Crône* Heinrichs von dem Türlin', unpublished doctoral dissertation, University of Kentucky, 1982.

Keller, Johannes, *Diu Crône Heinrichs von dem Türlin, Wunderketten, Gral und Tod* (Berne: Lang, 1997).

Kelly, Thomas E., *Le Haut Livre du Graal: Perlesvaus*, Histoire des Idées et Critique Littéraire 145 (Geneva: Droz, 1974).

Kennedy, Elspeth, *Lancelot and the Grail. A Study of the Prose 'Lancelot'* (Oxford: Clarendon, 1986).

————, 'The re-writing and re-reading of a text: the evolution of the Prose *Lancelot*', in *The Changing Face of Arthurian Romance. Essays on Arthurian Prose Romances in Honour of Cedric Pickford*, ed. Alison Adams (Woodbridge: Boydell & Brewer, 1986), pp. 1–9.

————, 'The narrative techniques used to give Arthurian romance a "historical" flavour', in *Conjunctions. Medieval Studies in Honor of Douglas Kelly*, ed. Keith Busby and Norris J. Lacy (Amsterdam: Rodopi, 1994), pp. 219–33.

Kern, Peter, 'Die Auseinandersetzung mit der Gattungstradition im *Wigalois* Wirnts von Gravenberg', in *Artusroman und Intertextualität*, ed. Friedrich Wolfzettel (Giessen: Wilhelm Schmidt, 1990), pp. 73–83.

————, 'Bewußtmachen von Artusromankonventionen in der *Crône* Heinrichs von dem Türlin', in *Erzählstrukturen der Artusliteratur. Forschungsgeschichte und neue Ansätze*, ed. Friedrich Wolfzettel (Tübingen: Niemeyer, 1999), pp. 199–218.

Kiekhefer, Richard, *Magic in the Middle Ages* (Cambridge: Cambridge U.P., 1990).

Kittredge, George Lyman, *A Study of Sir Gawain and the Green Knight* (Harvard U.P., 1916, repr. Gloucester, Massachusetts: Peter Smith, 1960).

Klaniczay, Gabor, *The Uses of Supernatural Power. The Transformation of Popular Religion in Medieval and Early Modern Europe*, trans. Susan Singerman (Cambridge: Polity Press, 1990).

Klarmann, Irma, 'Heinrich von dem Türlin: *Diu Krône*, Untersuchungen der Quellen', unpublished dissertation, University of Tübingen, 1944.

Knapp, Fritz-Peter, 'Virtus und Fortuna in der *Krone*': Zur Herkunft der ethischen Grundthese Heinrichs von dem Türlin', *ZfdA* 106 (1977), pp. 253–65.

————, 'Heinrich von dem Türlin: Literarische Beziehungen und mögliche Auftraggeber, dichterische Selbsteinschätzung und Zielsetzung', in *Die Mittelalterliche Literatur in Kärnten*, ed. A. Cella and P. Krämer, pp. 145–87.

————, 'Das Ideal des *chevalier errant* im französischen Prosa-*Lancelot* und in der *Krone* Heinrichs von dem Türlin', in *Artusrittertum im späten Mittelalter. Ethos und Ideologie*, ed. Friedrich Wolfzettel, Beiträge zur deutschen Philologie 57 (Giessen: Wilhelm Schmidt, 1984), pp. 138–45.

Knefelkamp, Ulrich, *Die Suche nach dem Reich des Priesterkönigs Johannes, dargestellt anhand von Reiseberichten und anderen ethnographischen Quellen des 12. bis 17. Jahrhunderts* (Gelsenkirchen: Andreas Müller Verlag, 1986).

Knoll, Hiltrud K., 'Studien zur realen und ausserrealen Welt im deutschen Artusroman (*Erec, Iwein, Lanzelet, Wigalois*)', dissertation, University of Bonn, 1966.

Kobbe, Peter, 'Funktion und Gestalt des Prologs in der mittelhochdeutschen nachklassischen Epik des 13. Jahrhunderts', *DVLG* 43 (1969), pp. 405–57.

Krämer, Peter and A. Cella, eds, *Die mittelalterliche Literatur in Kärnten*, Wiener Arbeiten zur germanischen Altertumskunde und Philologie 16 (Vienna: Halosar, 1981).

Kratz, Bernd, 'Rosengarten und Zwergenkönig in der *Crône* Heinrichs von dem Türlin', *Medievalia Bohemica* 1 (1969), pp. 21–29.

———, 'Zur Kompositionstechnik Heinrichs von dem Türlin', *ABäG* 5 (1973), pp. 141–53.

———, Gawein und Wolfdietrich', *Euphorion* 66 (1972), pp. 397–404.

———, 'Die Ambraser Mantel-Erzählung und ihr Autor,' *Euphorion* 71 (1977), pp. 1–17.

———, 'Die Geschichte vom Maultier ohne Zaum. Paien de Maisières, Heinrich von dem Türlin und Wieland', *Arcadia* 13 (1978), pp. 227–41.

———, 'Hippiatrisches in der *Crône* Heinrichs von dem Türlin', in *In hôhem prîse. A Festschrift in Honour of Ernst S. Dick on his 60th Birthday*, ed. Winder McConnell, GAG 480 (Göppingen: Kümmerle, 1989), pp. 223–34.

———, 'Ein zweites Acrostichon in der *Crône* Heinrichs von dem Türlin', *ZfdPh* 108 (1989), pp. 402–05.

Landau, Marcus, *Hölle und Fegfeuer in Volksglaube, Dichtung und Kirchenlehre* (Heidelberg: Winter, 1909).

Le Goff, Jacques, *The Birth of Purgatory*, trans. Arthur Goldhammer (Chicago: Chicago U.P., 1984).

Lerner, Luise, *Studien zur Komposition des höfischen Romans im 13. Jahrhundert*, Forschungen zur deutschen Sprache und Dichtung 7 (Münster in Westphalia: Aschendorff, 1936).

Lohbeck, Gisela, *Wigalois. Struktur der bezeichenunge* (Frankfurt am Main, Berne, New York, Paris: Lang, 1991).

Loomis, Roger S., ed., *Arthurian Literature in the Middle Ages* (Oxford: Clarendon, 1959).

Loomis, Roger S., 'More Celtic elements in *Gawain and the Green Knight*', *JEGP* 42 (1943), pp. 149–84.

Lyons, Faith, '*La Mort le Roi Artu*: an interpretation', in *The Legend of Arthur in the Middle Ages. Studies Presented to A. H. Diverres*, ed. P. B. Grout, R.A. Lodge, C. E. Pickford and E. K. C. Varty (Cambridge: D. S. Brewer, 1983), pp. 138–48.

Maddox, Donald, 'Levi-Strauss in Camelot: interrupted communication in Arthurian feudal fictions', in *Culture and the King. The Social Implications of the Arthurian Legend*, ed. Martin B. Schichtman and James P. Carley (Albany: State University of New York, 1994), pp. 35–53.

Maksymiuk, Stephen, 'Knowledge, politics and magic: the magician Gansguoter in Heinrich von dem Turlin's *Crône*', *The German Quarterly* 67 (1994), pp. 470–83.

———, *The Court Magician in Medieval German Romance*, Mikrokosmos 44 (Frankfurt: Lang, 1996).

Matarasso, Pauline, *The Quest of the Holy Grail* (Harmondsworth: Penguin, 1969).

Mauritz, Hans-Dieter, *Der Ritter im magischen Reich. Märchenelemente im französischen Abenteuerroman des 12. und. 13. Jahrhunderts*, Europäische Hochschulschriften series 13, vol. 23 (Berne: Lang, 1974).

McCarthy, Terence, *Reading the Morte Darthur* (Cambridge: D. S. Brewer, 1988).

McDannell, Colleen and Bernhard Lang, *Heaven: A History* (New Haven and London: Yale U.P., 1988).

Mentzel-Reuters, Arno, *Vröude. Artusbild, Fortuna- und Gralkonzeption in der 'Crône' des Heinrich von dem Türlin als Verteidigung des höfischen Lebensideals*, Europäische Hochschulschriften 1134 (Berne: Lang, 1989).

Mertens, Volker, ' "gewisse lêre". Zum Verhältnis von Fiktion und Didaxe im späten deutschen Artusroman', in *Artusroman und Intertextualitat*, ed. Friedrich Wolfzettel, pp. 85–106.

——, *Der deutsche Artusroman* (Stuttgart: Reclam, 1998).

——, and Friedrich Wolfzettel, ed., *Fiktionalität im Artusroman* (Tübingen: Niemeyer, 1993).

Meyer, Matthias, ' "So dunke ich mich ein werltgot." Überlegungen zum Verhältnis Autor-Erzähler-Fiktion im späten Artusroman', in *Fiktionalität im Artusroman*, ed. V. Mertens and F. Wolfzettel, pp. 185–202.

——, *Die Verfügbarkeit der Fiktion. Interpretationen und poetologische Untersuchungen zum Artusroman und zur aventiurehaften Dietrichepik des 13. Jahrhunderts* (Heidelberg: Carl Winter, 1994).

Micha, Alexandre, 'The Vulgate Merlin', in *Arthurian Literature in the Middle Ages. A Collaborative History*, ed. R. S. Loomis (Oxford: Clarendon, 1959), pp. 319–24.

Mills, Maldwyn, 'Christian significance and romance tradition in *Sir Gawain and the Green Knight*', in *Critical Studies of Sir Gawain and the Green Knight*, ed. Donald R. Howard and Christian Zacher (Notre Dame and London: University of Notre Dame Press, 1968), pp. 85–105.

Mitgau, Wolfgang, 'Nachahmung und Selbständigkeit Wirnts von Gravenberc in seinem *Wigalois*', *ZfdPh* 82 (1963), pp. 321–37.

Mohr, Wolfgang, 'Parzival und Gawan', *Euphorion* 52 (1958), pp. 1–22.

Morris, Colin, *The Discovery of the Individual* (New York: Harper and Row, 1973).

Morris, Rosemary, *The Character of King Arthur in Medieval Literature* (Cambridge: D. S. Brewer, 1982).

Nineham, Dennis, *Christianity Ancient and Modern. A Study in Religious Change* (London: SCM, 1993).

Nutt, Alfred, *Studies in the Legend of the Holy Grail*, Publications of the Folklore Society 23 (London, 1888).

——, *The Fairy Mythology of Shakespeare* (London: David Nutt, 1900).

Owen, D. D. R., *The Vision of Hell. Infernal Journeys in Medieval French Literature* (Edinburgh and London: Scottish Academic Press and Chatto and Windus, 1970).

Padel, Oliver, 'The nature of Arthur', *Cambrian Medieval Celtic Studies* 27 (1994), pp. 1–31.

Parins, Madelyn J., 'Scholarship, modern Arthurian', in *The New Arthurian Encyclopaedia*, ed. Norris J. Lacy (Chicago and London: St James Press, 1991), pp. 402–11.

Paris, Gaston, *Histoire Littéraire de la France* (Paris: Académie des Inscriptions et Belles-Lettres, 1888; repr. Nendeln, Liechtenstein: Kraus, 1971).

Pastré, Jean-Marc, 'Das Porträt der Amurfina in der *Crône* Heinrichs von dem Türlin', in *Von Otfrid von Weissenburg zum 15. Jahrhundert*, ed. Albrecht Classen, GAG 539 (Göppingen: Kümmerle, 1991), pp. 89–102.

Paton, Lucy A., *Studies in the Fairy Mythology of Arthurian Romance*, 2nd edn with a survey of Scholarship and Bibliography by R. S. Loomis (New York: Burt Franklin, 1970).

Paul, Hermann, *Mittelhochdeutsche Grammatik*, 21st edn, revised by Hugo Moser and Ingeborg Schröbler (Tübingen: Niemeyer, 1975).

Peters, Edward, *The Shadow King. Rex Inutilis in Medieval Law and Literature* (New Haven and London: Yale U.P., 1970).

Pratt, Karen, 'La Mort le Roi Artu as Tragedy', *Nottingham French Studies* 30 (1991), pp. 81–109.

Putter, Ad, 'Arthurian literature and the rhetoric of effeminacy', in *Arthurian Romance and Gender*, ed. F. Wolfzettel, pp. 34–49.

————, *Sir Gawain and the Green Knight and French Arthurian Romance* (Oxford: Clarendon, 1995).

Rahn, Bernhard, *Wolframs Sigunedichtung* (Zurich: Fretz and Wasmuth, 1958).

Raucheisen, Alfred, *Orient und Abendland. Ethisch-moralische Aspekte in Wolframs Epen 'Parzival' und 'Willehalm'*, Bremer Beiträge zur Literatur und Ideengeschichte 17 (Frankfurt: Lang, 1997).

Read, Ralph, 'Heinrich von dem Türlin's Diu Krône and Wolfram's Parzival', *Modern Language Quarterly* 35 (1974), pp. 129–39.

Reissenberger, Karl, *Zur Krone Heinrichs von dem Türlin* (Graz: Leuschner and Lubensky, 1879).

Renoir, Alain, 'Gawain and Parzival', *Studia Neophilologica* 31 (1958), pp. 155–58.

Richey, Margaret F., 'The German contribution to the matter of Britain with special reference to the legend of King Arthur and the Round Table', *Medium Aevum* 19 (1950), pp. 26–42.

Ruck, Elaine H., *An Index of Themes and Motifs in Twelfth-Century French Arthurian Poetry* (Cambridge: D. S. Brewer, 1991).

Sacker, Hugh, 'An interpretation of Hartmann's Iwein', *The Germanic Review* 36 (1961), pp. 5–26.

Salmon, Paul, *Literature in Medieval Germany* (London: Cresset, 1967).

Samples, Susann, 'The rape of Ginover in Heinrich von dem Türlin's Diu Crône', in *Arthurian Romance and Gender*, ed. F. Wolfzettel, pp. 196–205.

Sanders, Willy, *Glück. Zur Herkunft und Bedeutungsentwicklung eines mittelalterlichen Schicksalsbegriffs*, Niederdeutsche Studien 13 (Cologne and Graz: Böhlau, 1965).

Scharmann, Theodor, *Studien über die saelde in der ritterlichen Dichtung des 12. und 13. Jahrhunderts* (Würzburg: Konrad Triltsch, 1935).

Schiessl, Ute, 'Die Gawangestalt im Wigalois des Wirnt von Gravenberc', unpublished dissertation, University of Munich, 1968.

Schiewer, Hans-Jochen, 'Prädestination und Fiktionalität in Wirnts Wigalois', in *Fiktionalität im Artusroman*, ed. V. Mertens and F. Wolfzettel, pp. 146–59.

Schiprowski, P. E., *Merlin in der deutschen Dichtung* (Breslau: Antonius Verlag, 1933).

Schirok, Bernd, 'Artus der meienbaere man: Zum Stellenwert der "Artuskritik" im klassischen deutschen Artusroman', in *'Gotes und der werlte hulde'. Literatur in Mittelalter und Neuzeit. Festschrift fur Heinz Rupp zum 70 Geburtstag*, ed. Rüdiger Schnell (Berne and Stuttgart: Francke, 1989), pp. 58–82.

Schmid, Elizabeth, *Familiengeschichten und Heilsmythologie. Die Verwandschaftsstrukturen in den französischen und deutschen Gralromanen des 12. und 13. Jahrhunderts* (Tübingen: Niemeyer, 1986).

——, 'Text über Texte. Zur *Crône* des Heinrich von dem Türlin', *GRM* n.s. 44 (1994), pp. 266–87.

Schmidtke, Dietrich, *Das Wunderbare in der Mittelalterlichen Literatur*, GAG 606 (Göppingen: Kümmerle, 1994).

Shaw, Frank, 'Die Ginoverentführung in Hartmanns *Iwein*', *ZfdA* 104 (1975), pp. 32–40.

Schmidt, Klaus M., 'Der verschmähte Merlin. Mögliche Gründe für die mangelnde Merlin-Rezeption in Deutschland', in *Die deutsche Literatur des Mittelalters im europäischen Kontext*, ed. Rolf Bräuer, GAG 651 (Göppingen: Kümmerle, 1995), pp. 61–83.

Schmitt, Jean-Claude, *Ghosts in the Middle Ages. The Living and the Dead in Medieval Society*, trans. Teresa Lavender Fagan (Chicago and London: University of Chicago Press, 1998).

Schmolke-Hasselmann, Beate, *The Evolution of Arthurian Romance. The Verse Tradition from Chrétien to Froissart*, trans. Margaret and Roger Middleton (Cambridge: Cambridge U.P., 1998).

Schultz, James A., *The Shape of the Round Table. Structures of Middle High German Arthurian Romance* (Toronto: Toronto U.P., 1983).

Schouwink, Wilfried, *Fortuna im Alexanderroman Rudolf von Ems*, GAG 212 (Göppingen: Kümmerle, 1977).

Schröder, Werner, 'Zur Chronologie der drei grossen mittelhochdeutschen Epiker', *DVLG* 31 (1957), pp. 264–302.

——, 'Zur Literaturverarbeitung durch Heinrich von dem Türlin in seinem Gawein-Roman, *Diu Crône*', *ZfdA* 121 (1992), pp. 131–74.

Seznec, Jean, *The Survival of the Pagan Gods* (New York: Harper and Row, 1960).

Siberry, Elizabeth, *Criticism of Crusading 1095–1274* (Oxford: Clarendon, 1985).

Speckenbach, Klaus, 'Traum-Reisen in eine jenseitige Welt', in *Reisen und Welterfahrung in der deutschen Literatur des Mittelalters*, ed. Dietrich Huschenbett and John Margetts, Würzburger Beiträge zur deutschen Philologie 7 (Würzburg: Königshausen and Neumann, 1991), pp. 125–40.

Singer, Samuel, 'Heinrich von dem Türlin', in *Allgemeine Deutsche Biographie* 39 (Leipzig: Duncker and Humblot, 1895), pp. 20–22.

Stevens, Adrian, 'Heteroglossia and clerical narrative: on Wolfram's adaptation of Chrétien', in *Chrétien de Troyes and the German Middle Ages*, ed. Martin H. Jones and Roy Wisbey (Cambridge/London: D. S. Brewer and the Institute of Germanic Studies, 1993), pp. 241–55.

Stevens, John, *Medieval Romance* (London: Hutchinson, 1973).

Sumption, Jonathan, *Pilgrimage. An Image of Medieval Religion* (London: Faber and Faber, 1975).

Taylor, Jane, 'Order from accident: cyclic consciousness at the end of the Middle Ages', in *Cyclification. The Development of Narrative Cycles in the Chansons de Geste and the Arthurian Romances*, ed. Bart Besamusca, Willem P. Gerritsen, Corry Hogetoorn and Orlanda S. H. Lie (North-Holland, Amsterdam, Oxford, New York, Tokyo: Royal Netherlands Academy of Arts and Sciences, 1994), pp. 59–73.

Thomas, Keith, *Religion and the Decline of Magic* (New York: Scribners, 1971).

Thomas, Neil, 'Konrad von Stoffeln's *Gauriel von Muntabel*: a comment on Hartmann's *Iwein*?' *Oxford German Studies* 17 (1988), pp. 1–9.

————, 'Heinrich von dem Türlin's *Diu Crône*: an Arthurian fantasy?', *ABäG* 36 (1992), pp. 169–79.

————, *The Defence of Camelot. Ideology and Intertextuality in the 'post-Classical' German Romances of the Matter of Britain Cycle* (Berne: Lang, 1992).

————, 'The secularisation of myth: *Les Merveilles de Rigomer* as a *contrafactura* of the French Grail romances', in *Myth and its Legacy in European Literature*, ed. N. Thomas and F. Le Saux (Durham: Durham Modern Language Series, 1996), pp. 159–69.

Topsfield, Leslie T., *Chrétien de Troyes. A Study of the Arthurian Romances* (Cambridge: Cambridge U.P., 1981).

Vettermann, E., *Die Balendichtungen und ihre Quellen*, Beiheft zur *Zeitschrift für romanische Philologie* 40 (Halle am Saale: Niemeyer, 1918).

Uitti, Karl and Michelle Freeman, *Chrétien de Troyes Revisited* (New York: Twayne, 1995).

Vinaver, Eugene, 'The dolorous stroke', *Medium Aevum* 25 (1956), pp. 175–80.

————, *The Rise of Romance* (Oxford: Clarendon, 1971).

Wagner-Harken, Annegret, *Märchenelemente und ihre Funktion in der 'Crône' Heinrichs von dem Türlin. Ein Beitrag zur Unterscheidung zwischen 'klassischer' und 'nachklassischer' Artusepik*, Deutsche Literatur von den Anfängen bis 1700, 21 (Bern/Berlin/Frankfurt am Main/New York/Paris/Vienna: Lang, 1995).

Walker, D. P., *The Decline of Hell* (London: Routledge and Kegan Paul, 1964).

Wallbank, Rosemary, 'The composition of *Diu Crône*. Heinrich von dem Türlin's narrative technique', in *Medieval Miscellany presented to Eugène Vinaver*, ed. F. Whitehead, A. H. Diverres and F. E. Sutcliffe (Manchester: Manchester U.P., 1965), pp. 300–20.

————, 'Heinrichs von dem Türlin *Crône* und die irische Sage von Etain und Mider', in *Die mittelalterliche Literatur in Kärnten*, ed. Cella and Krämer, pp. 251–68.

————, 'König Artus und Frau Saelde in der *Crône* Heinrichs von dem Türlin', in *Geistliche und Weltliche Epik des Mittelalters in Österreich*, ed. David McLintock, Adrian Stevens and F. Wagner, GAG 446 (Göppingen: Kümmerle, 1987), pp. 129–36.

————, 'An Irish fairy in Austria: Vrou Giramphiel and Lady Fortune in *Diu Crône*', in *Connections. Essays in Honour of Eda Sagarra on the Occasion of her Sixtieth Birthday*, ed. Peter Skrine, Rosemary E. Wallbank-Turner and Jonathan West (Stuttgart: Hans Dieter Heinz, 1993), pp. 285–96.

Walshe, M. O'C., 'Heinrich von dem Türlin, Chrétien and Wolfram', in *Medieval German Studies Presented to Frederick Norman*, no editor (London: Publications of the Germanic Institute, 1965), pp. 204–18.

Wasielewski-Knecht, Claudia, *Studien zur Parzival-Rezeption in Epos und Drama des 18–20. Jahrhunderts* (Berne: Lang, 1993).

Webster, Kenneth G. T., *Guinevere. A History of her Abductions* (Milton, Massachusetts: Turtle Press, 1951).

Wehrli, Max, 'Antike Mythologie im christlichen Mittelalter', *DVLG* 57 (1983), pp. 18–32.

West, G. D., 'Grail problems I: Silimac the Stranger', *Romance Philology* 24 (1970/71), pp. 599–611.

——, 'Grail problems II: The Grail family in the Old French verse romances', *Romance Philology* 25 (1972), pp. 53–73.

Weiss, Adelaide, *Merlin in German Literature. A Study of the Merlin Legend in German Literature from Medieval Beginnings to the End of Romanticism*, Catholic University of America Studies in German 3 (Washington: Catholic University of America Publications, 1933).

Wellek, René and Austin Warren, *Theory of Literature* (Harmondsworth: Penguin, 1970).

Wells, Christopher J., *German. A Linguistic History to 1945* (Oxford: Clarendon, 1985).

Weston, Jessie L., *The Legend of Sir Gawain* (London: David Nutt, 1897).

——, *The Legend of Sir Perceval*, 2 vols (London: David Nutt, 1906).

——, *From Ritual to Romance* (Cambridge: Cambridge University Press, 1920, repr. Princeton N.J.: Princeton U.P., 1993, with Foreword by Robert A. Segal).

Wittmann-Klemm, Dorothee, *Studien zum 'Rappoltsteiner Parzifal'*. GAG 224 (Göppingen: Kümmerle, 1977).

Wolfzettel, Friedrich, ed., *Artusroman und Intertextualität* (Giessen: Wilhelm Schmitz, 1990).

——, *Arthurian Romance and Gender; Masculin/Feminin dans le Roman Arthurien Médiéval; Geschlechterrollen im mittelalterlichen Artusroman* (Amsterdam, Atlanta, GA: Rodopi, 1995).

——, *Erzählstrukturen der Artusliteratur. Forschungsgeschichte und neue Ansätze* (Tubingen: Niemeyer, 1999).

Worstbrock, Franz Josef, 'Über den Titel der *Krone* Heinrichs von dem Türlin', *ZfdA* 95 (1966), pp. 182–86.

Wynn, Marianne, 'The abduction of the queen in German Arthurian romance', in *Chevaliers errants, demoiselles et l'Autre: höfische und nachhöfische Literatur im europäischen Mittelalter (Festschrift fur Xenja von Ertzdorff)*, ed. Trude Ehlert, GAG 644 (Göppingen: Kümmerle, 1988), pp. 131–44.

Wyss, Ulrich, 'Wunderketten in der *Crône*', in *Die Mittelalterliche Literatur in Kärnten*, ed. A. Cella and P. Krämer, pp. 269–91.

Zach, Christine, *Die Erzählmotive der 'Crône' Heinrichs von dem Türlin und ihre altfranzösischen Quellen. Ein kommentiertes Register*, Passauer Schriften zu Sprache und Literatur 5 (Passau: Richard Rothe, 1990).

Zacharias, Rainer, 'Die Blutrache im Mittelalter', *ZfdA* 91 (1960/61), pp. 167–201.

Zimmer, Heinrich, 'Gawan beim grünen Ritter', in *Der arturische Roman*, ed. Kurt Wais, Wege der Forschung 157 (Darmstadt: Wissenschaftliche Buchgesellschaft, 1970,) pp. 282–300.

Zingerle, August, 'Wolfram von Eschenbach und Heinrich vom Türlein', *Germania* 5 (1860), pp. 468–79.

Zink, Georges, 'A propos d'un épisode de la *Crône* (v. 9129–9532)', in *Mélanges pour Jean Fourquet. 37 Essais de linguistique germanique et de littératures du moyen âge français et allemand*, ed. P. Valentin et G. Zink (Munich/Paris: Hueber, 1969), pp. 395–405.

Zumthor, Paul, *Merlin le Prophète. Un Thème Littéraire Polémique de l'Historiographie et des Romans* (Lausanne: Payot, 1943).

Index

ARTHURIAN STUDIES